The Oxford Book of Canadian Verse

The Oxford Book of Canadian Verse

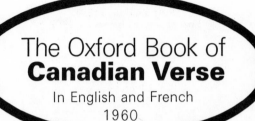

The Oxford Book of
Canadian Verse
In English and French
1960

Chosen and with an Introduction by
A. J. M. Smith

Toronto
Oxford University Press

First impression 1960
First paperback impression 1965

5 6 7 - 4 3

ISBU 0-19-540106-9

© Oxford University Press (Canadian Branch) 1960

Cover drawing by LEO RAMPEN

Printed in Canada by
HIGNELL PRINTING LIMITED

TO

E. J. PRATT AND A. M. KLEIN

IN HOMAGE

AND

WITH LOVE

CONTENTS

CONTENTS

CONTENTS

CONTENTS

CONTENTS

CONTENTS

CONTENTS

CONTENTS

CONTENTS

CONTENTS

xvi

CONTENTS

CONTENTS

CONTENTS

CONTENTS

CONTENTS

CONTENTS

INTRODUCTION

I

CANADIAN poetry is a branch of English or French poetry and
to some extent also, particularly in the work of contemporary
writers, of American poetry. It arose about a century and a
quarter ago—after the hard work of hacking a new home out
of the wilderness had been accomplished, and there was time
to catch one's breath before the task of consolidation and
unification began. When it became possible for the pioneer
to look beyond the harsh present and aspire to something more
gratifying than colonialism it became possible also—indeed,
it became imperative—to cultivate the arts, and particularly
poetry, the art that most directly and intimately expresses and
evaluates the compulsions of life and its environment. The
fact that Canadians were first Frenchmen or Englishmen or
Americans and that their language, whether French or Eng-
lish, already contained a rich poetic inheritance can be re-
garded as an advantage or a handicap according as one looks
for a continuation of the old tradition or hopes for something
entirely new. There is in American poetry as well as Canadian
a good deal more of the traditional and less of the original
than modern critics like to admit. Except for *Leaves of Grass*
and the unpublished lyrics of Emily Dickinson, American
poetry in the nineteenth century is in the European tradition
of the English romantics and the major Victorians, and so too
is Canadian poetry. Canada, it is true, produced no poet of
the stature of a Whitman, a Poe, or an Emerson; there are,
however, a number of writers as interesting, each in his own
way, as most of the other American poets, and there are
traces of local peculiarity and national individualism worth

INTRODUCTION

considering as something special that could only have developed in the unique circumstances obtaining in the British North American colonies that remained loyal to England.

What was at first a wilderness, then a battleground, and then a group of isolated colonies became in 1867 a federated autonomous nation and in the twentieth century an independent member of the British Commonwealth, a state whose voice, like India's, is listened to with respect in the council of nations. Conditions of mind and ways of feeling characteristic of each of these three stages—the colonial, the national, and the cosmopolitan—can be examined with peculiar convenience in the poetry of each period, for whatever else it may be Canadian poetry is and always has been a record of life in the new circumstances of a northern transplantation. And the record takes on significance and attains a more than local relevance as technical proficiency makes possible a more intense and accurate expression of sensibility.

From earliest times Canadian poets, both French and English, have held, consciously or unconsciously, to one of two distinct and sometimes divergent aims. One group has made an effort to express whatever is unique or local in Canadian life, while the other has concentrated on what it has in common with life everywhere. The poets of the first group sought to discover something distinctively and essentially 'Canadian' and thus come to terms with what was new in the natural, social, and political environment in which they found themselves or which they helped to create; the others made an effort to escape the limitations of provincialism or colonialism by entering into the universal civilizing culture of ideas. The first group was more homely, more natural, and sometimes more original, but it lacked, until the twentieth century, the technical proficiency necessary for real success. The danger for the second group was to be merely literary.

xxiv

INTRODUCTION

This is not a defect of the backwoods poets of the earliest period—perhaps because their model, when they had one, was Robert Burns or the popular broadsides of the eighteenth century. Their work has a solidity and tang that is emphasized and sharpened by the absence of polish and literary sophistication. Versifiers like Standish O'Grady and Alexander McLachlan, whose closeness to the soil and the forest clearing kept them from acquiring the smoothness and finish of the 'serious' poet, interpreted their environment and society with sharper insights than the literary poets who followed two generations later. This they did by shunning the abstract and the grandiose and concentrating with a sympathetic or angry eye upon the familiar and the local. The backwoods poet who is to make anything worthwhile out of his restricted material does so by facing it squarely and looking at it not with the sentimental glance of the local colourist but with the strict and penetrating vision of the realist. It is the pioneer poets' chief claim to serious consideration that this is exactly what they did. They were colonial poets to the extent that they could not forget their sturdy and almost instinctive sense of hearty British rightness, but this, more often than not, made them independent and resentful of interference from the governing classes of the mother country, and was one of the most powerful elements in the rise of Canadian national feeling. Indeed, it was the homesteader's vivid sense of the harsh necessities that confronted him in the wilderness which gave him the solid foundation on which to build a new national pride. This developed when he had at last conquered his environment and established himself in greater security and prosperity than he had ever known in the old country. When this was achieved his poetry—except as reminiscence—came to an end, and the literary poets of the Confederation period came into their own.

INTRODUCTION

There were, of course, from the beginning, a number of self-conscious literary poets, the earliest of whom, imitators of Lord Byron and Tom Moore, painted gaudy pictures of the noble red man and landscapes full of Alpine mountains and semi-tropical forests but produced nothing real enough to be of more than antiquarian interest. It is a curious and perhaps a significant fact that some of their volumes enjoyed a remarkable success among the colonists. W. F. Hawley's *Quebec, The Harp, and Other Poems* (1829) was awarded a gold medal by the Society for the Encouragement of the Arts and Sciences of Quebec, and Adam Kidd's *The Huron Chief* (1830) sold more than fifteen hundred copies within a year.

A quarter of a century later (after the rebellions of 1837, the establishment of responsible government, and the stimulation of a sense of national unity by the common fear of American annexationism) newspaper reviewers, magazine editors, and the public at large began to look for emotional and national inspiration from Canadian poets. As Standish O'Grady had written as early as 1842, 'This expanded and noble continent will no doubt furnish fit matter for the Muse. The diversity of climate, the richness of soil, the endearing qualities of a genial atmosphere must no doubt furnish a just excitement to the poetic mind, and arouse the energy correspondent with a richness of scenery, which the contemplative mind will studiously portray.' This enthusiasm is typical of the hopes and expectations that were held for the development of poetry in the new colonies. The Rev. Edward Hartley Dewart, who published a volume of selections from Canadian poets in 1864, wrote in his introduction that 'A national literature is an essential element in the formation of national character', and while outlining with considerable perspicacity the difficulties hindering the rise of an indigenous poetry he was able to single out a number of creditable

INTRODUCTION

achievements by Canadians, particularly the charming Spenserian stanzas of Sangster's *The St. Lawrence and the Saguenay* (1856), a somewhat Byronic sentimental journey down the two majestic rivers, and Heavysege's mammoth dramatic poem *Saul* (first edition 1857), both of which are actually more remarkable for their literary sophistication than for any native Canadian element. *Saul* particularly holds our attention—though not always in the way its author intended. The poem is a huge closet drama in blank verse, interspersed with lyrical interludes, a *tour de force* of linguistic adventures, an imitation of Webster and Tourneur by a self-taught, uncontrolled Beddoes. Heavysege is a strange 'sport'. There perhaps has never been in the poetry of the English-speaking peoples anywhere so curious a mixture of the grand and the grandiose, of the magnificent and the ridiculous as *Saul*. Both Sangster and Heavysege produced works of ambitious scope, and if there was actually little that was national in their poetry, there was a good deal—fragmentary and spasmodic though it was—that was poetry.

If, however, the claims of a national poetry can be satisfied by a minute and sometimes passionate delineation of landscape and of man's struggle to push into the heart of nature and make himself at home there, then two poets of a generation older than the famous Roberts–Lampman–Carman group of the nineties must be named as the creators of a new poetry in the seventies and eighties and the first distinguished members of a native Canadian school. These were Charles Mair and Isabella Valancy Crawford.

A good deal of Mair's verse is sentimental and verbose, but he has one claim to distinction—the sobriety and patience of his descriptions of the Canadian wilderness. In such poems as 'The Fireflies' and in descriptive passages in his historical drama *Tecumseh* (1886) he bends a careful and almost micro-

scopic glance upon the minutiae of the woods with their
animals, birds, and insects, changing in the varying moods of
the hours and the seasons. He watches the busy forms that
ply about the underbrush in the heat of late midsummer and
depicts their comings and goings with a loving care. His best
descriptive poems have a Vergilian rectitude, though their
diction and their rather stiff metrical regularity suggest a
transplanted eighteenth-century 'nature poet' like Cowper or
Thomson. When he turned to the western plains or the vast
stretches of unbroken forest, Mair's imagination caught fire
and his writing took on an intensity and power that anticipate
the more fervid spirit of the later poets. A few lines will show
this heightened quality:

> Great prairies swept beyond our aching sight
> Into the measureless West; uncharted realms,
> Voiceless and calm, save when tempestuous wind
> Rolled the rank herbage into billows vast
> And rushing tides which never found a shore . . .
> Flushed with fresh blooms, deep perfumed by the rose,
> And murmurous with flower-fed bird and bee.
> The deep-grooved bison-paths like furrows lay,
> Turned by the cloven hoofs of thundering herds. . . .
> There vainly sprung the affrighted antelope,
> Beset by glittering eyes and hurrying feet.
> The dancing grouse, at their insensate sport,
> Heard not the stealthy footstep of the fox;
> The gopher on his little earthwork stood,
> With folded arms, unconscious of the fate
> That wheeled in narrowing circles overhead;
> And the poor mouse, on heedless nibbling bent,
> Marked not the silent coiling of the snake.

It is in verses like these, at once traditional and full of accurate
observation, that Mair makes a genuine contribution to the
development of poetry in Canada. It is to be regretted that so
small a part of his work should have shown this solidity and

directness, yet the few passages where he attains his fullest power have a rectitude and clarity that anticipate Lampman.

Good as such poetry may be, however, it was excelled by that of a younger contemporary of Mair, Isabella Valancy Crawford, who died in 1887 at the age of thirty-seven. If we place beside even the best lines of Mair the wonderful second part of 'Malcolm's Katie' (1884) we shall see the difference between descriptive poetry which, though of a high order, is static and reflective, and impressionistic poetry that teems with energy and displays for the first time in Canadian writing an imaginative vitality commensurate with the western land itself and its challenge to the pioneer. 'Malcolm's Katie', undoubtedly Miss Crawford's finest achievement, is the product of an imagination that is curiously geographical and geological. It bases itself on an exact observation of minute detail, but its characteristic operation is to expand, amplify, and generalize—and in the process to utilize the most concrete and precise appeals to the senses. The coming of winter in the north woods is seen—and heard—like this, through the heightened sensibility, imaginatively apprehended, of the Red Man:

> The South Wind laid his moccasins aside,
> Broke his gay calumet of flow'rs, and cast
> His useless wampum, beaded with cool dews,
> Far from him, northward; his long, ruddy spear
> Flung sunward, whence it came, and his soft locks
> Of warm, fine haze grew silver as the birch. . .
>
> The late, last thunders of the summer crash'd,
> Where shrieked great eagles, lords of naked cliffs. . . .
>
> In this shrill moon the scouts of winter ran
> From the ice-belted north, and whistling shafts
> Struck maple and struck sumach—and a blaze
> Ran swift from leaf to leaf, from bough to bough,
> Till round the forest flash'd a belt of flame. . . .

INTRODUCTION

Miss Crawford's 'geographical animism' can be illustrated by many lines and images: 'Ancient billows that have torn the roots of cliffs and bitten at the golden lips of firm sleek beaches'; 'The round-eyed worlds that walk in the blank paths of space'; 'Lesser seas tossed from their rocking cup'; and, finally, a perfect line, classic in its formal beauty and filled with the richest of implications:

> Wrecks plunge, prow foremost, down still, solemn slopes.

For one reader this line has something of the magic of Rimbaud's 'Bateau Ivre' or Hart Crane's 'At Melville's Tomb'.

'Malcolm's Katie' is the first, and not one of the least, of the few poems that can be really called Canadian, because its language and its imagery, the sensibility it reveals and the vision it embodies is indigenously northern and western, a product not of England or the States but of Canada. We do not get this particular kind of success again until 'The Cachalot' (1923) and *Towards the Last Spike* (1952) of E. J. Pratt. With Isabella Valancy Crawford the early period of Canadian poetry in English comes to an end. Maturity had been achieved.

II

The earliest French poetry in Canada was produced in the city of Quebec before the conquest. It was minor occasional poetry in the neo-classic tradition. From the beginning it went hand in hand with journalism and had a social and often political function. After the victory of the English, the political function became a national one, religious and even racial in its scope. The habitants, led by European- and American-inspired intellectuals, tried to win the struggle for survival by force of arms in 1837 and 1838, and lost. They were to

INTRODUCTION

win it instead, as the century developed, by industry and the arts of peace. The study of the heroic past in the work of a national historian, François-Xavier Garneau, and a national poet, Octave Crémazie, gave an impetus to French-Canadian patriotism at the very moment it had become essential to survival. The national pride of the defeated and, as they felt, abandoned colonists of New France was stimulated and their wounds to some extent salved by the glowing pages of Garneau and the impassioned verse of Crémazie.

Crémazie is acknowledged to be the father of French-Canadian poetry. He was a man of wide culture, and though the theme of faithfulness to the courtly and Catholic ideals of pre-Revolutionary France was his chief inspiration, he was not himself provincial or even only national. He was well read in English and French, and like some later poets he studied Sanskrit. His first verses, published in 1854, hailed the partnership of Britain and France in the Crimean War. The immense enthusiasm aroused in Quebec, and indeed throughout the whole of Canada, by the visit of the French corvette *La Capricieuse* in 1856, marking the first time the flag of France had appeared in the St. Lawrence since the fall of New France, was shared also by Crémazie, and he wrote the first of a series of ambitious patriotic poems of which 'Le Drapeau de Carillon' is the most famous and the best.

Crémazie, however, was too intelligent a critic and too modest a man not to recognize the limitations and weaknesses of purely patriotic poetry, where rhetoric and hyperbole are the most effective instruments, and in his later years which he spent as a kind of Canadian exile in France, whence he had fled in 1862 from the financial catastrophe that had overtaken his efforts as a bookseller, he analysed with considerable acumen the difficulties, chiefly economic, of the writer in a colony and was able to make fun of his own popular and in French

Canada very influential verses. 'Il faut bien le dire', he wrote to his friend Abbé Casgrain, literary critic and editor, in 1867,

Il faut bien le dire, dans notre pays on n'a pas le goût très délicat en matière de poésie. Faites rimer un certain nombre de fois *gloire* avec *victoire*, *aïeux* avec *glorieux*, *France* avec *espérance*, entremêlez ces rimes de quelques mots sonores comme notre *religion*, notre *patrie*, notre *langue*, nos *lois*, le *sang de nos pères*; faites chauffer le tout à la flamme du patriotisme, et servez chaud. Tout le monde vous dira que c'est magnifique.

Crémazie outlined here not only his own worst defects, but those of one long-lived school of French-Canadian poetry. Only a very good poet can make something permanently valuable out of such material, and though it was his patriotic poetry that gave Crémazie his fame and his influence it is the melancholy 'Les Morts', in spite of echoes of Hugo and Lamartine, that testifies best to his poetic power. Perhaps the most satisfying example of early French-Canadian nationalism in poetry is the briefest and the simplest, the folk-song-like lyric by the novelist Antoine Gérin-Lajoie, 'Un Canadien errant', which celebrates the devotion of the exiled *patriotes* of 1837.

The mantle of Crémazie, who died in Le Havre in 1879, descended upon Louis Fréchette, a young law student of Lévis, across the river from Quebec. Fréchette associated with the older poet in his bookshop in Quebec City and published his first volume *Mes Loisirs* in 1865, poems emphasizing, as Crémazie had, the glorious past of French Canada. For three years in the late sixties Fréchette sought his fortune in Chicago and in *Voix d'un Exilé* he published some bitter attacks on the conditions that forced a young Canadian to leave his home for the more prosperous States. Later, after his return to Quebec, his participation in Canadian politics, and the acceptance of his poetry by his compatriots, he bought up and destroyed this volume. His poems published in Canada and in Paris during the late seventies were crowned by the French Academy, and it seemed at last as if something done in the North American dominion was meritorious enough to place beside the masterpieces of the old world. Fréchette acquired enormous prestige among his countrymen—English as well as French. He was winning recognition outside the narrow confines of his own province at the very moment that English-speaking poets in the Maritimes and Ontario—Roberts, Carman, Lampman, and Duncan Campbell Scott—were about to achieve something of the same sort of success in London and Boston. Fréchette's finest work was his *Légende d'un Peuple* (1887), which utilized the method of Victor Hugo to depict the heroic passages in the history of French Canada.

It is clear that both Crémazie and Fréchette had a divided aim and were attempting to do two somewhat incompatible things at once. They wished to express and interpret their native French-Canadian scene and to write a kind of Genesis and book of heroes; at the same time, they wished to demonstrate that poetry as good as, and therefore like, that produced in France could come out of the lost colony. It was this objective that prevented them from achieving a genuinely contemporary expression of the individual life of the province and limited their work, as so much of the thought and feeling of Quebec has been limited, to a nostalgic and static evocation of an idealized past. Nearly all of the contemporaries, rivals, and successors of Fréchette continued, as he did, the patriotic tradition of Crémazie, but all of them, in part of their work, developed a school of sober realism devoted to the minute delineation of the hard and homely life of the farmer and of the virtues of integrity and endurance that were really a part of the make-up of the *habitant*. Among these were Pamphile LeMay, the founder of the *terroir* school, William Chapman, and

Nérée Beauchemin. Beauchemin had written in the vein o *f* Crémazie in the nineties, but his best work was reserved for a volume of sonnets and lyrics of the soil published as late as 1928 and demonstrating the continuing vitality of the *terroir* poetry.

III

The success of Crémazie and Fréchette in the last thirty years of the nineteenth century was paralleled in English Canada by a group of remarkable poets born in the early sixties and producing a series of ambitious and successful volumes in the eighties and nineties. The acknowledged leader of the group was the New Brunswick poet Charles G. D. Roberts; closely associated with him were his cousin Bliss Carman and the Ontario poets Archibald Lampman, Wilfred Campbell, and Duncan Campbell Scott. These men were all classically educated, were lovers of nature (in the Wordsworthian sense), were filled with something of the same local and national pride that animated their French confrères, and were stimulated by such contemporary English poets as Arnold, the pre-Raphaelites, and Swinburne. Though the romantic spirit which animates their classical forms is out of fashion just now, it cannot be denied that they established a national school of reflective nature poetry and achieved a standard of technical excellence unattained in Canada before and only rarely equalled since.

The work of these poets was stimulated by the spirit of rather blatant national sentiment that preceded and followed Confederation, but it served to humanize and refine that spirit. It was Roberts, quite consciously, and Campbell, Lampman, and Scott implicitly, who demonstrated for the benefit of those who wished to see the new Dominion unified and strengthened by the rise of a national literature that the poets at least were willing to try. Yet only Roberts was openly and obviously a patriotic poet dedicated to the national theme (as Crémazie and Fréchette had been dedicated to *their* national theme). But patriotic enthusiasm did not provide him with his finest poetry. This is to be found in what is really a close equivalent to the poetry of the *terroir*, the homely sonnets and lyrics collected in *Songs of the Common Day* (1893) and *The Book of the Native* (1896). It was the local scene and nature treated realistically or with classical restraint that gave him his most enduring subjects. His finest poetry is not to be found in his ambitious odes on Confederation or in his pseudo-mystical transcendental pieces but in the verses that most faithfully and soberly present the life of the farmer, the fisherman, and the woodsman going about their eternal tasks under the changing skies of the four seasons.

In his best work Roberts kept his feet solidly on earth, but Carman soared, or tried to soar, into the 'intense inane'. His gift was purely lyrical, and though it achieved some beautiful successes it proved dangerous and eventually enervating. Carman reflected in his own special way the glow of Swinburnian lyricism and at the same time a good deal of the heartiness of the cult of the open road, that stemmed from Whitman through Stevenson, Henley, and the American poet Richard Hovey, with whom Carman collaborated in the well-known series of *Songs from Vagabondia* in the early years of the new century. Carman's gift of song was an ambiguous one. It is impossible not to see him as a kind of sorcerer's apprentice. He has the power to burst forth in song but not the taste or intelligence to know when to stop. There are few of his poems that are not too long, and too many of them trail away after a fine beginning into a glib and tenuous vacuity. Yet in his small number of perfectly successful lyrics and in many scattered lines and occasional stanzas there is an unforgettable quality that makes itself felt as a strange and troubling mixture of the beautiful and the sinister. It is the product of an acute and quivering sensibility, and it testifies to the presence of a genuine and original emotion. 'Low Tide on Grand Pré' and 'Daphne' express an awareness of the mystery and beauty of life and at the same time of its frustrations and disillusionments. It is unfortunate that so pure a lyricist should, in his later career, have fallen under influences that diluted and distorted the spirit of his work and caused him to fritter away much of his talent in the pursuit of an attenuated transcendentalism that was neither very new nor, intellectually speaking, very reputable.

Associated with these two New Brunswick poets were three men in Ontario: Archibald Lampman, Duncan Campbell Scott, and Wilfred Campbell. They were born within a year or two of one another and all began their careers in the late eighties and early nineties. All were inheritors of the English romantic movement, but its influence on them was modified and tempered by a classical education and, at least in Lampman and Scott, by an enthusiasm for Matthew Arnold and Robert Bridges and for Keats and William Morris rather than for Shelley or Swinburne. While they learned their craft from their predecessors and contemporaries among the English poets they did not cease to keep the immediate Canadian scene before their eyes, and they continued, with more art than Mair if not with more intensity than Miss Crawford, to interpret nature and the impingement of nature upon the sensitive mind in ways that were peculiar to their northern locale.

Lampman, like Roberts and Carman, was of loyalist descent and was the son of an Anglican clergyman. He was educated at Trinity College, Toronto, and after a brief spell of schoolmastering he went into the civil service in Ottawa where he remained until his early death in 1899. In such finely etched pictures as the delicate and perfect 'Heat' and in such very different, but again perfect, sonnets as 'Solitude', 'A Sunset at Les Éboulements', or 'Winter Evening' Lampman displays his fine painter's eye for significant detail and his poet's power of striking the unforgettable phrase or cadence, and demonstrates that a recognizably distinct eastern Canadian landscape can be presented with the artistry of a Keats or a Bridges. It is in his nature poems and poems of pure landscape that Lampman is generally most himself; when he attempted to philosophize or moralize he became dull and unoriginal, and he had little gift for narrative. In one poem, however, the remarkable 'City of the End of Things', Lampman transcended his usual themes and became for once a poet of vision and prophecy.

Duncan Campbell Scott, the friend of Lampman and editor of his *Collected Poems*, served in the Department of Indian Affairs at Ottawa and was brought into close contact with the wilderness and the life of the Red Man. It was this that gave him one of his most characteristic themes—the conflict between the heroic or the primitive and the new commercial world with its superior arms and its superior cunning. But Scott in his poems of the forest settlements and the Indian is far from being a romantic primitivist. His evocations of the cruelty and magic power of the wild, whether in man or nature, were unsentimental and accurately observed. As a result, some of his tragic narratives of Indian life—'The Forsaken' and 'At Gull Lake, August 1810' are the best—are among the most original and valid of Canadian poems. But this was not the only theme of Scott's poetry, and his manner was more varied than that of any other poet of his generation except Roberts. His first volume had been published in London in 1893, and it showed in about equal proportions the somewhat feverish emotionalism of the aesthetic movement and the formal fastidiousness of classicism. Such a fusion appears too in the strange, intense evocations of night and storm that introduce a note of cruelty at the heart of beauty into many of his descriptive and narrative poems—a troubling perception that is found also, perhaps only half consciously, in his early love poems. In his best work Scott is as sensitive and intense as Carman, and far more accurate; as accurate as Lampman or Roberts, and more truly passionate than either.

The last poet of the group, Wilfred Campbell, sought to make himself a kind of unofficial laureate of the Dominion and the Empire, but he is interesting and significant in only one volume, *Lake Lyrics*, his first, which appeared in 1889. Here, in poems like 'How One Winter Came In the Lake Region' and 'The Winter Lakes', he caught the spirit of the Georgian Bay region of northern Ontario in a way that anticipated the starkness of the Group of Seven painters of some thirty years later. A close attention to details of landscape and weather, an insistent rhythm, and a relevant and powerful emotion that rises in some of the winter pieces to terror and hysteria give Campbell's best lyrics their special claim to distinction.

The influence of this school of poets had a dazzling and, it must be admitted, rather stupefying effect on their successors for two generations. In the sincere and often competent work of Theodore Goodridge Roberts, the younger brother of Charles, Francis Sherman, and, more recently, Audrey Alexandra Brown, the tradition of romantic nature poetry tended to lose its grip on the immediate and the local, and much of its energy was dissipated in rather attenuated reflections of various European movements such as Pre-Raphaelitism and the Celtic Twilight. An exception must be made, however, for the best of Theodore Roberts' pieces and for a handful of the lyrics of Marjorie Pickthall, which sound a note of singular purity that lifts them above the work of any of her contemporaries, at least among the English-Canadian poets. A sharp perceptiveness of the beauty and transience of life and a passionate longing for escape into God give to her poems 'Resurgam' and 'Quiet' a quality not much inferior, if at all, to that of Christina Rossetti. In striking contrast to the delicacy of feeling and suavity of expression in the work of Marjorie Pickthall is the hearty Bohemianism in the Villon-esque ballades and rondeaus of the West Coast poet, Tom MacInnes, who developed the cult of the open road and dramatized the figure of the happy vagabond, which had been one of the most energetic aspects of Carman before him. At about the same time also, Robert W. Service, who can be considered only as a visiting Englishman, produced his immensely popular synthetic ballads. The fame of these was to be equalled a little later, during the first World War, by John McCrae with his widely quoted lyric 'In Flanders Fields', published originally in *Punch*.

IV

In French poetry also, the decade of the nineties was a sort of 'golden age', and here its influence was to extend fruitfully into the two first decades of the new century. Beginning with the establishment in 1895 of the *École Littéraire de Montréal* the patriotic themes of the Quebec masters Crémazie and Fréchette were replaced by a more cosmopolitan emphasis on craftsmanship, personal emotion, and variety. The Montreal School was established by two young law students, Jean Charbonneau and Paul de Martigny, and regular meetings of poets, critics, scholars, and journalists were soon being held in the Château de Ramezay, the old head-

quarters of the French governors of Montreal. The proceed-
ings of some of the meetings and new work by the poets
belonging to the group were published in 1900, including also
a contribution by Fréchette, who was honoured if not imitated
by the succeeding generation. The new poets were inspired
in their experiments with form and in their more emotional
and original themes by the various poetic movements in
France, particularly Parnassianism and Symbolism. Among
these poets must be named Gonzalve Désaulniers, one of the
oldest, who much later, in 1930, turned back to the homely
task of depicting in brief realistic descriptions the scenes of his
native province; Charles Gill, the painter poet who planned
a series of ambitious descriptive and historical tableaux of the
river St. Lawrence; the critical and sceptical Charles Dantin;
the invalid Albert Lozeau; and the tragic figure of Émile
Nelligan. The last two made the most impressive and enduring
contribution to Canadian poetry.

From the age of eighteen Lozeau had been confined to his
bed with a form of spinal paralysis. Forced to relinquish any
attempt to interpret the life of his *beau pays Canadien*, which
he confessed he did not and could not know, he became instead
the poet of the closed-in life. With great elegance, charm, and
modesty—'Je suis resté neuf ans les pieds à la hauteur de la
tête', he wrote once, 'cela m'a enseigné l'humilité'—he
developed a narrow but pure talent for the inner life of sensi-
bility and reverie, which provided him with material for three
volumes of verse between 1907 and 1916.

The career of Émile Nelligan was briefer and more brilliant.
His poetry, which introduced Baudelairism and Verlainism
into the opening circles of the French-Canadian literary con-
sciousness, was hailed with enthusiasm by the poets and critics
of the Montreal School, and the reciting by the young poet
of his 'Romance du vin' at one of the *soirées* of the Château de

Ramezay was a memorable event. Technical virtuosity, aspirations of more than local scope, and a passionate, if feverish, sensibility combined to produce some of the finest poems ever written in Canada. A new, surprising, and, for French Canada, extremely salutary movement was being inaugurated at the moment it could be most useful, a movement that was at once aesthetic, passionate, cosmopolitan, and exotic, and that gave an immense impetus to the *other*, the non-native tradition in Canadian literature. It was later poets, however, Paul Morin and René Chopin particularly, who were to carry on the movement. Nelligan, like Chatterton or Rimbaud, was a marvellous boy, whose work was done before he reached twenty. In 1899 his mind collapsed, and though he did not die until 1941 he remained hopelessly insane, one of the most tragic figures in the history of North American letters.

One or two poets of lesser stature belonging to the Montreal School indicate almost as clearly as Lozeau and Nelligan the new winds that were blowing into the closed garden of Quebec culture. Louis Dantin, in such ambiguous poems as 'Noël intime', sounds the familiar note of religious scepticism, a scepticism, however, which is actually a painful, if inescapable, shadow of faith. Albert Ferland, who later, however, was to become a poet of the French-Canadian soil, wrote with bitter irony in 'La Patrie au poète' what amounts to a repudiation of the earlier school of patriotic poetry:

> Va, Barde primitif des vierges Laurentides,
> Va-t'en pleurer ton cœur comme un fou dans les bois,
> Fidèle au souvenir des héros d'autrefois,
> Tandis que l'or vainqueur fait les hommes avides!
>
> Poète, mon enfant, tu me chantes en vain.
> Je suis la Terre ingrate où rêva Crémazie;
> Célèbre si tu veux ma grave poésie;
> Mais pour toi, mon enfant, je n'aurai pas de pain!

INTRODUCTION

Joseph-Arthur Lapointe, at one time president of l'École de Montréal, produced in the nine lines of 'Les Pauvres' a poem of social indignation and pity worthy of Thomas Hardy. Paul Morin, who published two volumes, *Le Paon d'émail* in 1911 and *Poèmes de Cendre et d'Or* in 1922, was a leader of the aesthetic and exotic school. He had frequented the salon of la Comtesse de Noailles in Paris and had travelled in Greece, the Levant, and North Africa. His poetry was polished, brightly coloured, heavily jewelled, and with a Byzantine glitter that was in itself something of a criticism of the provincialism and piety of so much French-Canadian poetry. Morin was accused of dilettantism and coldness, of exoticism and paganism; but the perfection of his forms and the dedicated spirit of his devotion to art answered for him even more effectively than his own humble reply in the poem 'A ceux de mon pays'.

V

The modern movement in Canada began a little later in English poetry than in French, perhaps because it began in France before it did in England. The significant dates are the publication of E. J. Pratt's 'little epics', *The Witches' Brew* in 1925 and 'The Cachalot' and 'The Great Feud' in 1926. There was a great flurry of new poetry also in the magazines, particularly in the undergraduate journal *The McGill Fortnightly Review* (1925–7), which introduced the work of some of the poets who were later to become influential. Among them were A. M. Klein, Leo Kennedy, F. R. Scott, and A. J. M. Smith. These joined with the Toronto poet Robert Finch and the well-established Pratt to produce a group anthology, *New Provinces*, which did not appear, however, until 1936. The new poets themselves did not publish volumes until the early forties, when certain Toronto publishing houses suddenly became receptive to work in the modern manner, and the poetic revival which was to distinguish the forties and fifties was at last under way.

Of contemporary poets, the oldest and the first to be established, E. J. Pratt, has been the most ambitious, the most self-confident, and in some ways the most adventurous; and he has reached the widest audience. He is, with the exception of the younger West-Coast poet, Earle Birney, the only English-Canadian poet whose gift is mainly for narrative and who has created on a large scale. His main contribution has been a series of dynamic narrative poems, some fabulous, some heroic, some humorous, some historical, and some (during the war) topical, but all filled with vitality and power. Pratt was born in Newfoundland, and the sea and the rocky coast are in his blood. The poems of 1925 and 1926 are fantastic, fabulous, and humorous—miniature epics that dramatize man's struggle with nature or, in 'The Great Feud', tell of the suicidal war to extinction between monsters of the primeval slime. These narratives present a philosophical or quasi-religious attitude toward the problem of man's survival and of man's significance. They are essentially parables, but their success is due to the fact that the poet never stoops to moralize or allows his action to bog down in exposition: everything is concrete and active. During the thirties Pratt wrote two soberly realistic narratives, *The Roosevelt and the Antinoë* and *The Titanic*, and a compassionate 'novel in verse', *Brébeuf and His Brethren* (1940). Pratt's most recen work, *Towards the Last Spike*, is sub-titled 'a verse panorama of the building of the Canadian Pacific Railway'. The poem is a brilliantly original treatment of the theme that recurs frequently in Pratt's poetry—the theme of power and its analysis into factors of good and evil. The ironic solution to the conflict is that man triumphs over his antagonist, the

Laurentian Shield and the Rocky Mountains, by a fusion with it or a merging into it. Here, as in other poems, Pratt's attitude towards Power, whether natural, human, or demonic, is complex and ambiguous, and the emotions it arouses in him are ambiguous also—exaltation, terror, and ultimately compassion. The irony implicit in this attitude gives Pratt's poetry its intellectual tang; compassion humanizes it and gives it its final calm.

In his poems of the sea and the war Pratt has an affinity with Masefield and in his fantastic imaginative pieces with Roy Campbell. Although he is not well known outside Canada, in neither case need he fear the comparison. His very virtues, however, have tended to separate him from his younger contemporaries of the thirties and forties. His energy, enthusiasm, and faith, and the expansiveness of his good humour, are all somewhat alien to the divided and disillusioned spirit of the new generation.

Only one modern Canadian poet has shown a similar boldness and a similar ability to create on a large scale. He is Robert Choquette, who was born in 1905 and who launched his first volume *A travers les vents* in 1925 when Pratt was producing his earliest original work. Choquette repudiated the aestheticism of Nelligan and the exoticism of Paul Morin and cultivated instead, not a poetry of the soil or the village but a universal and emotional poetry that was to be at once national and filled with energy and thought.

Nous avons grandi [he wrote] parmi la nature la plus virile, la plus âpre, la plus pathétiquement sauvage que porte la terre; nos plaines, nos lacs, nos fleuves, nos forêts donnent le vertige aux imaginations européennes: nous sentons remuer dans nos corps la vigueur d'une race pleine de sève et vierge et neuve comme nos sapins verts; et voici qu'au lieu de chanter à pleins poumons des hymnes d'amour et d'enthousiasme, voici que nous apportous au peuple de petites soies fines ou des barres de métal poli.

Expressed thus rhetorically this enthusiasm does not sound very convincing. These are sentiments that might have been heard from the earliest of the patriotic and romantic Canadian poets and reviewers, English and French alike. Parallel quotations can be found in Standish O'Grady, Sangster, and Dr. Dewart, as well as in Garneau and Crémazie. But there is a difference. Choquette, a romantic though he may be, whose rhythms recall those of Hugo and Lamartine, is a child of the twentieth century, and it is a modern consciousness that expresses itself in his best and most ambitious poems *Metropolitan Museum* (1933) and the long and beautifully sustained *Suite marine* (1953).

VI

The modern spirit in Canadian poetry, indeed, has developed, as it has in Europe and the United States, in a progressive and orderly revolution. There was first a widening of the subject-matter of poetry to include all aspects of contemporary life, especially the homely, the familiar, and the urban, treated realistically or with irony. At the same time there was a simplification of poetic language and an expansion of its scope to include the colloquial and the ordinary. This was part of the worldwide reaction against the rhetoric of the nineteenth century and academic doctrines of poetic diction. The free-verse movement in France and imagism in England and America were part of this technical revolution. Influences which made for simplicity and inclusiveness were felt by all the serious Canadian poets after the First World War, and particularly by the writers of the native tradition. These were mainly poets who experienced the left-wing political impulses of the post-depression years and, among the French, young revivalists of the school of *le terroir*. Dorothy Livesay, Anne

INTRODUCTION

Marriott, and Earle Birney in the west, and Raymond Souster and Louis Dudek in Toronto and Montreal are representative of the poets of this school writing in English; Alfred Des-Rochers, particularly in the final edition of *A l'ombre d'Orford* (1948), is the best of its French adherents. Two poets somewhat older than any of these, W. W. E. Ross and Raymond Knister, who was drowned in 1932, represent this realistic and imagistic aspect of modernism more purely and with a narrower but possibly sharper vision. In any case, the accurately pinpointed and rigidly objective 'laconics' of Ross and the brief vivid farm poems of Knister have an originality and native flavour that is lacking in the work of more ambitious poets. Some of Knister's earliest poems and stories were published in *transition* under the editorship of Eugene Jolas, and Ross's work was admired by Marianne Moore and printed in *The Dial*.

The metaphysical revolution effected by Eliot was reflected as early as the mid-twenties by the English-speaking poets of a new 'Montreal school', Scott, Klein, Kennedy, and Smith, while the theories of T. E. Hulme and Ezra Pound had an invigorating effect on the whole community of new poets. The Jewish poet, Abraham Klein, has a unique and special interest that derives from more than the energy and spirited bravura of his technical achievements. He throws a surprising and penetrating light on the problem of nationalism—a problem that has remained unsolved from the beginning of Canadian literature. Klein is the most successful and intensely dedicated of national poets, but the nationalism that stirs him is not a Canadian but a Jewish nationalism. Steeped in the ancient lore and ritual of Judaism, he is a Jewish poet in the sense that Claudel was a Catholic poet, and while his first two volumes, *Hath not a Jew ...* (1940) and *Poems* (1944), concern themselves with the traditions and aspirations of his own people, his last book, *The Rocking Chair* (1948), is a brilliant and sympathetic interpretation of the province of Quebec. The patriarchal, ecclesiastical, and conservative structure of the French-speaking province, with its own language, its own laws, and its own religion, is something that his Hebraic conservatism envies and understands, though he has a bitter awareness also of the folly and racial intolerance that sometimes corrupt it.

The other poets of the group were more firmly committed to a cosmopolitan tradition, and sometimes with irony and sometimes with more uncomplicated emotions they assimilated the methods of the symbolists and the modern metaphysicals. During the war years of the forties poetry centred on little magazines in Montreal and on the West Coast, and the editors, the late John Sutherland, of *First Statement* and *Northern Review*, and Alan Crawley, of *Contemporary Verse*, deserve great credit for their part in the contemporary revival. Among the poets themselves, an Englishman, Patrick Anderson, was a dynamic and inspiring source of energy. He had come to Canada on a Commonwealth Fellowship from Oxford and became a Canadian citizen, working first as a schoolmaster in Montreal and later as a lecturer at McGill University. From 1940 to 1950 he remained in Montreal and in association with F. R. Scott, P. K. Page, Neufville Shaw, Bruce Ruddick, and others edited the experimental literary journal *Preview*. Anderson is a gifted and fluent writer. Adopting the manner now of Auden, now of Macneice, and now of Barker or Dylan Thomas, and inspired both by Marx and Freud, he turned his attention with refreshing gusto to the problem of Canadian identity. His 'Poem on Canada' (1946) has much that is individual and penetrating, while lyrics like 'Sleigh-ride' and 'Camp' indicate the influence of nature in Canada upon a sophisticated European sensibility. The most brilliant poet of the group, however, is Miss P. K. Page, whose sympathies are warmer than Anderson's and whose flair is psychological rather than political. Her style is characterized by subjective but exceedingly concrete images and witty conceits that sometimes are both verbal and visual. In 'The Stenographers', for instance, she looks into the harassed eyes of her fellow workers in a government office under war-time pressure, and expresses her sense of horror and breakdown in a characteristic conceit:

> In their eyes I have seen
> the pin-men of madness in marathon trim
> race round the track of the stadium pupil.

'I lie in the long *parenthesis* of arms', she writes in another poem, and achieves a conciseness and ambiguity that would please Mr. Empson, while in such poems as 'Man with One Small Hand' and 'Arras', strangeness and terror grow naturally out of the familiar, as they do in dreams.

There is a good deal of psychological subtlety in the work of all these English-Canadian poets of the forties and fifties, but for spiritual insight we must turn to two of their French compatriots, Saint-Denys-Garneau, a descendant of Canada's first historian, and his cousin, Anne Hébert. Saint-Denys-Garneau, who was born in 1916 and died in 1943, was the master of an abstract and symbolic poetry that mirrors a metaphysical anguish. The poems in his *Régards et jeux dans l'espace* (1938), though they have an affinity with the *method* of Rimbaud and recall sometimes the *subject* of Rilke or Kafka, are nevertheless quite individual and original. Their unifying theme is the problem of responsibility and guilt. The perceptions of childhood, of nature, and finally of death and nothingness are explored in an effort to recover lost innocence. Anne Hébert is perhaps less adventurous, but her sensibility and her style are even purer, if that is possible.

xlviii

INTRODUCTION

Her poems collected in *Les Songes en équilibre* (1942) and *Le Tombeau des rois* (1953) deal also with childhood, loneliness, memory, and death. They show an awareness that sometimes approaches mysticism. Solitude, reverie, and the enclosed life are valued in their personal aspect. In some of her poems, however, notably 'Vie de Château', she expresses a sense of the stifling atmosphere created by the enclosed, backward-looking, ancestor-worshipping, earthbound spirit of French-Canadian nationalism. It is a new and more critical attitude that is replacing the patriotic and religious poetry of the school of *le terroir* in the work of the French poets of the forties and fifties. Sometimes the transcending of provincial limitations is found in the cosmopolitan modernism of the technique rather than explicitly in the subject-matter—Pierre Trottier's 'Femme aux couleurs de mon pays' is a good illustration of this—and certain poets, notably Alain Grandbois, have introduced the methods of surrealism into Canadian poetry. His 'Fermons l'armoire' is explicit enough in its rejection of the old spirit, and so are the later poems of François Hertel, a Jesuit priest who, having for a number of years in the late thirties and forties exercised a considerable influence as poet, critic, and editor, underwent a spiritual crisis, came to doubt his vocation and even his faith, and exiled himself to France, a colonial, a hopeless outsider, proclaiming himself in his prose memoirs a new *Canadien errant*, 'porc parmi les porcs'. Of the many young French poets of the new cosmopolitanism Gilles Hénault, Roland Giguère, and Jean-Guy Pilon may be allowed to represent the adventurousness of style and the resolute seeking for a new faith to replace the old, no longer satisfying, objects of respect.

A somewhat similar progression can be seen in the poetry of the English-Canadians, though the story is less one of definable literary movements than the simultaneous emergence of a number of brilliant and independent talents. The poetic revival of the forties was continued throughout the fifties without diminution. Perhaps the most striking figure of the new decade was Irving Layton. A holdover from the early days of *First Statement* and *Northern Review*, Layton had written a series of shrill and strident volumes of left-wing poetry and had had some success in shocking the bourgeoisie with the verbal frankness of his love poems and social satires. But with the publication in 1954 of *In the Midst of my Fever*, and of *The Cold Green Element* in 1955, he suddenly revealed himself as one of the most original poets of his generation in North America. The self-confidence that looked like arrogance in the early verse and the savage indignation that had looked like mere contempt had here ripened and grown sharp and relevant. The qualities that distinguish the later poems—and that won the praise of William Carlos Williams, whom along with Whitman, Blake, Lawrence, and the Hebrew prophets Layton looks upon as a master—are both technical and what one must not be afraid to call spiritual. Our pleasure in such a poem as 'The Cold Green Element', for instance, depends on many things: the elegance of the writing, the neatness of the stanza pattern, the emotional variety and energy, and the myth-making creativeness that draws its materials as easily from drugstore shelves as from the myth of Orpheus.

It is the fusion of the modern world with the archetypal patterns of myth and psychology rather than with Christianity or patriotism that gives a characteristic cosmopolitan flavour to much of the poetry of the fifties in Canada. We find various aspects of such a fusion in the exotic and deceptively innocent infantilism of James Reaney, in the metaphysical intensity of Anne Wilkinson's revitalization of ballad and pastoral, in the gnomic suggestiveness of Jay Macpherson's finely chiselled lyrics, and in the toughness of mind and tenderness of spirit revealed in Margaret Avison's difficult poetry. The themes that engage these writers are not local or even national; they are cosmopolitan and, indeed, universal. The bewildering multiplicity of scientific, moral, and metaphysical data with which the poet must now come to terms, and the burden of guilt, fancied or real, which the disintegration of values in religion, politics, and morals places on his unsupported shoulders, make it very difficult, if not impossible, for him to be anything but complex, divided, erudite, allusive, and sometimes obscure. These, of course, are the characteristics of modernity in the poetry of Europe and the United States as well as of Canada. But the Canadian poet has one advantage—an advantage that derives from his position of separateness and semi-isolation. He can draw upon French, British, and American sources in language and literary convention; at the same time he enjoys a measure of detachment that enables him to select and adapt what is relevant and useful. This gives to contemporary Canadian poetry in either language a distinctive quality—its eclectic detachment. This can be, and has been, a defect of timidity and mediocrity; but it can also be, as it is hoped this book will show, a virtue of intelligence and discrimination.

A. J. M. SMITH

ACKNOWLEDGEMENTS

An *Oxford Book of Canadian Verse* edited by Wilfred Campbell was published in 1912, but it has long since been out of date and out of print; and it contained nothing in French. More than two-thirds of the poems in the present volume, indeed, have been written since the first *Oxford Book* appeared.

It is a pleasure to acknowledge the assistance that was generously given by a number of authorities and friends. With the difficult task of choosing the French poems I was helped by the advice of Mr. Guy Sylvestre, of the Parliamentary Library, Ottawa, whose *Anthologie de la poésie canadienne d'expression française* has become a classic, and of W. E. Collin, professor of Romance Languages at the University of Western Ontario. Mr. F. R. Scott read the Introduction, while Professors Malcolm Ross and Northrop Frye gave me the benefit of their taste and learning in a number of pleasant conversations. My colleague Professor Georges Joyaux was of help with a number of textual problems. I have been fortunate in having the assistance of my wife, not only in reading proofs but in selecting the poems. I must hasten to add, however, that all the errors of judgement, lapses of taste, and sins of omission that no anthologist can hope entirely to escape are mine alone.

A. J. M. S.

ACKNOWLEDGEMENTS

Thanks for permission to include copyright poems by the following authors are due to the copyright-holders listed:

PATRICK ANDERSON: Mr. Anderson and The Ryerson Press.

MARGARET AVISON: Miss Avison.

ALFRED GOLDSWORTHY BAILEY: McClelland and Stewart Limited.

NÉRÉE BEAUCHEMIN: Mr. Germain Beauchemin.

EARLE BIRNEY: Dr. Birney and The Ryerson Press.

ARTHUR S. BOURINOT: Mr. Bourinot.

ELIZABETH BREWSTER: Miss Brewster.

CHARLES BRUCE: The Macmillan Company of Canada Limited.

WILFRED CAMPBELL: The Ryerson Press.

BLISS CARMAN: The University of New Brunswick, McClelland and Stewart Limited, and Dodd, Mead and Company, New York.

RENÉ CHOPIN: Mr. Bernard Moore.

ROBERT CHOQUETTE: Mr. Choquette.

LEONARD COHEN: Mr. Cohen.

ROY DANIELLS: McClelland and Stewart Limited.

GONZALVE DESAULNIERS: Librairie Beauchemin Limitée, Montreal.

ALFRED DESROCHERS: La Corporation des Éditions Fides, Montreal.

KILDARE DOBBS: Mr. Dobbs.

LOUIS DUDEK: Mr. Dudek and The Ryerson Press.

ROBERT FINCH: Mr. Finch, McClelland and Stewart Limited, and the Oxford University Press, Canadian Branch.

SAINT-DENYS-GARNEAU: La Corporation des Éditions Fides, Montreal.

ROLAND GIGUÈRE: Mr. Giguère.

JOHN GLASSCO: Mr. Glassco and McClelland and Stewart Limited.

RALPH GUSTAFSON: Mr. Gustafson.

liv

ACKNOWLEDGEMENTS

RONALD HAMBLETON: The Ryerson Press.

ANNE HÉBERT: Miss Hébert.

GILLES HÉNAULT: Mr. Hénault and Les Éditions Erta, Montreal.

FRANÇOIS HERTEL: Mr. Hertel.

DARYL HINE: Mr. Hine.

LEO KENNEDY: Mr. Kennedy.

A. M. KLEIN: Mr. Klein and The Ryerson Press.

RAYMOND KNISTER: The Ryerson Press.

FREDERICK E. LAIGHT: Mr. Laight.

RINA LASNIER: Miss Lasnier.

IRVING LAYTON: Mr. Layton.

PAMPHILE LEMAY: Miss Cécile Saint-Jorre.

DOUGLAS LE PAN: Chatto and Windus Limited, London.

KENNETH LESLIE: The Ryerson Press.

NORMAN LEVINE: Mr. Levine.

DOROTHY LIVESAY: The Ryerson Press.

MALCOLM LOWRY: Mrs. Lowry.

J. E. H. MACDONALD: The Ryerson Press.

TOM MACINNES: The Ryerson Press.

L. A. MACKAY: Mr. Mackay and The Ryerson Press.

JAY MACPHERSON: The Oxford University Press, Canadian Branch.

CHARLES MAIR: The Ryerson Press.

E. W. MANDEL: Dr. Mandel.

ANNE MARRIOTT: the author.

JOHN MCCRAE: the Proprietors of *Punch*, London.

FLORIS CLARK MCLAREN: Mrs. McLaren.

ÉMILE NELLIGAN: Mr. Maurice Corbeil.

P. K. PAGE: the author and McClelland and Stewart Limited.

MARJORIE PICKTHALL: McClelland and Stewart Limited.

JEAN-GUY PILON: Mr. Pilon.

E. J. PRATT: The Macmillan Company of Canada Limited and Alfred A. Knopf, Inc., New York

ACKNOWLEDGEMENTS

JAMES REANEY: the author's representatives and The Macmillan Company of Canada Limited.

MYRA VON RIEDEMANN: Miss von Riedemann.

SIR CHARLES G. D. ROBERTS: The Ryerson Press.

THEODORE GOODRIDGE ROBERTS: The Ryerson Press.

W. W. E. ROSS: Mr. Ross.

SIMONE ROUTIER: Miss Routier.

DUNCAN CAMPBELL SCOTT: McClelland and Stewart Limited and The Ryerson Press.

F. R. SCOTT: Mr. Scott and The Ryerson Press.

FREDERICK GEORGE SCOTT: Mr. F. R. Scott.

A. J. M. SMITH: Mr. Smith, Michigan State University Press, and The Ryerson Press.

KAY SMITH: Miss Smith.

RAYMOND SOUSTER: Mr. Souster.

HEATHER SPEARS: The author.

PIERRE TROTTIER: Les Éditions de l'Hexagone.

MIRIAM WADDINGTON: The Ryerson Press.

BERTRAM WARR: Mrs. B. H. Warr.

WILFRED WATSON: Faber and Faber Limited, London, and Farrar, Straus, and Cudahy, Inc., New York.

PHYLLIS WEBB: Miss Webb and McClelland and Stewart Limited.

ANNE WILKINSON: Mrs. Wilkinson and The Macmillan Company of Canada Limited.

There are a few poems whose copyright owners have not been located after diligent inquiry. The publishers would be grateful for information enabling them to make suitable acknowledgements in future editions.

STANDISH O'GRADY

1793–1841

I

From *The Emigrant*

[*Winter in Lower Canada*]

Thou barren waste; unprofitable strand,
Where hemlocks brood on unproductive land,
Whose frozen air on one bleak winter's night
Can metamorphose *dark brown hares to white!*

Here forests crowd, unprofitable lumber,
O'er fruitless lands indefinite as number;
Where birds scarce light, and with the north winds veer
On wings of wind, and quickly disappear,
Here the rough Bear subsists his winter year,
And licks his paw and finds *no better fare.*

.   .   .

One month we hear birds, shrill and loud and harsh,
The plaintive bittern sounding from the marsh;
The next we see the fleet-winged swallow,
The duck, the woodcock, and the ice-birds follow;
Then comes drear clime, the lakes all stagnant grow,
And the wild wilderness is rapt in snow.

The lank Canadian eager trims his fire,
And all around their simpering stoves retire;
With fur-clad friends their progenies abound,
And thus regale their buffaloes around;
Unlettered race, how few the number tells,
Their only pride a *cariole and bells!*

To mirth or mourning, thus by folly led,
To mix in pleasure or to chaunt the dead!
To seek the chapel prostrate to adore,
Or leave their fathers' coffins at the door!
Perchance they revel; still around they creep,
And talk, and smoke, and spit, and drink, and sleep!

.   .   .

With sanguine sash and eke with Indian's mogs,
Let Frenchmen feed on fricassees or frogs;
Brave Greenland winters, seven long months to freeze,
With naught of verdure save their Greenland trees;
Bright veiled amid the drapery of night,
In ice-wrought tapestry of gorgeous white,
No matter here in this sad soil who delves;
Still leave their *lower province* to themselves.

2   *Old Nick in Sorel*

Old Nick took a fancy, as many men tell,
To come for a winter to live in Sorel.
Yet the snow fell so deep as he came in his sleigh,
That his fingers and toes were frost-nipt on the way.

In truth, saith the demon, who'd ever suppose,
I must go back again with the loss of all those;
In either extreme, sure it matters me not,
If I freeze upon earth or at home I'm too hot;

So he put back his sleigh, for he thought it amiss,
His clime to compare to a climate like this;
And now 'tis resolved that this frightful new-comer
Will winter in hell and be here in the summer.

OLIVER GOLDSMITH

1794–1861

From *The Rising Village*

3

(i)

What noble courage must their hearts have fired,
How great the ardour which their souls inspired,
Who, leaving far behind their native plain,
Have sought a home beyond the western main;
And braved the terrors of the stormy seas,
In search of wealth, of freedom, and of ease!
Oh! none can tell but they who sadly share
The bosom's anguish, and its wild despair,
What dire distress awaits the hardy bands
That venture first on bleak and desert lands;
How great the pain, the danger, and the toil
Which mark the first rude culture of the soil.
When, looking round, the lonely settler sees
His home amid a wilderness of trees:
How sinks his heart in those deep solitudes,
Where not a voice upon his ear intrudes;
Where solemn silence all the waste pervades,
Heightening the horror of its gloomy shades.

4

(ii)

Not fifty summers yet have passed thy clime—
How short a period in the page of time—
Since savage tribes, with terror in their train,
Rushed o'er thy fields, and ravaged all thy plain.
But some few years have rolled in haste away
Since, through thy vales, the fearless beast of prey,
With dismal yell and loud appalling cry,
Proclaimed his midnight reign of terror nigh.

And now how changed the scene! the first afar
Have fled to wilds beneath the northern star;
The last has learned to shun man's dreaded eye,
And, in his turn, to distant regions fly.
While the poor peasant, whose laborious care
Scarce from the soil could wring his scanty fare,
Now in the peaceful arts of culture skilled,
Sees his wide barn with ample treasures filled;
Now finds his dwelling, as the year goes round,
Beyond his hopes, with joy and plenty crowned.

5   (*iii*)

How sweet it is, at first approach of morn,
Before the silvery dew has left the lawn,
When warring winds are sleeping yet on high,
Or breathe as softly as the bosom's sigh,
To gain some easy hill's ascending height
Where all the landscape brightens with delight,
And boundless prospects stretched on every side
Proclaim the country's industry and pride.
Here the broad marsh extends its open plain,
Until its limits touch the distant main;
There verdant meads along the uplands spring,
And grateful odours to the breezes fling;
Here crops of grain in rich luxuriance rise,
And wave their golden riches to the skies;
There smiling orchards interrupt the scene
Of gardens bounded by some fence of green;
The farmer's cottage, bosomed 'mong the trees,
Whose spreading branches shelter from the breeze;
The winding stream that turns the busy mill,
Whose clanking echoes o'er the distant hill;

OLIVER GOLDSMITH

The neat white church beside whose wall are spread
The grass-clad hillocks of the sacred dead,
Where rude-cut stones or painted tablets tell,
In laboured verse, how youth and beauty fell;
How worth and hope were hurried to the grave,
And torn from those who had no power to save.

SUSANNA MOODIE

1803–1885

6   *The Canadian Herd-Boy*

A SONG OF THE BACKWOODS

Through the deep woods, at peep of day,
The careless herd-boy wends his way,
By piny ridge and forest stream,
To summon home his roving team:
Cobos! Cobos! from distant dell
Sly echo wafts the cattle-bell.

A blithe reply he whistles back,
And follows out the devious track,
O'er fallen tree and mossy stone,
A path to all save him unknown:
Cobos! Cobos! far down the dell
More faintly falls the cattle-bell.

See, the dark swamp before him throws
A tangled maze of cedar boughs;
On all around deep silence broods
In Nature's boundless solitudes:
Cobos! Cobos! the breezes swell
As nearer floats the cattle-bell.

He sees them now; beneath yon trees
His motley herd recline at ease;
With lazy pace and sullen stare
They slowly leave their shady lair:
Cobos! Cobos! far up the dell
Quick jingling comes the cattle-bell.

W. F. HAWLEY

1804–1855

A Love Song

Yes, I will love thee when the sun
  Throws light upon a thousand flowers;
When winter's biting breath is gone,
  And spring leads on the smiling hours.
And I will call thee beautiful—
  More beautiful than May's bright wreaths—
Tho' all the air with sweets be full,
  Tho' every bird his soft tone breathes.

And I will love thee when the earth
  Is bright with summer's rich attire;
When morn to seas of gold gives birth,
  And eve to brighter wreaths of fire;
When the broad moon and burning stars
  Are riding thro' the lucid air
On snow-white fleecy clouds for cars—
  Then will I dream of thee, my fair!

I'll love thee when the autumn winds
  Sweep heavily the misty plain;
When the last flower its cold bed finds,
  And birds are far away again:

W. F. HAWLEY

When the last pale and withered leaf
    Along the swollen stream floats on—
One thought of thee shall give relief,
    Tho' bright and lovely things are gone.

And I will shield thee when the breath
    Of winter beats upon the earth;
And we will laugh at nature's death,
    Content with love and festive mirth.
The tale and sportive song shall be
    Only of soft and fairy things;
Young Love shall rest with us, and we
    Will give old Time his silken wings.

CHARLES HEAVYSEGE

1816–1876

From *Saul*

8   *[Zaph Describes the Haunts of Malzah]*

The Jewish king now walks at large and sound,
Yet of our emissary Malzah hear we nothing:
Go now, sweet spirit, and, if need be, seek
This world all over for him:—find him out,
Be he within the bounds of earth and hell.
He is a most erratic spirit, so
May give thee trouble (as I give thee time)
To find him, for he may be now diminished,
And at the bottom of some silken flower,
Wherein, I know, he loves, when evening comes,
To creep, and lie all night, encanopied
Beneath the manifold and scented petals;

7

Fancying, he says, he bids the world adieu,
And is again a slumberer in heaven:
Or, in some other vein, perchance thou'lt find him
Within the walls or dens of some famed city.
Give thou a general search, in open day,
I' the town and country's ample field; and next
Seek him in dusky cave, and in dim grot;
And in the shadow of the precipice,
Prone or supine extended motionless;
Or, in the twilight of o'erhanging leaves,
Swung at the nodding arm of some vast beech.
By moonlight seek him on the mount, at noon
In the translucent waters salt or fresh;
Or near the dank-marged fountain, or clear well,
Watching the tadpole thrive on suck of venom;
Or where the brook runs o'er the stones, and smooths
Their green locks with its current's crystal comb.
Seek him in rising vapours, and in clouds
Crimson or dun; and often on the edge
Of the grey morning and of tawny eve;
Search in the rocky alcove and woody bower;
And in the crows'-nest look, and into every
Pilgrim-crowd-drawing Idol, wherein he
Is wont to sit in darkness and be worshipped.
If thou shouldst find him not in these, search for him
By the lone melancholy tarns of bitterns;
And in the embosomed dells, whereunto maidens
Resort to bathe within the tepid pool.
Look specially there, and, if thou seest peeping
Satyr or fawn, give chase and call out 'Malzah!'

CHARLES HEAVYSEGE

[Malzah's Song]

There was a devil and his name was I;
From out Profundus he did cry:
He changed his note as he changed his coat,
And his coat was of a varying dye.
It had many a hue: in hell 'twas blue,
'Twas green i' the sea, and white i' the sky.
O, do not ask me, ask me why
'Twas green i' the sea, and white i' the sky;
Why from Profundus he did cry:
Suffice that he wailed with a chirruping note,
And quaintly cut was his motley coat.—

I have forgot the rest. Would I could sleep;
Would I could sleep away an age or so,
And let Saul work out his own weal or woe:
All that I ask is to be let alone.

O, to be let alone! to be let alone!
To laugh if I list; if I list to groan;
Despairing, yet knowing God's anger o'erblown.
O, why should God trouble me?
Why should he double my
Sorrow, pursuing me when he has thrown
Me out of his favour? O, why should he labour
Down lower ever thrusting me into hell's zone?
O let me alone! O let me alone!
O leave me, Creator, Tormentor, alone!

10   *The Winter Galaxy*

The stars are glittering in the frosty sky,
Frequent as pebbles on a broad sea-coast,
And o'er the vault the cloud-like galaxy
Has marshalled its innumerable host.
Alive all heaven seems! with wondrous glow
Tenfold refulgent every star appears,
As if some wide, celestial gale did blow,
And thrice illume the ever-kindled spheres.
Orbs, with glad orbs rejoicing, burning, beam,
Ray-crowned, with lambent lustre in their zones,
Till o'er the blue, bespangled spaces seem
Angels and great archangels on their thrones;
A host divine, whose eyes are sparkling gems,
And forms more bright than diamond diadems.

11   *Night*

'Tis solemn darkness; the sublime of shade;
Night, by no stars nor rising moon relieved;
The awful blank of nothingness arrayed,
O'er which my eyeballs roll in vain, deceived.
Upward, around, and downward I explore,
E'en to the frontiers of the ebon air;
But cannot, though I strive, discover more
Than what seems one huge cavern of despair.
Oh, Night, art thou so grim, when, black and bare
Of moonbeams, and no cloudlets to adorn,
Like a nude Ethiop 'twixt two houris fair,
Thou stand'st between the evening and the morn?
I took thee for an angel, but have wooed
A cacodæmon in mine ignorant mood.

ALEXANDER McLACHLAN

1818–1896

From *The Emigrant*

[*Song*]

Old England is eaten by knaves,
  Yet her heart is all right at the core,
May she ne'er be the mother of slaves,
  Nor a foreign foe land on her shore.

I love my own country and race,
  Nor lightly I fled from them both,
Yet who would remain in a place
  Where there's too many spoons for the broth?

The squire's preserving his game.
  He says that God gave it to him,
And he'll banish the poor without shame,
  For touching a feather or limb.

The Justice he feels very big,
  And boasts what the law can secure,
But has two different laws in his wig,
  Which he keeps for the rich and the poor.

The Bishop he preaches and prays,
  And talks of a heavenly birth,
But somehow, for all that he says,
  He grabs a good share of the earth.

Old England is eaten by knaves,
  Yet her heart is all right at the core,
May she ne'er be the mother of slaves,
  Nor a foreign foe land on her shore.

13   ## *We Live in a Rickety House*

We live in a rickety house,
  In a dirty dismal street,
Where the naked hide from day,
  And thieves and drunkards meet.

And pious folks with their tracts,
  When our dens they enter in,
They point to our shirtless backs,
  As the fruits of beer and gin.

And they quote us texts to prove
  That our hearts are hard as stone,
And they feed us with the fact
  That the fault is all our own.

It will be long ere the poor
  Will learn their grog to shun
While it's raiment, food and fire,
  And religion all in one.

I wonder some pious folks
  Can look us straight in the face,
For our ignorance and crime
  Are the Church's shame and disgrace.

We live in a rickety house,
  In a dirty dismal street,
Where the naked hide from day,
  And thieves and drunkards meet.

1822–1893

14   From *The St. Lawrence and the
Saguenay*

[*The Thousand Islands*]

The bark leaps love-fraught from the land; the sea
Lies calm before us. Many an isle is there,
Clad with soft verdure; many a stately tree
Uplifts its leafy branches through the air;
The amorous current bathes the islets fair,
As we skip, youth-like, o'er the limpid waves;
White cloudlets speck the golden atmosphere,
Through which the passionate sun looks down, and graves
His image on the pearls that boil from the deep caves,

And bathe the vessel's prow. Isle after isle
Is passed, as we glide tortuously through
The opening vistas, that uprise and smile
Upon us from the ever-changing view.
Here nature, lavish of her wealth, did strew
Her flocks of panting islets on the breast
Of the admiring River, where they grew,
Like shapes of Beauty, formed to give a zest
To the charmed mind, like waking Visions of the Blest.

The silver-sinewed arms of the proud Lake,
Love-wild, embrace each islet tenderly,
The zephyrs kiss the flowers when they wake
At morn, flushed with a rare simplicity;
See how they bloom around yon birchen tree,
And smile along the bank, by the sandy shore,
In lovely groups—a fair community!
The embossed rocks glitter like golden ore,
And here, the o'erarching trees form a fantastic bower.

Red walls of granite rise on either hand,
Rugged and smooth; a proud young eagle soars
Above the stately evergreens, that stand
Like watchful sentinels on these God-built towers;
And near yon beds of many coloured flowers
Browse two majestic deer, and at their side
A spotted fawn all innocently cowers;
In the rank brushwood it attempts to hide,
While the strong-antlered stag steps forth with lordly stride,

And slakes his thirst, undaunted, at the stream.
Isles of o'erwhelming beauty! surely here
The wild enthusiast might live, and dream
His life away. No Nymphic trains appear,
To charm the pale Ideal Worshipper
Of Beauty; nor Neriads from the deeps below;
Nor hideous Gnomes, to fill the breast with fear:
But crystal streams through endless landscapes flow,
And o'er the clustering Isles the softest breezes blow.

.   .   .

And now 'tis Night. A myriad stars have come
To cheer the earth, and sentinel the skies.
The full-orbed moon irradiates the gloom,
And fills the air with light. Each Islet lies
Immersed in shadow, soft as thy dark eyes;
Swift through the sinuous path our vessel glides,
Now hidden by the massive promontories,
Anon the bubbling silver from its sides
Spurning, like a wild bird, whose home is on the tides.

Here Nature holds her Carnival of Isles.
Steeped in warm sunlight all the merry day,
Each nodding tree and floating greenwood smiles,
And moss-crowned monsters move in grim array;

All night the Fisher spears his finny prey;
The piney flambeaux reddening the deep,
Past the dim shores, or up some mimic bay:
Like grotesque banditti they boldly sweep
Upon the startled prey, and stab them while they sleep.

Many a tale of legendary lore
Is told of these romantic Isles. The feet
Of the Red Man have pressed each wave-zoned shore,
And many an eye of beauty oft did greet
The painted warriors and their birchen fleet,
As they returned with trophies of the slain.
That race has passed away; their fair retreat
In its primeval loneness smiles again,
Save where some vessel snaps the isle-enwoven chain:

Save where the echo of the huntsman's gun
Startles the wild duck from some shallow nook,
Or the swift hounds' deep baying, as they run,
Rouses the lounging student from his book;
Or where, assembled by some sedgy brook,
A pic-nic party, resting in the shade,
Spring pleasedly to their feet, to catch a look
At the strong steamer, through the watery glade
Ploughing, like a huge serpent from its ambuscade.

15   From *Pleasant Memories*

         [*The Meadow-Field*]

Do you remember the meadow-field,
Where the red-ripe strawberries lay concealed,
Close to the roots of the scented grass,
That bowed to let the sunbeams pass

To smile on the buttercups clustering over
The drooping heads of honied clover?
Or the golden dandelions, milky-stemmed,
With which the spring fields were begemmed?
Do you remember the hawthorn hedge,
 In its virginal bloom
 Breathing perfume
Far along the water-worn ledge;
The crows, with their signals of raven-like caws,
Like Ethiope sentinels over the haws?
 The wild roses flinging
 Their sweets to the breeze,
 While perched on the trees
 The sparrow sat, singing
Its plain, homely melody, and the brown thrush
Flung mellowy peals from thickets of rush,
As the blackbird piped from his vocal throat
His one soft-syllabled, graceful note?
 Gentlier breezes never blew,
 Lovelier roses never grew,
 Honeysuckles nowhere ever
 Had a more delicious flavour,
 Never hedge that ever budded
 Was more delicately studded,
 Never buttercups more yellow,
 Clover sweeter or more mellow,
 Than along this bank of flowers . . .
  Mary, do you remember?

16   *Un Canadien errant*

1838

Un Canadien errant,
Banni de ses foyers,
Parcourait en pleurant
Des pays étrangers.

Un jour, triste et pensif,
Assis au bord des flots,
Au courant fugitif
Il adressa ces mots:

'Si tu vois mon pays,
Mon pays malheureux,
Va, dis à mes amis
Que je me souviens d'eux.

' Ô jours si pleins d'appas,
Vous êtes disparus,
Et ma patrie, hélas!
Je ne la verrai plus.

'Non, mais en expirant,
Ô mon cher Canada,
Mon regard languissant
Vers toi se portera.'

17   From *Le Drapeau de Carillon*

Pensez-vous quelquefois à ces temps glorieux,
Où seuls, abandonnés par la France, leur mère,
Nos aïeux défendaient son nom victorieux
Et voyaient devant eux fuir l'armée étrangère?
Regrettez-vous encor ces jours de Carillon,
Où, sous le drapeau blanc enchaînant la victoire,
Nos pères se couvraient d'un immortel renom,
Et traçaient de leur glaive une héroïque histoire?

Regrettez-vous ces jours où, lâchement vendus
Par le faible Bourbon qui régnait sur la France,
Les héros canadiens, trahis, mais non vaincus,
Contre un joug ennemi se trouvaient sans défense?
D'une grande épopée ô triste et dernier chant
Où la voix de Lévis retentissait sonore,
Plein de hautes leçons, ton souvenir touchant
Dans nos cœurs oublieux sait-il régner encore?

Montcalm était tombé comme tombe un héros,
Enveloppant sa mort dans un rayon de gloire,
Au lieu même où le chef des conquérants nouveaux,
Wolfe, avait rencontré la mort et la victoire.
Dans un effort suprême en vain nos vieux soldats
Cueillaient sous nos remparts des lauriers inutiles;
Car un roi sans honneur avait livré leurs bras,
Sans donner un regret à leurs plaintes stériles.

. . . .

Sur les champs refroidis jetant son manteau blanc,
Décembre était venu. Voyageur solitaire,
Un homme s'avançait d'un pas faible et tremblant
Aux bords du lac Champlain. Sur sa figure austère

OCTAVE CRÉMAZIE

Une immense douleur avait posé sa main.
Gravissant lentement la route qui s'incline,
De Carillon bientôt il prenait le chemin,
Puis enfin s'arrêtait sur la haute colline.

Là, dans le sol glacé fixant un étendard,
Il déroulait au vent les couleurs de la France.
Planant sur l'horizon, son triste et long regard
Semblait trouver des lieux chéris de son enfance.
Sombre et silencieux il pleura bien longtemps,
Comme on pleure au tombeau d'une mère adorée.
Puis à l'écho sonore envoyant ses accents,
Sa voix jeta le cri de son âme éplorée:

'Ô Carillon, je te revois encore,
Non plus, hélas! comme en ces jours bénis
Où dans tes murs la trompette sonore
Pour te sauver nous avait réunis.
Je viens à toi, quand mon âme succombe
Et sent déjà son courage faiblir.
Oui, près de toi, venant chercher ma tombe,
Pour mon drapeau je viens ici mourir.

'Mes compagnons, d'une vaine espérance
Berçant encor leurs cœurs toujours français,
Les yeux tournés du côté de la France,
Diront souvent: reviendront-ils jamais?
L'illusion consolera leur vie;
Moi, sans espoir, quand mes jours vont finir,
Et sans entendre une parole amie,
Pour mon drapeau je viens ici mourir.

'Cet étendard qu'au grand jour des batailles,
Noble Montcalm, tu plaças dans ma main,
Cet étendard qu'aux portes de Versailles,
Naguère, hélas! je déployais en vain,
Je le remets aux champs où de la gloire
Vivra toujours l'immortel souvenir,
Et dans ma tombe emportant ta mémoire,
Pour mon drapeau je viens ici mourir.

'Qu'ils sont heureux ceux qui dans la mêlée
Près de Lévis moururent en soldats!
En expirant, leur âme consolée
Voyait la gloire adoucir leur trépas.
Vous qui dormez dans votre froide bière,
Vous que j'implore à mon dernier soupir,
Réveillez-vous! Apportant ma bannière,
Sur vos tombeaux, je viens ici mourir. . . .'

18   *Les Morts*

III

Quand le doux rossignol a quitté les bocages,
Quand le ciel gris d'automne, amassant ses nuages,
Prépare le linceul que l'hiver doit jeter
Sur les champs refroidis, il est un jour austère
Où nos cœurs, oubliant les vains soins de la terre,
Sur ceux qui ne sont plus aiment à méditer.

C'est le jour où les morts, abandonnant leurs tombes,
Comme on voit s'envoler de joyeuses colombes,
S'échappent un instant de leurs froides prisons;
En nous apparaissant, ils n'ont rien qui repousse;
Leur aspect est rêveur et leur figure est douce,
Et leur œil fixe et creux n'a pas de trahisons.

OCTAVE CRÉMAZIE

Quand ils viennent ainsi, quand leur regard contemple
La foule qui pour eux implore dans le temple
La clémence du ciel, un éclair de bonheur,
Pareil au pur rayon qui brille sur l'opale,
Vient errer un instant sur leur front calme et pâle,
Et dans leur cœur glacé verse un peu de chaleur.

Tous les élus du ciel, toutes les âmes saintes,
Qui portent leur fardeau sans murmure et sans plaintes
Et marchent tout le jour sous le regard de Dieu,
Dorment toute la nuit sous la garde des anges,
Sans que leur œil troublé de visions étranges
Aperçoive en rêvant des abîmes de feu;

Tous ceux dont le cœur pur n'écoute sur la terre
Que les échos du ciel, qui rendent moins amère
La douloureuse voie où l'homme doit marcher,
Et, des biens d'ici-bas reconnaissant le vide,
Déroulent leur vertu comme un tapis splendide,
Et marchent sur le mal sans jamais le toucher;

Quand les hôtes plaintifs de la cité dolente,
Qu'en un rêve sublime entrevit le vieux Dante,
Paraissent parmi nous en ce jour solennel,
Ce n'est que pour ceux-là. Seuls ils peuvent entendre
Les secrets de la tombe. Eux seuls savent comprendre
Ces pâles mendiants qui demandent le ciel.

Les cantiques sacrés du barde de Solyme,
Accompagnant de Job la tristesse sublime,
Au fond du sanctuaire éclatent en sanglots;
Et le son de l'airain, plein de sombres alarmes,
Jette son glas funèbre et demande des larmes
Pour les spectres errants, nombreux comme les flots.

OCTAVE CRÉMAZIE

Donnez donc, en ce jour où l'Église pleurante
Fait entendre pour eux une plainte touchante;
Pour calmer vos regrets, peut-être vos remords,
Donnez, du souvenir ressuscitant la flamme,
Une fleur à la tombe, une prière à l'âme,
Ces doux parfums du ciel qui consolent les morts.

Priez pour vos amis, priez pour votre mère,
Qui vous fit d'heureux jours dans cette vie amère,
Pour les parts de vos cœurs dormant dans les tombeaux.
Hélas! tous ces objets de vos jeunes tendresses
Dans leur étroit cercueil n'ont plus d'autres caresses
Que les baisers du ver qui dévore leurs os.

Priez pour l'exilé, qui, loin de sa patrie,
Expira sans entendre une parole amie;
Isolé dans sa vie, isolé dans sa mort,
Personne ne viendra donner une prière,
L'aumône d'une larme à la tombe étrangère:
Qui pense à l'inconnu qui sous la terre dort?

Priez encor pour ceux dont les âmes blessées
Ici-bas n'ont connu que les sombres pensées
Qui font les jours sans joie et les nuits sans sommeil;
Pour ceux qui, chaque jour, bénissant l'existence,
N'ont trouvé le matin, au lieu de l'espérance,
A leurs rêves dorés qu'un horrible réveil.

Ah! pour ces parias de la famille humaine,
Qui, lourdement chargés de leur fardeau de peine,
Ont monté jusqu'au bout l'échelle de douleur,
Que votre cœur touché vienne donner l'obole
D'un pieux souvenir, d'une sainte parole,
Qui découvre à leurs yeux la face du Seigneur.

OCTAVE CRÉMAZIE

Apportez ce tribut de prière et de larmes,
Afin qu'en ce moment terrible et plein d'alarmes,
Où de vos jours le terme enfin sera venu,
Votre nom, répété par la reconnaissance
De ceux dont vous aurez abrégé la souffrance,
En arrivant là-haut, ne soit pas inconnu.

Et prenant ce tribut, un ange aux blanches ailes,
Avant de le porter aux sphères éternelles,
Le dépose un instant sur les tombeaux amis;
Et les mourantes fleurs du sombre cimetière,
Se ranimant soudain au vent de la prière,
Versent tous leurs parfums sur les morts endormis.

JOHN HUNTER DUVAR

1830–1899

19   From *De Roberval: a Drama*

[*La Belle Sauvage*]

DE ROBERVAL

Ha! are there wood-ghosts in this solitude,
Such as we read of in *roman de rou?*
No, it is Dian, or Diana's maid,
And fully armed with arrow, belt and bow,
Though tricked out in a somewhat antic guise.

By heathen Venus, what a shape it has!
If nymph it be, and not an airy form

Evoked from out the rainbows of the place:[1]
Small head well set, arched neck, svelt frame and limbs,
Lissome as steel, as active as a deer,
And skin no duskier than I oft have seen
Among the peasant maids of warm Provence,
At time of grapes, when browned by vintage sun;
It lives, it moves, it answers to my gaze,
Yet I have heard these Dryades are dumb;
If this should be a woman, now, and she
An average sample of the belle sauvage,
'Twould be no task to populate the land.

.   .   .

A SOLDIER

If this same salvage chit were whitewashed now,
She'd look the very picture of Christine,
A peasant girl I knew down in Cognac,
'Tis true Christine was rather fat and squab,
And I bethink me now, was bandy-legged,
While this wild jade is slender as a reed,
And on her pins stands like a fugleman.

ANOTHER

I saw a savage once from Africa;
Black as a lump of charcoal, kettle black,
But fat as any high Church dignitary,
And greasy as a friar mendicant;
Bohemians bought her for a kind of show,
As a descendant of the Queen of Sheba.

.   .   .

[1] Near the cataract of Niagara.

JOHN HUNTER DUVAR

RELIGIEUSE

There is a savage maiden who comes here . . .
Pray have her seized when next she comes again,
And given over to our sisterhood,
Where she shall be placed under discipline,
And after short novitiate may be
Sent as an emissary to her tribe,
By name of Martha Bridget Ursula.

DE ROBERVAL

Trebly euphonious, and appropriate
As 'chick-a-bid' would be to a young eagle . . .
I will not have this girl converted. No!
I will take this one's soul in my own hands.
What would you have? The Christian graces are
Modesty, credulence and faithfulness,
A touch of gratitude, a sense of truth,
And some dependence on the deity.
She has them all. She shall not be converted.

Come hither, child. Tell me, Ohnawa 'mie,
Wilt thou abjure thy god, give up thy faith,
And be baptized for Him who died on tree,
The Christian Three-in-one?

OHNAWA

                The Great Spirit,
Master of Life, is good; he sends the rain
And sun that makes the yellow corn to grow,
And when the ice breaks up, makes fish to swim,
And game return at time of opening leaves.
We are the creatures of His unseen hand.

JOHN HUNTER DUVAR

Our God has never died, but lives. We hear
His whispered orders speaking in our hearts,
And though he knows, to show we reverence him
We cast shells in the streams and burn sweet weeds;
In war our warriors offer sacrifice.
He loves the Red Man. When the lamp goes out
From forth our bodies, if we do His will
He will relight the light of life again,
And lead us to the happier hunting woods.

PAMPHILE LEMAY

1837–1918

20   *La Laitière*

Le sarrasin fleuri verse un parfum de miel,
Et le moineau, gorgé des blés mûrs qu'il saccage,
Vole à son nid. L'érable et le pin du bocage
Dentellent, au ponant, les champs pourpres du ciel.

C'est le soir. Dans l'air pur monte un vibrant appel,
Et soudain le troupeau qu'on a mis au pacage,
Par la sente connue ou par le marécage,
Accourt lécher la main d'où s'égraine le sel.

La génisse rumine auprès de la barrière.
Avec un bruit de source, au fond d'une chaudière,
De sa lourde mamelle il tombe un flot de lait.

La laitière caresse un rêve. Elle présume
Qu'avec deux fois le prix de cette blanche écume
Elle peut étrenner un joli mantelet.

PAMPHILE LEMAY

21 *La Sucrerie*

Les chemins sont durcis comme par le rouleau,
Et la lune les montre en des éclairs de glaive.
La neige des tapis, que nul vent ne soulève,
Donne une teinte chaste au sylvestre tableau.

Une vaste chaudière où déjà chante l'eau
Verse un grisant arome et la cuisson s'achève.
Écoutez le babil de la goutte de sève
Qui tombe de l'érable en l'auge de bouleau.

Et la cabane est là, sous l'épaisse ramée.
J'aime son toit moussu d'où monte la fumée,
Et sa table sans nappe avec ses bols d'étain.

Si vous mordez ensemble aux cristaux de la *tire*,
Elles et vous, les gars, alors faut-il le dire?
La bouche est imprudente et le baiser, certain.

CHARLES MAIR

1838–1927

22 *Winter*

When gadding snow makes hill-sides white,
    And icicles form more and more;
When niggard Frost stands all the night,
    And taps at snoring Gaffer's door;
When watch-dogs bay the vagrant wind,
    And shiv'ring kine herd close in shed;
When kitchens chill, and maids unkind,
    Send rustic suitors home to bed—
      Then do I say the winter cold,
      It seems to me, is much too bold.

When winking sparks run up the stalk,
   And faggots blaze within the grate,
And, by the ingle-cheek, I talk
   With shadows from the realm of fate;
When authors old, yet ever young,
   Look down upon me from the walls,
And songs by spirit-lips are sung
    To pleasant tunes and madrigals,—
      Then do I say the winter cold
      Brings back to me the joys of old.

When morn is bleak, and sunshine cool,
   And trav'llers' beards with rime are grey;
When frost-nipt urchins weep in school,
   And sleighs creak o'er the drifted way;
When smoke goes quick from chimney-top,
   And mist flies through the open hatch;
When snow-flecks to the window hop,
    And children's tongues cling to the latch,—
      Then do I sigh for summer wind,
      And wish the winter less unkind.

When merry bells a-jingling go,
   And prancing horses beat the ground;
When youthful hearts are all aglow,
   And youthful gladness rings around;
When gallants praise, and maidens blush
   To hear their charms so loudly told,
Whilst echoing vale and echoing bush
    Halloo their laughter, fold on fold,—
      Then do I think the winter meet,
      For gallants free and maidens sweet.

CHARLES MAIR

When great pines crack with mighty sound,
   And ice doth rift with doleful moan;
When luckless wanderers are found
   Quite stiff in wooded valleys lone;
When ragged mothers have no sheet
   To shield their babes from winter's flaw;
When milk is frozen in the teat,
   And beggars shiver in their straw,—
     Then do I hate the winter's cheer,
     And weep for springtime of the year.

When ancient hosts their guests do meet,
   And fetch old jorums from the bin;
When viols loud and dancers' feet
   In lofty halls make mickle din;
When jokes pass round, and nappy ale
   Sends pleasure mounting to the brain;
When hours are filched from night so pale,
   And youngsters sigh and maids are fain,—
     Then do I hail the wintry breeze
     Which brings such ripened joys as these.

But, when the winter chills my friend,
   And steals the heart-fire from his breast;
Or woos the ruffian wind to send
   One pang to rob him of his rest—
All gainless grows the Christmas cheer,
   And gloomy seems the new year's light,
For joy but lives when friends are near,
   And dies when they do quit the sight,—
     Then, winter, do I cry, 'Thy greed
     Is great, ay, thou art cold indeed!'

CHARLES MAIR

From *Tecumseh*

(i)

There was a time on this fair continent
When all things throve in spacious peacefulness.
The prosperous forests unmolested stood,
For where the stalwart oak grew there it lived
Long ages, and then died among its kind.
The hoary pines—those ancients of the earth—
Brimful of legends of the early world,
Stood thick on their own mountains unsubdued.
And all things else illumined by the sun,
Inland or by the lifted wave, had rest.
The passionate or calm pageants of the skies
No artist drew; but in the auburn west
Innumerable faces of fair cloud
Vanished in silent darkness with the day.
The prairie realm—vast ocean's paraphrase-
Rich in wild grasses numberless, and flowers
Unnamed save in mute Nature's inventory,
No civilized barbarian trenched for gain.
And all that flowed was sweet and uncorrupt
The rivers and their tributary streams,
Undammed, wound on forever, and gave up
Their lonely torrents to weird gulfs of sea,
And ocean wastes unshadowed by a sail.
And all the wild life of this western world
Knew not the fear of man; yet in those woods,
And by those plenteous streams and mighty lakes,
And on stupendous steppes of peerless plain,
And in the rocky gloom of canyons deep,
Screened by the stony ribs of mountains hoar
Which steeped their snowy peaks in purging cloud,

And down the continent where tropic suns
Warmed to her very heart the mother earth,
And in the congeal'd north where silence self
Ached with intensity of stubborn frost,
There lived a soul more wild than barbarous;
A tameless soul—the sunburnt savage free—
Free, and untainted by the greed of gain:
Great Nature's man content with Nature's food.

24   (*ii*)

LEFROY We left
The silent forest, and, day after day,
Great prairies swept beyond our aching sight
Into the measureless West; uncharted realms,
Voiceless and calm, save when tempestuous wind
Rolled the rank herbage into billows vast,
And rushing tides which never found a shore.
And tender clouds, and veils of morning mist,
Cast flying shadows, chased by flying light,
Into interminable wildernesses,
Flushed with fresh blooms, deep perfumed by the rose,
And murmurous with flower-fed bird and bee.
The deep-grooved bison-paths like furrows lay,
Turned by the cloven hoofs of thundering herds
Primeval, and still travelled as of yore.
And gloomy valleys opened at our feet—
Shagged with dusk cypresses and hoary pine;
And sunless gorges, rummaged by the wolf,
Which through long reaches of the prairie wound,
Then melted slowly into upland vales,
Lingering, far-stretched amongst the spreading hills.

CHARLES MAIR

BROCK What charming solitudes! And life was there!

LEFROY Yes, life was there! inexplicable life,
Still wasted by inexorable death.
There had the stately stag his battle-field—
Dying for mastery among his hinds.
There vainly sprung the affrighted antelope,
Beset by glittering eyes and hurrying feet.
The dancing grouse, at their insensate sport,
Heard not the stealthy footstep of the fox;
The gopher on his little earthwork stood,
With folded arms, unconscious of the fate
That wheeled in narrowing circles overhead;
And the poor mouse, on heedless nibbling bent,
Marked not the silent coiling of the snake.
At length we heard a deep and solemn sound—
Erupted moanings of the troubled earth
Trembling beneath innumerable feet.
A growing uproar blending in our ears,
With noise tumultuous as ocean's surge,
Of bellowings, fierce breath and battle shock,
And ardour of unconquerable herds.
A multitude whose trampling shook the plains,
With discord of harsh sound and rumblings deep
As if the swift revolving earth had struck,
And from some adamantine peak recoiled,
Jarring. At length we topped a high-browed hill—
The last and loftiest of a file of such—
And, lo! before us lay the tameless stock,
Slow wending to the northward like a cloud!
A multitude in motion, dark and dense—
Far as the eye could reach, and farther still,
In countless myriads stretched for many a league.

25　　　　　From *The Fireflies*

How dreamy-dark it is!
Men yawn for weariness, and hoard their gains,
While careful housewives drown the kitchen fires. . . .
The plodding oxen, dragging creaky wains
O'er bosky roads, their ancient horns entwine,
Lick their huge joles, and think of bedded stalls,
And munching of sweet corn. The lick'rous swine
Huddled in routed turf, neglect the calls
And pinches of their young, and hide their dugs,
Swoll'n with a lazy milk, whilst timid sheep,
Far from their winter-folds of knotty fir,
Dream of lean wolves and bleatings in their sleep.

Yet there are those that oft the silence mock,
For life wings through the darkness everywhere,
And night's dull, ugly brood is all astir.
The flapping bat and hungry-snapping hawk
Now glut themselves with innocent, droning flies,
Whisked from the dingy commonwealth of air.
The loathsome toad, which foul infection breeds
And lep'rous sores, hops o'er the dusty walk,
And, in the hollows where the river lies,
The hoarse frogs sprawl among the bedded reeds,
And croak harsh ditties to their uncouth mates. . . .

This is the hour
When fire-flies flit about each lofty crag,
And down the valleys sail on lucid wing. . . .
I see them glimmer where the waters lag
By winding bays, and to the willows sing;
And, far away, where stands the forest dim,

Huge-built of old, their tremulous lights are seen.
High overhead they gleam like trailing stars,
Then sink adown, until their emerald sheen
Dies in the darkness like an evening hymn—
Anon to float again in glorious bars
Of streaming rapture, such as man may hear
When the soul casts its slough of mortal fear.
And now they make rich spangles in the grass,
Gilding the night-dew on the tender blade;
Then hover o'er the meadow-pools to gaze
At their bright forms shrined in the dreamy glass
Which earth, and air, and bounteous rain have made.
One moment, and the thicket is ablaze
With twinkling lamps which swing from bough to bough:
Another, and like sylphids they descend
To cheer the brook-side where the bell-flow'rs grow.
Near and more near they softly come, until
Their little life is busy at my feet;
They glow around me, and my fancies blend
Capriciously with their delight, and fill
My wakeful bosom with unwonted heat.
One lights upon my hand, and there I clutch
With an alarming finger its quick wing:
Erstwhile so free, it pants, the tender thing!
And dreads its captor and his handsel touch.

1839–1908

Renouveau

I

Il faisait froid. J'errais dans la lande déserte,
Songeant, rêveur distrait, aux beaux jours envolés;
De givre étincelant la route était couverte,
Et le vent secouait les arbres désolés.

Tout à coup, au détour du sentier, sous les branches
D'un buisson dépouillé, j'aperçus, entr'ouvert,
Un nid, débris informe où quelques plumes blanches
Tourbillonnaient encor sous la bise d'hiver.

Je m'en souviens: — c'était le nid d'une linotte
Que j'avais, un matin du mois de mai dernier,
Surprise, éparpillant sa merveilleuse note
Dans les airs tout remplis d'arôme printanier.

Ce jour-là, tout riait; la lande ensoleillée
S'enveloppait au loin de reflets radieux;
Et, sous chaque arbrisseau, l'oreille émerveillée
Entendait bourdonner des bruits mélodieux.

Le soleil était chaud, la brise caressante;
De feuilles et de fleurs les rameaux étaient lourds ...
La linotte chantait sa gamme éblouissante
Près du berceau de mousse où dormaient ses amours.

Alors, au souvenir de ces jours clairs et roses,
Qu'a remplacés l'automne avec son ciel marbré,
Mon cœur, — j'ai quelquefois de ces heures moroses, —
Mon cœur s'émut devant ce vieux nid délabré.

Et je songeai longtemps à mes jeunes années,
Frêles fleurs dont l'orage a tué les parfums,
A mes illusions que la vie a fanées,
Au pauvre nid brisé de mes bonheurs défunts !

Car quelle âme ici-bas n'eut sa flore nouvelle,
Son doux soleil d'avril et ses tièdes saisons ?
Épanouissement du cœur qui se révèle !
Des naïves amours mystiques floraisons !

Ô jeunesse ! tu fuis comme un songe d'aurore . . .
Et que retrouve-t-on, quand ton rêve est fini ?
Quelques plumes, hélas ! qui frissonnent encore
Aux branches où le cœur avait bâti son nid.

II

Et je revins chez moi, ce soir-là, sombre et triste . . .
Mais quand la douce nuit m'eut versé son sommeil,
Dans un tourbillon d'or, de pourpre et d'améthyste,
Je vis renaître au loin le beau printemps vermeil.

Je vis, comme autrefois, la lande, ranimée,
Étaler au soleil son prisme aux cent couleurs;
Des vents harmonieux jasaient dans la ramée,
Et des rayons dorés pleuvaient parmi les fleurs !

La nature avait mis sa robe des dimanches . . .
Et je vis deux pinsons, sous le feuillage vert,
Qui tapissaient leur nid avec ces plumes blanches
Dont les lambeaux flottaient naguère au vent d'hiver.

Ô Temps! courant fatal où vont nos destinées,
De nos plus chers espoirs aveugle destructeur,
Sois béni! car, par toi, nos amours moissonnées
Peuvent encor revivre, ô grand consolateur!

Dans l'épreuve, par toi, l'espérance nous reste . . .
Tu fais, après l'hiver, reverdir les sillons;
Et tu verses toujours quelque baume céleste
Aux blessures que font tes cruels aiguillons.

Au découragement n'ouvrons jamais nos portes:
Après les jours de froid viennent les jours de mai;
Et c'est souvent avec ses illusions mortes
Que le cœur se refait un nid plus parfumé!

27   *La Découverte du Mississipi*

I

Le grand fleuve dormait couché dans la savane.
Dans les lointains brumeux passaient en caravane
De farouches troupeaux d'élans et de bisons.
Drapé dans les rayons de l'aube matinale,
Le désert déployait sa splendeur virginale
      Sur d'insondables horizons.

Juin brillait. Sur les eaux, dans l'herbe des pelouses,
Sur les sommets, au fond des profondeurs jalouses,
L'Été fécond chantait ses sauvages amours.
Du Sud à l'Aquilon, du Couchant à l'Aurore,
Toute l'immensité semblait garder encore
      La majesté des premiers jours.

Travail mystérieux ! les rochers aux fronts chauves,
Les pampas, les bayous, les bois, les antres fauves,
Tout semblait tressaillir sous un souffle effréné;
On sentait palpiter les solitudes mornes,
Comme au jour où vibra, dans l'espace sans bornes,
  L'hymne du monde nouveau-né.

L'Inconnu trônait là dans sa grandeur première,
Splendide, et tacheté d'ombres et de lumière,
Comme un reptile immense au soleil engourdi,
Le vieux Meschacébé, vierge encor de servage,
Déployait ses anneaux de rivage en rivage
  Jusques aux golfes du Midi.

Écharpe de Titan sur le globe enroulée,
Le grand fleuve épanchait sa nappe immaculée
Des régions de l'Ourse aux plages d'Orion,
Baignant le steppe aride et les bosquets d'orange,
Et mariant ainsi, dans un hymen étrange,
  L'Équateur au Septentrion.

Fier de sa liberté, fier de ses flots sans nombre,
Fier du grand pin touffu qui lui verse son ombre,
Le Roi-des-Eaux n'avait encore, en aucun lieu
Où l'avait promené sa course vagabonde,
Déposé le tribut de sa vague profonde,
  Que devant le soleil et Dieu ! . . .

II

Jolliet ! Jolliet ! quel spectacle féerique
Dut frapper ton regard, quand ta nef historique
Bondit sur les flots d'or du grand fleuve inconnu !

LOUIS FRÉCHETTE

Quel sourire d'orgueil dut effleurer ta lèvre!
Quel éclair triomphant, à cet instant de fièvre,
    Dut resplendir sur ton front nu !

Le voyez-vous, là-bas, debout comme un prophète,
Le regard rayonnant d'audace satisfaite,
La main tendue au loin vers l'Occident bronzé,
Prendre possession de ce domaine immense,
Au nom du Dieu vivant, au nom du roi de France,
    Et du monde civilisé !

Puis, bercé par la houle, et bercé par ses rêves,
L'oreille ouverte aux bruits harmonieux des grèves,
Humant l'âcre parfum des grands bois odorants,
Rasant les îlots verts et les dunes d'opale,
De méandre en méandre, au fil de l'onde pâle,
    Suivre le cours des flots errants !

A son aspect, du sein des flottantes ramures,
Montait comme un concert de chants et de murmures;
Des vols d'oiseaux marins s'élevaient des roseaux,
Et, pour montrer la route à la pirogue frêle,
S'enfuyaient en avant, traînant leur ombre grêle
    Dans le pli lumineux des eaux.

Et, pendant qu'il allait voguant à la dérive,
L'on aurait dit qu'au loin les arbres de la rive,
En arceaux parfumés penchés sur son chemin,
Saluaient le héros dont l'énergique audace
Venait d'inscrire encor le nom de notre race
    Aux fastes de l'esprit humain !

III

O grand Meschacébé! — Voyageur taciturne,
Bien des fois, au rayon de l'étoile nocturne,
Sur tes bords endormis je suis venu m'asseoir;
Et là, seul et rêveur, perdu sous les grands ormes,
J'ai souvent du regard suivi d'étranges formes
  Glissant dans les brumes du soir.

Tantôt je croyais voir, sous les vertes arcades,
Du fatal de Soto passer les cavalcades,
En jetant au désert un défi solennel!
Tantôt c'était Marquette errant dans la prairie,
Impatient d'offrir un monde à sa patrie,
  Et des âmes à l'Éternel!

Parfois, sous les taillis, ma prunelle trompée
Croyait voir de La Salle étinceler l'épée;
Et parfois, groupe informe allant je ne sais où,
Devant une humble croix, ô puissance magique!
De farouches guerriers à l'œil sombre et tragique
  Passer en pliant le genou!

Et puis, berçant mon âme aux rêves des poètes,
J'entrevoyais aussi de blanches silhouettes,
Doux fantômes flottant dans le vague des nuits,
Atala, Gabriel, Chactas, Évangéline,
Et l'ombre de René, debout sur la colline,
  Pleurant ses immortels ennuis.

Et j'endormais ainsi mes souvenirs moroses . . .
Mais de ces visions poétiques et roses
Celle qui plus souvent venait frapper mon œil,

C'était, passant au loin dans un reflet de gloire,
Ce hardi pionnier dont notre jeune histoire
    Redit le nom avec orgueil.

IV

Jolliet! Jolliet! deux siècles de conquêtes,
Deux siècles sans rivaux ont passé sur nos têtes,
Depuis l'heure sublime où, de ta propre main,
Tu jetas, d'un seul trait, sur la carte du monde
Ces vastes régions, zone immense et féconde,
    Futur grenier du genre humain!

Deux siècles sont passés depuis que ton génie
Nous fraya le chemin de la terre bénie
Que Dieu fit avec tant de prodigalité,
Qu'elle garde toujours dans les plis de sa robe,
Pour les déshérités de tous les coins du globe,
    Du pain avec la liberté!

Oui, deux siècles ont fui! La solitude vierge
N'est plus là! Du progrès le flot montant submerge
Les vestiges derniers d'un passé qui finit.
Où le désert dormait grandit la métropole;
Et le fleuve asservi courbe sa large épaule
    Sous l'arche aux piliers de granit!

Plus de forêts sans fin: la vapeur les sillonne!
L'astre des jours nouveaux sur tous les points rayonne;
L'enfant de la nature est évangélisé;
Le soc du laboureur fertilise la plaine;
Et le surplus doré de sa gerbe trop pleine
      Nourrit le vieux monde épuisé!

v

Des plus purs dévoûments merveilleuse semence !
Qui de vous eût jamais rêvé cette œuvre immense,
Ô Jolliet, et vous apôtres ingénus,
Humbles soldats de Dieu, sans reproche et sans crainte,
Qui portiez le flambeau de la vérité sainte
      Dans ces parages inconnus ?

Des volontés du ciel exécuteurs dociles,
Vous fûtes les jalons qui rendent plus faciles
Les durs sentiers où doit marcher l'humanité . . .
Gloire à vous tous ! du Temps franchissant les abîmes
Vos noms environnés d'auréoles sublimes
      Iront à l'immortalité !

Et toi, de ces héros généreuse patrie,
Sol canadien, que j'aime avec idolâtrie,
Dans l'accomplissement de tous ces grands travaux,
Quand je pèse la part que le ciel t'a donnée,
Les yeux sur l'avenir, terre prédestinée,
      J'ai foi dans tes destins nouveaux !

28   *Les Oiseaux de neige*

Quand le rude équinoxe, avec son froid cortège,
Quitte nos horizons moins inhospitaliers,
Sur nos champs de frimas s'abattent par milliers
Ces visiteurs ailés qu'on nomme oiseaux de neige.

Des graines nulle part ! nul feuillage aux halliers !
Contre la giboulée et nos vents de Norvège,
Seul le regard d'en haut les abrite, et protège
Ces courriers du soleil en butte aux oiseliers.

Chers petits voyageurs, sous le givre et la grêle,
Vous voltigez gaîment, et l'on voit sur votre aile
Luire un premier rayon du printemps attardé.

Allez, tourbillonnez autour des avalanches;
Sans peur, aux flocons blancs mêlez vos plumes blanches:
Le faible que Dieu garde est toujours bien gardé!

29 *Le Cap Éternité*

C'est un bloc écrasant dont la crête surplombe
Au-dessus des flots noirs, et dont le front puissant
Domine le brouillard, et défie en passant
L'aile de la tempête ou le choc de la trombe.

Énorme pan de roc, colosse menaçant
Dont le flanc narguerait le boulet et la bombe,
Qui monte d'un seul jet dans la nue, et retombe
Dans le gouffre insondable où sa base descend!

Quel caprice a dressé cette sombre muraille?
Caprice! qui le sait? Hardi celui qui raille
Ces aveugles efforts de la fécondité!

Cette masse nourrit mille plantes vivaces;
L'hirondelle des monts niche dans ses crevasses;
Et ce monstre farouche a sa paternité!

1850–1887

30   *The Canoe*

My masters twain made me a bed
Of pine-boughs resinous, and cedar;
Of moss, a soft and gentle breeder
Of dreams of rest; and me they spread
With furry skins, and laughing said,
'Now she shall lay her polish'd sides,
As queens do rest, or dainty brides,
Our slender lady of the tides!'

My masters twain their camp-soul lit,
Streamed incense from the hissing cones,
Large, crimson flashes grew and whirl'd,
Thin, golden nerves of sly light curl'd
Round the dun camp, and rose faint zones,
Half way about each grim bole knit,
Like a shy child that would bedeck
With its soft clasp a Brave's red neck;
Yet sees the rough shield on his breast,
The awful plumes shake on his crest,
And fearful drops his timid face,
Nor dares complete the sweet embrace.

Into the hollow hearts of brakes,
Yet warm from sides of does and stags,
Pass'd to the crisp dark river flags;
Sinuous, red as copper snakes,
Sharp-headed serpents, made of light,
Glided and hid themselves in night.

44

ISABELLA VALANCY CRAWFORD

My masters twain the slaughter'd deer
Hung on fork'd boughs—with thongs of leather.
Bound were his stiff, slim feet together—
His eyes like dead stars cold and drear;
The wand'ring firelight drew near
And laid its wide palm, red and anxious,
On the sharp splendour of his branches;
On the white foam grown hard and sere
   On flank and shoulder.
Death—hard as breast of granite boulder,
   And under his lashes
Peer'd thro' his eyes at his life's grey ashes.

My masters twain sang songs that wove
(As they burnish'd hunting blade and rifle)
A golden thread with a cobweb trifle—
Loud of the chase, and low of love.

'O Love, art thou a silver fish?
Shy of the line and shy of gaffing,
Which we do follow, fierce, yet laughing,
Casting at thee the light-wing'd wish,
And at the last shall we bring thee up
From the crystal darkness under the cup
   Of lily folden,
   On broad leaves golden?

'O Love! art thou a silver deer,
Swift thy starr'd feet as wing of swallow
While we with rushing arrows follow;
And at the last shall we draw near,

And over thy velvet neck cast thongs—
Woven of roses, of stars, of songs?
  New chains all moulden
  Of rare gems olden!'

They hung the slaughter'd fish like swords
On saplings slender—like scimitars
Bright, and ruddied from new-dead wars,
Blaz'd in the light—the scaly hordes.

They pil'd up boughs beneath the trees,
Of cedar-web and green fir tassel;
Low did the pointed pine tops rustle,
The camp fire blush'd to the tender breeze.

The hounds laid dew-laps on the ground,
With needles of pine sweet, soft and rusty—
Dream'd of the dead stag stout and lusty;
A bat by the red flames wove its round.

The darkness built its wigwam walls
Close round the camp, and at its curtain
Press'd shapes, thin woven and uncertain,
As white locks of tall waterfalls.

From *Malcolm's Katie*

31   (*i*)

The South Wind laid his moccasins aside,
Broke his gay calumet of flow'rs, and cast
His useless wampum, beaded with cool dews,
Far from him, northward; his long, ruddy spear

Flung sunward, whence it came, and his soft locks
Of warm, fine haze grew silver as the birch.
His wigwam of green leaves began to shake;
The crackling rice-beds scolded harsh like squaws;
The small ponds pouted up their silver lips;
The great lakes ey'd the mountains, whisper'd 'Ugh!
Are ye so tall, O chiefs? Not taller than
Our plumes can reach.' And rose a little way,
As panthers stretch to try their velvet limbs,
And then retreat to purr and bide their time.
At morn the sharp breath of the night arose
From the wide prairies, in deep-struggling seas,
In rolling breakers, bursting to the sky;
In tumbling surfs, all yellow'd faintly thro'
With the low sun—in mad, conflicting crests,
Voic'd with low thunder from the hairy throats
Of the mist-buried herds; and for a man
To stand amid the cloudy roll and moil,
The phantom waters breaking overhead,
Shades of vex'd billows bursting on his breast,
Torn caves of mist wall'd with a sudden gold,
Reseal'd as swift as seen—broad, shaggy fronts,
Fire-ey'd and tossing on impatient horns
The wave impalpable—was but to think
A dream of phantoms held him as he stood.
The late, last thunders of the summer crash'd,
Where shriek'd great eagles, lords of naked cliffs.
The pulseless forest, lock'd and interlock'd
So closely, bough with bough, and leaf with leaf,
So serf'd by its own wealth, that while from high
The moons of summer kiss'd its green-gloss'd locks;
And round its knees the merry West Wind danc'd;
And round its ring, compacted emerald;

47

The south wind crept on moccasins of flame;
And the red fingers of th' impatient sun
Pluck'd at its outmost fringes—its dim veins
Beat with no life—its deep and dusky heart,
In a deep trance of shadow, felt no throb
To such soft wooing answer: thro' its dream
Brown rivers of deep waters sunless stole;
Small creeks sprang from its mosses, and amaz'd,
Like children in a wigwam curtain'd close
Above the great, dead heart of some red chief,
Slipp'd on soft feet, swift stealing through the gloom,
Eager for light and for the frolic winds.
In this shrill moon the scouts of winter ran
From the ice-belted north, and whistling shafts
Struck maple and struck sumach—and a blaze
Ran swift from leaf to leaf, from bough to bough;
Till round the forest flash'd a belt of flame
And inward lick'd its tongues of red and gold
To the deep, tranced inmost heart of all.
Rous'd the still heart—but all too late, too late.
Too late, the branches welded fast with leaves,
Toss'd, loosen'd, to the winds—too late the sun
Pour'd his last vigour to the deep, dark cells
Of the dim wood. The keen, two-bladed Moon
Of Falling Leaves roll'd up on crested mists
And where the lush, rank boughs had foil'd the sun
In his red prime, her pale, sharp fingers crept
After the wind and felt about the moss,
And seem'd to pluck from shrinking twig and stem
The burning leaves—while groan'd the shudd'ring wood.
Who journey'd where the prairies made a pause,
Saw burnish'd ramparts flaming in the sun,
With beacon fires, tall on their rustling walls.

And when the vast, horn'd herds at sunset drew
Their sullen masses into one black cloud,
Rolling thund'rous o'er the quick pulsating plain,
They seem'd to sweep between two fierce red suns
Which, hunter-wise, shot at their glaring balls
Keen shafts, with scarlet feathers and gold barbs,
By round, small lakes with thinner forests fring'd,
More jocund woods that sung about the feet
And crept along the shoulders of great cliffs;
The warrior stags, with does and tripping fawns,
Like shadows black upon the throbbing mist
Of Evening's rose, flash'd thro' the singing woods—
Nor tim'rous, sniff'd the spicy, cone-breath'd air;
For never had the patriarch of the herd
Seen limn'd against the farthest rim of light
Of the low-dipping sky, the plume or bow
Of the red hunter; nor when stoop'd to drink,
Had from the rustling rice-beds heard the shaft
Of the still hunter hidden in its spears;
His bark canoe close-knotted in its bronze,
His form as stirless as the brooding air,
His dusky eyes, too, fix'd, unwinking fires;
His bow-string tighten'd till it subtly sang
To the long throbs, and leaping pulse that roll'd
And beat within his knotted, naked breast. . . .

32   (*ii*)

  'Bite deep and wide, O Axe, the tree,
  What doth thy bold voice promise me?'

  'I promise thee all joyous things,
  That furnish forth the lives of kings!

'For ev'ry silver ringing blow,
Cities and palaces shall grow!'

'Bite deep and wide, O Axe, the tree,
Tell wider prophecies to me.'

'When rust hath gnaw'd me deep and red,
A nation strong shall lift his head!

'His crown the very Heav'ns shall smite,
Æons shall build him in his might!'

'Bite deep and wide, O Axe, the tree;
Bright Seer, help on thy prophecy!'

Max smote the snow-weigh'd tree and lightly laugh'd.
'See, friend,' he cried to one that look'd and smil'd,
'My axe and I—we do immortal tasks—
We build up nations—this my axe and I!'
'O,' said the other with a cold, short smile,
'Nations are not immortal! is there now
One nation thron'd upon the sphere of earth,
That walk'd with the first Gods, and saw
The budding world unfold its slow-leav'd flow'r?
Nay; it is hardly theirs to leave behind
Ruins so eloquent, that the hoary sage
Can lay his hand upon their stones, and say:
"These once were thrones!" The lean, lank lion peals
His midnight thunders over lone, red plains,
Long-ridg'd and crested on their dusty waves,
With fires from moons red-hearted as the sun;
And deep re-thunders all the earth to him.
For, far beneath the flame-fleck'd, shifting sands,

Below the roots of palms, and under stones
Of younger ruins, thrones, tow'rs and cities
Honeycomb the earth. The high, solemn walls
Of hoary ruins—their foundings all unknown
(But to the round-ey'd worlds that walk
In the blank paths of Space and blanker Chance)
At whose stones young mountains wonder, and the seas'
New-silv'ring, deep-set valleys pause and gaze—
Are rear'd upon old shrines, whose very Gods
Were dreams to the shrine-builders, of a time
They caught in far-off flashes—as the child
Half thinks he can remember how one came
And took him in her hand and shew'd him that
He thinks she call'd the sun. Proud ships rear high
On ancient billows that have torn the roots
Of cliffs, and bitten at the golden lips
Of firm, sleek beaches, till they conquer'd all,
And sow'd the reeling earth with salted waves.
Wrecks plunge, prow foremost, down still, solemn slopes,
And bring their dead crews to as dead a quay;
Some city built before that ocean grew,
By silver drops from many a floating cloud,
By icebergs bellowing in their throes of death,
By lesser seas toss'd from their rocking cups,
And leaping each to each; by dew-drops flung
From painted sprays, whose weird leaves and flow'rs
Are moulded for new dwellers on the earth,
Printed in hearts of mountains and of mines.
Nations immortal? where the well-trimm'd lamps
Of long-past ages, when Time seem'd to pause
On smooth, dust-blotted graves that, like the tombs
Of monarchs, held dead bones and sparkling gems?
She saw no glimmer on the hideous ring

Of the black clouds; no stream of sharp, clear light
From those great torches, pass'd into the black
Of deep oblivion. She seem'd to watch, but she
Forgot her long-dead nations. When she stirr'd
Her vast limbs in the dawn that forc'd its fire
Up the black East, and saw the imperious red
Burst over virgin dews and budding flow'rs,
She still forgot her moulder'd thrones and kings,
Her sages and their torches, and their Gods,
And said, "This is my birth—my primal day!"
She dream'd new Gods, and rear'd them other shrines,
Planted young nations, smote a feeble flame
From sunless flint, re-lit the torch of mind;
Again she hung her cities on the hills,
Built her rich towers, crown'd her kings again,
And with the sunlight on her awful wings
Swept round the flow'ry cestus of the earth,
And said, "I build for Immortality!"
Her vast hand rear'd her tow'rs, her shrines, her thrones;
The ceaseless sweep of her tremendous wings
Still beat them down and swept their dust abroad;
Her iron finger wrote on mountain sides
Her deeds and prowess—and her own soft plume
Wore down the hills! Again drew darkly on
A night of deep forgetfulness; once more
Time seem'd to pause upon forgotten graves—
Once more a young dawn stole into her eyes—
Again her broad wings stirr'd, and fresh clear airs
Blew the great clouds apart;—again Time said,
"This is my birth—my deeds and handiwork
Shall be immortal." Thus and so dream on
Fool'd nations, and thus dream their dullard sons.
Naught is immortal save immortal—Death!'

Max paus'd and smil'd: 'O, preach such gospel, friend,
To all but lovers who most truly love;
For *them*, their gold-wrought scripture glibly reads,
All else is mortal but immortal—Love!'

33   From *Gisli, the Chieftain*

The Song of the Arrow

What know I,
As I bite the blue veins of the throbbing sky;
To the quarry's breast,
Hot from the sides of the sleek smooth nest?

What know I
Of the will of the tense bow from which I fly!
What the need or jest,
That feathers my flight to its bloody rest.

What know I
Of the will of the bow that speeds me on high?
What doth the shrill bow
Of the hand on its singing soul-string know?

Flame-swift speed I—
And the dove and the eagle shriek out and die;
Whence comes my sharp zest
For the heart of the quarry? the Gods know best.

Deep pierc'd the red gaze of the eagle
The breast of a cygnet below him;
Beneath his dun wing from the eastward
Shrill-chaunted the long shaft of Gisli!

Beneath his dun wing from the westward
Shook a shaft that laugh'd in its biting—
Met in the fierce breast of the eagle
ˎThe arrows of Gisli and Brynhild!

WILLIAM CHAPMAN

1850–1917

34 *Notre Langue*

Notre langue naquit aux lèvres des Gaulois.
Ses mots sont caressants, ses règles sont sévères,
Et, faite pour chanter les gloires d'autrefois,
Elle a puisé son souffle aux refrains des trouvères.

Elle a le charme exquis du timbre des Latins,
Le séduisant brio du parler des Hellènes,
Le chaud rayonnement des émaux florentins,
Le diaphane et frais poli des porcelaines.

Elle a les sons moelleux du luth éolien,
Le doux babil du vent dans les blés et les seigles,
La clarté de l'azur, l'éclair olympien,
Les soupirs du ramier, l'envergure des aigles.

Elle chante partout pour louer Jéhova,
Et, dissipant la nuit où l'erreur se dérobe,
Elle est la messagère immortelle qui va
Porter de la lumière aux limites du globe.

La première, elle dit le nom de l'Éternel
Sous les bois canadiens noyés dans le mystère.

WILLIAM CHAPMAN

La première, elle fit monter vers notre ciel
Les hymnes de l'amour, l'élan de la prière.

La première, elle fit tout à coup frissonner
Du grand Meschacébé la forêt infinie,
Et l'arbre du rivage a paru s'incliner
En entendant vibrer cette langue bénie.

Langue de feu, qui luit comme un divin flambeau
Elle éclaire les arts et guide la science;
Elle jette, en servant le vrai, le bien, le beau,
A l'horizon du siècle une lueur immense.

Un jour, d'âpres marins, vénérés parmi nous,
L'apportèrent du sol des menhirs et des landes,
Et nos mères nous ont bercés sur leurs genoux
Aux vieux refrains dolents des ballades normandes.

Nous avons conservé l'idiome légué
Par ces héros quittant pour nos bois leurs falaises,
Et, bien que par moments on le crût subjugué,
Il est encore vainqueur sous les couleurs anglaises.

Et nul n'osera plus désormais opprimer
Ce langage aujourd'hui si ferme et si vivace . . .
Et les persécuteurs n'ont pu le supprimer,
Parce qu'il doit durer autant que notre race.

Essayer d'arrêter son élan, c'est vouloir
Empêcher les bourgeons et les roses d'éclore;
Tenter d'anéantir son charme et son pouvoir,
C'est rêver d'abolir les rayons de l'aurore.

Brille donc à jamais sous le regard de Dieu,
Ô langue des anciens! Combats et civilise,
Et sois toujours pour nous la colonne de feu
Qui guidait les Hébreux vers la Terre promise!

35 *Le Laboureur*

Derrière deux grands bœufs ou deux lourds percherons,
L'homme marche courbé, dans le pré solitaire,
Ses poignets musculeux rivés aux mancherons
De la charrue ouvrant le ventre de la terre.

Au pied d'un coteau vert noyé dans les rayons,
Les yeux toujours fixés sur la glèbe si chère,
Grisé du lourd parfum qu'exhale la jachère,
Avec calme et lenteur il trace ses sillons.

Et, rêveur, quelquefois il ébauche un sourire:
Son oreille déjà croit entendre bruire
Une mer d'épis d'or sous un soleil de feu;

Il s'imagine voir le blé gonfler sa grange;
Il songe que ses pas sont comptés par un ange,
Et que le laboureur collabore avec Dieu.

36 *Janvier*

Il fait froid. Les *blizzards* soufflent, et nul rayon
Ne dore des forêts les blancheurs infinies;
Mais Noël sur nos cœurs laissa comme un sillon
De clartés, de parfums, de paix et d'harmonie.

WILLIAM CHAPMAN

Et sur l'épais verglas des chemins *boulineux*,
Sur les trottoirs glissants et clairs comme l'agate,
Dans les logis obscurs, sous les toits lumineux,
L'allégresse loquace et tapageuse éclate.

En vain la neige à flots tombe des cieux brouillés,
En vain le grand réseau polaire nous enlace,
En vain le fouet du vent nous flagelle la face,
Nos cœurs ont la chaleur des bords ensoleillés.

Les somptueux salons sont ruisselants de flammes,
Et sous le flamboiement des lustres de cristal,
Comme un écho divin, la musique du bal
Emporte en son repli prestigieux les âmes.

Dans tout cercle du soir plus vive est la gaieté,
Pendant que sur les toits sanglote la rafale,
Ou qu'au ciel éclairci l'aurore boréale
Déroule les splendeurs de son voile enchanté.

NÉRÉE BEAUCHEMIN

1850-1931

37   *Fleurs d'aurore*

Comme au printemps de l'autre année,
Au mois des fleurs, après les froids,
Par quelque belle matinée,
Nous irons encore sous bois.

Nous y verrons les mêmes choses,
Le même glorieux réveil,
Et les mêmes métamorphoses
De tout ce qui vit au soleil.

NÉRÉE BEAUCHEMIN

Nous y verrons les grands squelettes
Des arbres gris ressusciter,
Et les yeux clos des violettes
A la lumière palpiter.

Sous le clair feuillage vert tendre,
Les tourterelles des buissons,
Ce jour-là, nous feront entendre
Leurs lentes et molles chansons.

Ensemble nous irons encore
Cueillir dans les prés, au matin,
De ces bouquets couleur d'aurore
Qui fleurent la rose et le thym.

Nous y boirons l'odeur subtile,
Les capiteux aromes blonds
Que, dans l'air tiède et pur, distille
La flore chaude des vallons.

Radieux, secouant le givre
Et les frimas de l'an dernier,
Nos chers espoirs pourront revivre
Au bon vieux soleil printanier.

En attendant que tout renaisse,
Que tout aime et revive un jour,
Laisse nos rêves, ô jeunesse,
S'envoler vers tes bois d'amour !

Chère idylle, tes primevères
Éclosent en toute saison;
Elles narguent les froids sévères
Et percent la neige à foison.

Éternel renouveau, tes sèves
Montent même aux cœurs refroidis
Et tes capiteuses fleurs brèves
Nous grisent comme au temps jadis.

Oh ! oui, nous cueillerons encore,
Aussi frais que l'autre matin,
Ces fins bouquets couleur d'aurore
Qui fleurent la rose et le thym.

38   *La Glaneuse*

Dans l'encadrement clair de la grand' porte ouverte,
Que le géranium odorant fleurit
De son aigrette rouge et de sa feuille verte,
La glaneuse robuste apparaît, et sourit.

Debout, le buste droit, la poitrine gonflée
Du souffle que dilate et rythme le travail,
Elle attend, tout de toile et de laine habillée,
Le départ pour les champs des gens et du bétail.

Et la cour de la ferme et la longue rangée
Des bâtiments, fenils et granges, ont frémi,
Aux rustiques rumeurs dont la brise est chargée,
Par un matin joyeux d'avoir longtemps dormi.

Bonjour à toi, bonjour, à la fois semblent dire
Les blés dont la rosée achève le roui;
Et les herbes des prés que le vent fait bruire
Semblent balbutier un poème inouï.

NÉRÉE BEAUCHEMIN

A toi, tout le cristal dont mon eau se fait gloire,
Dit le puits. C'est pour toi, c'est pour ton riche amour,
Ô reine des moissons, que j'offre et donne à boire,
A ton homme, à ta fille, à tes fils, tout le jour.

Mais voici que soudain, frappant toutes les choses,
Et les êtres qu'enchaîne encore le sommeil,
Gloire à toi, dit l'Aurore; à toi, toutes mes roses!
Femme, à toi, tout mon or, répond le grand Soleil.

GEORGE FREDERICK CAMERON

1854–1885

39 *The Future*

O poet of the future! I,
 Of the dead present, bid thee hail!
Come forth and speak,—our speech shall die:
 Come forth and sing,—our song shall fail:
Our speech, our song fall barren,—we go by!

Our heart is weak. In vain it swells
 And beats to bursting at the wrong:
There never sets a sun but tells
 Of weak ones trampled down by strong,
Of Truth and Justice both immured in cells.

We would aspire, but round us lies
 A maze of high desires and aims;
Would seek a prize, but, ah! our eyes
 Fail as we face the fallen fames
Of the great world's Olympian games.

Seeing the victors vanquished, we
  Grow heartsick at the sight, and choose
To hold in fee what things there be
  Rather than in the hazard use,—
Than stake the all we have—to lose!

We all are feeble. Still we tread
  An ever-upward sloping way;
Deep chasms and dark are round us spread
  And bale-fires beckon us astray:
But thou shalt stand upon the mountain head.

But thou wilt look with gladdened eyes
  And see the mist of error flee,
And see the happy suns arise
  Of happier days that are to be,—
On greener, gladder earth, and clearer skies.

We, of the Morning, but behold
  The dawn afar: thine eyes shall see
The full and perfect day unfold,—
  The full and perfect day to be,
When Justice shall return as lovely as of old.

Thou, with unloosened tongue, shalt speak
  In words of subtle, silver sound,—
In words not futile now, nor weak,
  To all the nations listening round
Until they seek the light,—nor vainly seek!

We only ask it as our share,
  That, when your day-star rises clear,—
A perfect splendour in the air,—
  A glory ever, far and near,—
Ye write such words—*as these of those who were!*

40 *Standing on Tiptoe*

Standing on tiptoe ever since my youth
   Striving to grasp the future just above,
I hold at length the only future—Truth,
   And Truth is Love.

I feel as one who being awhile confined
   Sees drop to dust about him all his bars:—
The clay grows less, and, leaving it, the mind
   Dwells with the stars.

WILLIAM HENRY DRUMMOND

1854–1907

41 *The Wreck of the* Julie Plante

A LEGEND OF LAC ST. PIERRE

On wan dark night on Lac St. Pierre,
   De win' she blow, blow, blow,
An' de crew of de wood-scow *Julie Plante*
   Got scar't an' run below—
For de win' she blow lak' hurricane,
   Bimeby she blow some more,
An' de scow bus' up on Lac St. Pierre
   Wan arpent from de shore.

De captinne walk on de front deck,
   An' walk de hin' deck too—
He call de crew from up de hole,
   He call de cook also.

De cook she's name was Rosie,
  She come from Montreal,
Was chambre maid on lumber-barge
  On de Grande Lachine Canal.

De win' she blow from nor'-eas'-wes',
  De sout' win' she blow too,
W'en Rosie cry, 'Mon cher captinne,
  Mon cher, w'at I shall do?'
De captinne t'row de beeg ankerre,
  But still de scow she dreef:
De crew he can't pass on de shore
  Becos' he los' hees skeef.

De night was dark lak' wan black cat,
  De wave run high an' fas',
W'en de captinne tak' de Rosie girl
  An' tie her to de mas'.
Den he also tak' de life-preserve,
  An' jomp off on de lak',
An' say, 'Good-bye, my Rosie dear,
  I go drown for your sak'!'

Nex' mornin' very early
  'Bout ha'f pas' two—t'ree—four—
De captinne—scow—an' de poor Rosie
  Was corpses on de shore.
For de win' she blow lak' hurricane,
  Bimeby she blow some more,
An' de scow bus' up on Lac St. Pierre
  Wan arpent from de shore.

WILLIAM HENRY DRUMMOND

Moral

Now all good wood-scow sailor-man,
    Tak' warning by dat storm
An' go an' marry some nice French girl
    An' leev on wan beeg farm.
De win' can blow lak' hurricane,
    An' s'pose she blow some more,
You can't get drown' on Lac St. Pierre
    So long you stay on shore.

SIR CHARLES G. D. ROBERTS

1860–1944

42   *The Solitary Woodsman*

When the grey lake-water rushes
Past the dripping alder-bushes,
    And the bodeful autumn wind
In the fir-tree weeps and hushes,—

When the air is sharply damp
Round the solitary camp,
    And the moose-bush in the thicket
Glimmers like a scarlet lamp,—

When the birches twinkle yellow,
And the cornel bunches mellow,
    And the owl across the twilight
Trumpets to his downy fellow,—

When the nut-fed chipmunks romp
Through the maples' crimson pomp,
    And the slim viburnum flushes
In the darkness of the swamp,—

SIR CHARLES G. D. ROBERTS

When the blueberries are dead,
When the rowan clusters red,
    And the shy bear, summer-sleekened,
In the bracken makes his bed,—

On a day there comes once more
To the latched and lonely door,
    Down the wood-road striding silent,
One who has been here before.

Green spruce branches for his head,
Here he makes his simple bed,
    Couching with the sun, and rising
When the dawn is frosty red.

All day long he wanders wide
With the grey moss for his guide,
    And his lonely axe-stroke startles
The expectant forest-side.

Toward the quiet close of day
Back to camp he takes his way,
    And about his sober footsteps
Unafraid the squirrels play.

On his roof the red leaf falls,
At his door the bluejay calls,
    And he hears the wood-mice hurry
Up and down his rough log walls;

Hears the laughter of the loon
Thrill the dying afternoon;
    Hears the calling of the moose
Echo to the early moon.

And he hears the partridge drumming,
The belated hornet humming,—
  All the faint, prophetic sounds
That foretell the winter's coming.

And the wind about his eaves
Through the chilly night-wet grieves,
  And the earth's dumb patience fills him,
Fellow to the falling leaves.

43   *The Tantramar Revisited*

Summers and summers have come, and gone with the flight
    of the swallow;
Sunshine and thunder have been, storm, and winter, and frost;
Many and many a sorrow has all but died from remembrance,
Many a dream of joy fall'n in the shadow of pain.
Hands of chance and change have marred, or moulded, or
    broken,
Busy with spirit or flesh, all I most have adored;
Even the bosom of Earth is strewn with heavier shadows,—
Only in these green hills, aslant to the sea, no change!
Here where the road that has climbed from the inland valleys
    and woodlands,
Dips from the hill-tops down, straight to the base of the
    hills,—
Here, from my vantage-ground, I can see the scattering
    houses,
Stained with time, set warm in orchards, meadows, and wheat,
Dotting the broad bright slopes outspread to southward and
    eastward,
Wind-swept all day long, blown by the south-east wind.

Skirting the sunbright uplands stretches a riband of meadow,
Shorn of the labouring grass, bulwarked well from the sea,
Fenced on its seaward border with long clay dikes from the turbid
Surge and flow of the tides vexing the Westmoreland shores.
Yonder, toward the left, lie broad the Westmoreland marshes,—
Miles on miles they extend, level, and grassy, and dim,
Clear from the long red sweep of flats to the sky in the distance,
Save for the outlying heights, green-rampired Cumberland Point;
Miles on miles outrolled, and the river-channels divide them,—
Miles on miles of green, barred by the hurtling gusts.

Miles on miles beyond the tawny bay is Minudie.
There are the low blue hills; villages gleam at their feet.
Nearer a white sail shines across the water, and nearer
Still are the slim, grey masts of fishing boats dry on the flats.
Ah, how well I remember those wide red flats, above tide-mark,
Pale with scurf of the salt, seamed and baked in the sun!
Well I remember the piles of blocks and ropes, and the net-reels
Wound with the beaded nets, dripping and dark from the sea!
Now at this season the nets are unwound; they hang from the rafters
Over the fresh-stowed hay in upland barns, and the wind
Blows all day through the chinks, with the streaks of sunlight, and sways them
Softly at will; or they lie heaped in the gloom of a loft.

Now at this season the reels are empty and idle; I see them
Over the lines of the dikes, over the gossiping grass.
Now at this season they swing in the long strong wind, thro'
    the lonesome
Golden afternoon, shunned by the foraging gulls.
Near about sunset the crane will journey homeward above
    them;
Round them, under the moon, all the calm night long,
Winnowing soft grey wings of marsh-owls wander and
    wander,
Now to the broad, lit marsh, now to the dusk of the dike.
Soon, thro' their dew-wet frames, in the live keen freshness
    of morning,
Out of the teeth of the dawn blows back the awakening wind.
Then, as the blue day mounts, and the low-shot shafts of the
    sunlight
Glance from the tide to the shore, gossamers jewelled with dew
Sparkle and wave, where late sea-spoiling fathoms of drift-net,
Myriad-meshed, uploomed sombrely over the land.

Well I remember it all. The salt, raw scent of the margin;
While, with men at the windlass, groaned each reel, and the
    net,
Surging in ponderous lengths, uprose and coiled in its station;
Then each man to his home,—well I remember it all!

Yet, as I sit and watch, this present peace of the landscape,—
Stranded boats, these reels empty and idle, the hush,
One grey hawk slow-wheeling above yon cluster of hay-
    stacks,—
More than the old-time stir this stillness welcomes me home.

Ah, the old-time stir, how once it stung me with rapture,—
Old-time sweetness, the winds freighted with honey and salt!

Yet will I stay my steps and not go down to the marshland,—
Muse and recall far off, rather remember than see,—
Lest on too close sight I miss the darling illusion,
Spy at their task even here the hands of chance and change.

44   *The Sower*

    A brown, sad-coloured hillside, where the soil
Fresh from the frequent harrow, deep and fine,
Lies bare; no break in the remote sky-line,
Save where a flock of pigeons streams aloft,
Startled from feed in some low-lying croft,
Or far-off spires with yellow of sunset shine;
And here the Sower, unwittingly divine,
Exerts the silent forethought of his toil.
Alone he treads the glebe, his measured stride
Dumb in the yielding soil; and though small joy
Dwell in his heavy face, as spreads the blind
Pale grain from his dispensing palm aside,
This plodding churl grows great in his employ;—
Godlike, he makes provision for mankind.

45   *The Pea-Fields*

    These are the fields of light, and laughing air,
And yellow butterflies, and foraging bees,
And whitish, wayward blossoms winged as these,
And pale green tangles like a seamaid's hair.

Pale, pale the blue, but pure beyond compare,
And pale the sparkle of the far-off seas
A-shimmer like these fluttering slopes of peas,
And pale the open landscape everywhere.
From fence to fence a perfumed breath exhales
O'er the bright pallor of the well-loved fields,—
My fields of Tantramar in summer-time;
And, scorning the poor feed their pasture yields,
Up from the bushy lots the cattle climb
To gaze with longing through the grey, mossed rails.

46 *The Mowing*

This is the voice of high midsummer's heat.
    The rasping vibrant clamour soars and shrills
    O'er all the meadowy range of shadeless hills,
As if a host of giant cicadae beat
The cymbals of their wings with tireless feet,
    Or brazen grasshoppers with triumphing note
    From the long swath proclaimed the fate that smote
The clover and timothy-tops and meadowsweet.

The crying knives glide on; the green swath lies.
    And all noon long the sun, with chemic ray,
    Seals up each cordial essence in its cell,
That in the dusky stalls, some winter's day,
    The spirit of June, here prisoned by his spell,
    May cheer the herds with pasture memories.

SIR CHARLES G. D. ROBERTS

47   *Ice*

When Winter scourged the meadow and the hill
And in the withered leafage worked his will,
The water shrank, and shuddered, and stood still,—
Then built himself a magic house of glass,
Irised with memories of flowers and grass,
Wherein to sit and watch the fury pass.

48   *The Brook in February*

A snowy path for squirrel and fox,
   It winds between the wintry firs.
Snow-muffled are its iron rocks,
   And o'er its stillness nothing stirs.

But low, bend low a listening ear!
   Beneath the mask of moveless white
A babbling whisper you shall hear
   Of birds and blossoms, leaves and light.

ARCHIBALD LAMPMAN

1861–1899

49   *Heat*

From plains that reel to southward, dim,
   The road runs by me white and bare;
Up the steep hill it seems to swim
   Beyond, and melt into the glare.

ARCHIBALD LAMPMAN

Upward half-way, or it may be
   Nearer the summit, slowly steals
A hay-cart, moving dustily
   With idly clacking wheels.

By his cart's side the wagoner
   Is slouching slowly at his ease,
Half-hidden in the windless blur
   Of white dust puffing to his knees.
This wagon on the height above,
   From sky to sky on either hand,
Is the sole thing that seems to move
   In all the heat-held land.

Beyond me in the fields the sun
   Soaks in the grass and hath his will;
I count the marguerites one by one;
   Even the buttercups are still.
On the brook yonder not a breath
   Disturbs the spider or the midge.
The water-bugs draw close beneath
   The cool gloom of the bridge.

Where the far elm-tree shadows flood
   Dark patches in the burning grass,
The cows, each with her peaceful cud,
   Lie waiting for the heat to pass.
From somewhere on the slope near by
   Into the pale depth of the noon
A wandering thrush slides leisurely
   His thin revolving tune.

In intervals of dream, I hear
   The cricket from the droughty ground;
The grasshoppers spin into mine ear
   A small innumerable sound.
I lift mine eyes sometimes to gaze;
   The burning sky-line blinds my sight;
The woods far off are blue with haze;
   The hills are drenched in light.

And yet to me not this or that
   Is always sharp or always sweet:
In the sloped shadow of my hat
   I lean at rest and drain the heat;
Nay more, I think some blessèd power
   Hath brought me wandering idly here:
In the full furnace of this hour
   My thoughts grow keen and clear.

50   *Solitude*

How still it is here in the woods. The trees
Stand motionless, as if they did not dare
To stir, lest it should break the spell. The air
Hangs quiet as spaces in a marble frieze.
Even this little brook, that runs at ease,
Whispering and gurgling in its knotted bed,
Seems but to deepen, with its curling thread
Of sound, the shadowy sun-pierced silences.
Sometimes a hawk screams or a woodpecker
Startles the stillness from its fixéd mood
With his loud careless tap. Sometimes I hear
The dreamy white-throat from some far-off tree
Pipe slowly on the listening solitude,
His five pure notes succeeding pensively.

51 *A Sunset at Les Éboulements*

Broad shadows fall. On all the mountain side
The scythe-swept fields are silent. Slowly home
By the long beach the high-piled hay-carts come,
Splashing the pale salt shallows. Over wide
Fawn-coloured wastes of mud the slipping tide,
Round the dun rocks and wattled fisheries,
Creeps murmuring in. And now by twos and threes,
O'er the slow spreading pools with clamorous chide,
Belated crows from strip to strip take flight.
Soon will the first star shine; yet ere the night
Reach onward to the pale-green distances,
The sun's last shaft beyond the grey sea-floor
Still dreams upon the Kamouraska shore,
And the long line of golden villages.

52 *Temagami*

Far in the grim Northwest beyond the lines
That turn the rivers eastward to the sea,
Set with a thousand islands, crowned with pines,
Lies the deep water, wild Temagami:
Wild for the hunter's roving, and the use
Of trappers in its dark and trackless vales,
Wild with the trampling of the giant moose,
And the weird magic of old Indian tales.
All day with steady paddles toward the west
Our heavy-laden long canoe we pressed:
All day we saw the thunder-travelled sky
Purpled with storm in many a trailing tress,
And saw at eve the broken sunset die
In crimson on the silent wilderness.

In November

With loitering step and quiet eye,
Beneath the low November sky,
I wandered in the woods, and found
A clearing, where the broken ground
Was scattered with black stumps and briers,
And the old wreck of forest fires.
It was a bleak and sandy spot,
And, all about, the vacant plot
Was peopled and inhabited
By scores of mulleins long since dead.
A silent and forsaken brood
In that mute opening of the wood,
So shrivelled and so thin they were,
So grey, so haggard, and austere,
Not plants at all they seemed to me,
But rather some spare company
Of hermit folk, who long ago,
Wandering in bodies to and fro,
Had chanced upon this lonely way,
And rested thus, till death one day
Surprised them at their compline prayer,
And left them standing lifeless there.

There was no sound about the wood
Save the wind's secret stir. I stood
Among the mullein-stalks as still
As if myself had grown to be
One of their sombre company,
A body without wish or will.
And as I stood, quite suddenly,
Down from a furrow in the sky

The sun shone out a little space
Across that silent sober place,
Over the sand heaps and brown sod,
The mulleins and dead goldenrod,
And passed beyond the thickets grey,
And lit the fallen leaves that lay,
Level and deep within the wood,
A rustling yellow multitude.

And all around me the thin light,
So sere, so melancholy bright,
Fell like the half-reflected gleam
Or shadow of some former dream;
A moment's golden reverie
Poured out on every plant and tree
A semblance of weird joy, or less,
A sort of spectral happiness;
And I, too, standing idly there,
With muffled hands in the chill air,
Felt the warm glow about my feet,
And shuddering betwixt cold and heat,
Drew my thoughts closer, like a cloak,
While something in my blood awoke,
A nameless and unnatural cheer,
A pleasure secret and austere.

54   *A January Morning*

The glittering roofs are still with frost; each worn
Black chimney builds into the quiet sky
Its curling pile to crumble silently.
Far out to westward on the edge of morn,

ARCHIBALD LAMPMAN

The slender misty city towers up-borne
Glimmer faint rose against the pallid blue;
And yonder on those northern hills, the hue
Of amethyst, hang fleeces dull as horn.

And here behind me come the woodmen's sleighs
With shouts and clamorous squeakings; might and main
Up the steep slope the horses stamp and strain,
Urged on by hoarse-tongued drivers—cheeks ablaze,
Iced beards and frozen eyelids—team by team,
With frost-fringed flanks, and nostrils jetting steam.

55   *Winter Evening*

To-night the very horses springing by
Toss gold from whitened nostrils. In a dream
The streets that narrow to the westward gleam
Like rows of golden palaces; and high
From all the crowded chimneys tower and die
A thousand aureoles. Down in the west
The brimming plains beneath the sunset rest,
One burning sea of gold. Soon, soon shall fly
The glorious vision, and the hours shall feel
A mightier master; soon from height to height,
With silence and the sharp unpitying stars,
Stern creeping frosts, and winds that touch like steel,
Out of the depth beyond the eastern bars,
Glittering and still shall come the awful night.

56　　　　　*Midnight*

From where I sit, I see the stars,
　　And down the chilly floor
The moon between the frozen bars
　　Is glimmering dim and hoar.

Without in many a peakéd mound
　　The glinting snowdrifts lie;
There is no voice or living sound;
　　The embers slowly die.

Yet some wild thing is in mine ear;
　　I hold my breath and hark;
Out of the depth I seem to hear
　　A crying in the dark;

No sound of man or wife or child,
　　No sound of beast that groans,
Or of the wind that whistles wild,
　　Or of the tree that moans:

I know not what it is I hear;
　　I bend my head and hark:
I cannot drive it from mine ear,
　　That crying in the dark.

57　　　　*The City of the End of Things*

Beside the pounding cataracts
Of midnight streams unknown to us
'Tis builded in the leafless tracts
And valleys huge of Tartarus.

ARCHIBALD LAMPMAN

Lurid and lofty and vast it seems;
It hath no rounded name that rings,
But I have heard it called in dreams
The City of the End of Things.

Its roofs and iron towers have grown
None knoweth how high within the night,
But in its murky streets far down
A flaming terrible and bright
Shakes all the stalking shadows there,
Across the walls, across the floors,
And shifts upon the upper air
From out a thousand furnace doors;
And all the while an awful sound
Keeps roaring on continually,
And crashes in the ceaseless round
Of a gigantic harmony.
Through its grim depths re-echoing
And all its weary height of walls,
With measured roar and iron ring,
The inhuman music lifts and falls.
Where no thing rests and no man is,
And only fire and night hold sway;
The beat, the thunder and the hiss
Cease not, and change not, night nor day.
And moving at unheard commands,
The abysses and vast fires between,
Flit figures that with clanking hands
Obey a hideous routine;
They are not flesh, they are not bone,
They see not with the human eye,
And from their iron lips is blown
A dreadful and monotonous cry;

And whoso of our mortal race
Should find that city unaware,
Lean Death would smite him face to face,
And blanch him with its venomed air:
Or caught by the terrific spell,
Each thread of memory snapt and cut,
His soul would shrivel and its shell
Go rattling like an empty nut.

It was not always so, but once,
In days that no man thinks upon,
Fair voices echoed from its stones,
The light above it leaped and shone:
Once there were multitudes of men,
That built that city in their pride,
Until its might was made, and then
They withered age by age and died.
But now of that prodigious race,
Three only in an iron tower,
Set like carved idols face to face,
Remain the masters of its power;
And at the city gate a fourth,
Gigantic and with dreadful eyes,
Sits looking toward the lightless north,
Beyond the reach of memories;
Fast rooted to the lurid floor,
A bulk that never moves a jot,
In his pale body dwells no more,
Or mind or soul,—an idiot!
But sometime in the end those three
Shall perish and their hands be still,
And with the master's touch shall flee
Their incommunicable skill.

ARCHIBALD LAMPMAN

A stillness absolute as death
Along the slacking wheels shall lie,
And, flagging at a single breath,
The fires shall moulder out and die.
The roar shall vanish at its height,
And over that tremendous town
The silence of eternal night
Shall gather close and settle down.
All its grim grandeur, tower and hall,
Shall be abandoned utterly,
And into rust and dust shall fall
From century to century;
Nor ever living thing shall grow,
Nor trunk of tree, nor blade of grass;
No drop shall fall, no wind shall blow,
Nor sound of any foot shall pass:
Alone of its accurséd state,
One thing the hand of Time shall spare,
For the grim Idiot at the gate
Is deathless and eternal there.

WILFRED CAMPBELL

1861–1918

58   *Indian Summer*

Along the line of smoky hills
    The crimson forest stands,
And all the day the blue-jay calls
    Throughout the autumn lands.

Now by the brook the maple leans
   With all his glory spread,
And all the sumachs on the hills
   Have turned their green to red.

Now by great marshes wrapt in mist,
   Or past some river's mouth,
Throughout the long, still autumn day
   Wild birds are flying south.

59   *How One Winter Came in the
Lake Region*

For weeks and weeks the autumn world stood still,
   Clothed in the shadow of a smoky haze;
The fields were dead, the wind had lost its will,
And all the lands were hushed by wood and hill,
   In those grey, withered days.

Behind a mist the blear sun rose and set,
   At night the moon would nestle in a cloud;
The fisherman, a ghost, did cast his net;
The lake its shores forgot to chafe and fret,
   And hushed its caverns loud.

Far in the smoky woods the birds were mute,
   Save that from blackened tree a jay would scream,
Or far in swamps the lizard's lonesome lute
Would pipe in thirst, or by some gnarled root
   The tree-toad trilled his dream.

From day to day still hushed the season's mood,
    The streams stayed in their runnels shrunk and dry;
Suns rose aghast by wave and shore and wood,
And all the world, with ominous silence, stood
    In weird expectancy.

When one strange night the sun like blood went down,
    Flooding the heavens in a ruddy hue;
Red grew the lake, the sere fields parched and brown,
Red grew the marshes where the creeks stole down,
    But never a wind-breath blew.

That night I felt the winter in my veins,
    A joyous tremor of the icy glow;
And woke to hear the North's wild vibrant strains,
While far and wide, by withered woods and plains,
    Fast fell the driving snow.

60   *The Winter Lakes*

Out in a world of death, far to the northward lying,
    Under the sun and the moon, under the dusk and the day;
Under the glimmer of stars and the purple of sunsets dying,
    Wan and waste and white, stretch the great lakes away.

Never a bud of spring, never a laugh of summer,
    Never a dream of love, never a song of bird;
But only the silence and white, the shores that grow chiller
    and dumber,
    Wherever the ice-winds sob, and the griefs of winter are
    heard.

WILFRED CAMPBELL

Crags that are black and wet out of the grey lake looming,
   Under the sunset's flush, and the pallid, faint glimmer of
     dawn;
Shadowy, ghost-like shores, where midnight surfs are booming
   Thunders of wintry woe over the spaces wan.

Lands that loom like spectres, whited regions of winter,
   Wastes of desolate woods, deserts of water and shore;
A world of winter and death, within these regions who enter,
   Lost to summer and life, go to return no more.

Moons that glimmer above, waters that lie white under,
   Miles and miles of lake far out under the night;
Foaming crests of waves, surfs that shoreward thunder,
   Shadowy shapes that flee, haunting the spaces white.

Lonely hidden bays, moon-lit, ice-rimmed, winding,
   Fringed by forests and crags, haunted by shadowy shores;
Hushed from the outward strife, where the mighty surf is
     grinding
   Death and hate on the rocks, as sandward and landward it
     roars.

BLISS CARMAN

1861–1929

61   *Low Tide on Grand Pré*

    The sun goes down, and over all
      These barren reaches by the tide
    Such unelusive glories fall,
      I almost dream they yet will bide
      Until the coming of the tide.

And yet I know that not for us,
　　By any ecstasy of dream,
He lingers to keep luminous
　　A little while the grievous stream,
　　Which frets, uncomforted of dream—

A grievous stream, that to and fro
　　Athrough the fields of Acadie
Goes wandering, as if to know
　　Why one beloved face should be
　　So long from home and Acadie.

Was it a year or lives ago
　　We took the grasses in our hands,
And caught the summer flying low
　　Over the waving meadow lands,
　　And held it there between our hands?

The while the river at our feet—
　　A drowsy inland meadow stream—
At set of sun the after-heat
　　Made running gold, and in the gleam
　　We freed our birch upon the stream.

There down along the elms at dusk
　　We lifted dripping blade to drift,
Through twilight scented fine like musk,
　　Where night and gloom awhile uplift,
　　Nor sunder soul and soul adrift.

And that we took into our hands
　　Spirit of life or subtler thing—
Breathed on us there, and loosed the bands

Of death, and taught us, whispering,
The secret of some wonder-thing.

Then all your face grew light, and seemed
To hold the shadow of the sun;
The evening faltered, and I deemed
That time was ripe, and years had done
Their wheeling underneath the sun.

So all desire and all regret,
And fear and memory, were naught;
One to remember or forget
The keen delight our hands had caught;
Morrow and yesterday were naught.

The night has fallen, and the tide . . .
Now and again comes drifting home,
Across these aching barrens wide,
A sigh like driven wind or foam:
In grief the flood is bursting home.

62   *Daphne*

I know that face!
In some lone forest place,
When June brings back the laurel to the hills,
Where shade and sunlight lace,

Where all day long
The brown birds make their song—
A music that seems never to have known
Dismay nor haste nor wrong—

I once before
Have seen thee by the shore,
As if about to shed the flowery guise
And be thyself once more.

Dear, shy, soft face,
With just the elfin trace
That lends thy human beauty the last touch
Of wild, elusive grace!

Can it be true,
A god did once pursue
Thy gleaming beauty through the glimmering wood,
Drenched in the Dorian dew,

Too mad to stay
His hot and headstrong way,
Demented by the fragrance of thy flight,
Heedless of thy dismay?

But I to thee
More gently fond would be,
Nor less a lover woo thee with soft words
And woodland melody;

Take pipe and play
Each forest fear away;
Win thee to idle in the leafy shade
All the long Summer day;

Tell thee old tales
Of love, that still avails
More than all mighty things in this great world,
Still wonder works nor fails;

Teach thee new lore,
How to love more and more,
And find the magical delirium
In joys unguessed before.

I would try over
And over to discover
Some wild, sweet, foolish, irresistible
New way to be thy lover—

New, wondrous ways
To fill thy golden days,
Thy lovely pagan body with delight,
Thy loving heart with praise.

For I would learn,
Deep in the brookside fern,
The magic of the syrinx whispering low
With bubbly fall and turn;

Mock every note
Of the green woodbird's throat,
Till some wild strain, impassioned yet serene,
Should form and float

Far through the hills,
Where mellow sunlight fills
The world with joy, and from the purple vines
The brew of life distils.

Ah, then indeed
Thy heart should have no need
To tremble at a footfall in the brake,
And bid thy bright limbs speed,

But night would come,
And I should make thy home
In the deep pines, lit by a yellow star
Hung in the dark blue dome—

A fragrant house
Of woven balsam boughs,
Where the great Cyprian mother should receive
Our warm unsullied vows.

Songs of the Sea-Children

63

LIV

I see the golden hunter go,
With his hound star close at heel,
Through purple fallows above the hill,
When the large autumn night is still
And the tide of the world is low.

And while to their unwearied quest
The sister Pleiads pass,
The seventh loveliest and lost
Desire of all the orient host
Is here upon my breast.

64

LXVI

What is it to remember?
How white the moonlight poured into the room,
That summer long ago!
How still it was
In that great solemn midnight of the North,
A century ago!

And how I wakened trembling
At soft love-whispers warm against my cheek,
And laughed it was no dream?
Then far away,
The troubled, refluent murmur of the sea,
A sigh within a dream!

65 *Lord of my Heart's Elation*

Lord of my heart's elation,
Spirit of things unseen,
Be thou my aspiration
Consuming and serene!

Bear up, bear out, bear onward
This mortal soul alone,
To selfhood or oblivion,
Incredibly thine own,—

As the foamheads are loosened
And blown along the sea,
Or sink and merge forever
In that which bids them be.

I, too, must climb in wonder,
Uplift at thy command,—
Be one with my frail fellows
Beneath the wind's strong hand,

A fleet and shadowy column
Of dust or mountain rain,
To walk the earth a moment
And be dissolved again.

Be thou my exaltation
Or fortitude of mien,
Lord of the world's elation,
Thou breath of things unseen!

FREDERICK GEORGE SCOTT

1861–1944

66 *Easter Island*

There lies a lone isle in the tropic seas,—
A mountain isle, with beaches shining white,
Where soft stars smile upon its sleep by night,
And every noonday fans it with a breeze.
Here on a cliff, carved upward from the knees,
Three uncouth statues of gigantic height,
Upon whose brows the circling sea-birds light,
Stare out to ocean over the tall trees.

For ever gaze they at the sea and sky,
For ever hear the thunder of the main,
For ever watch the ages die away;
And ever round them rings the phantom cry
Of some lost race that died in human pain,
Looking towards heaven, yet seeing no more than they.

67 *The Sting of Death*

'Is Sin, then, fair?'
  Nay, love, come now,
Put back the hair
  From his sunny brow;

FREDERICK GEORGE SCOTT

See, here, blood-red
Across his head
A brand is set,
The word—'Regret'.

'Is Sin so fleet
   That while he stays,
Our hands and feet
   May go his ways?'
Nay, love, his breath
Clings round like death,
He slakes desire
With liquid fire.

'Is Sin Death's sting?'
   Ay, sure he is,
His golden wing
   Darkens man's bliss;
And when Death comes,
Sin sits and hums
A chaunt of fears
Into man's ears.

'How slayeth Sin?'
   First, God is hid,
And the heart within
   By its own self chid;
Then the maddened brain
Is scourged by pain
To sin as before
And more and more,
   For evermore.

DUNCAN CAMPBELL SCOTT

1862–1947

68   *Off Rivière du Loup*

O ship incoming from the sea
   With all your cloudy tower of sail,
Dashing the water to the lee,
   And leaning grandly to the gale;

The sunset pageant in the west
   Has filled your canvas curves with rose,
And jewelled every toppling crest
   That crashes into silver snows!

You know the joy of coming home,
   After long leagues to France or Spain;
You feel the clear Canadian foam
   And the gulf water heave again.

Between these sombre purple hills
   That cool the sunset's molten bars,
You will go on as the wind wills,
   Beneath the river's roof of stars.

You will toss onward toward the lights
   That spangle over the lonely pier,
By hamlets glimmering on the heights,
   By level islands black and clear.

You will go on beyond the tide,
   Through brimming plains of olive sedge,
Through paler shallows light and wide,
   The rapids piled along the ledge.

At evening off some reedy bay
　　You will swing slowly on your chain,
And catch the scent of dewy hay,
　　Soft blowing from the pleasant plain.

69　　　　*A Night in June*

The world is heated seven times,
　　The sky is close above the lawn,
　　An oven when the coals are drawn.

There is no stir of air at all,
　　Only at times an inward breeze
　　Turns back a pale leaf in the trees.

Here the syringa's rich perfume
　　Covers the tulip's red retreat,
　　A burning pool of scent and heat.

The pallid lightning wavers dim
　　Between the trees, then deep and dense
　　The darkness settles more intense.

A hawk lies panting in the grass,
　　Or plunges upward through the air,
　　The lightning shows him whirling there.

A bird calls madly from the eaves,
　　Then stops, the silence all at once
　　Disturbed, falls dead again and stuns.

A redder lightning flits about,
    But in the north a storm is rolled
    That splits the gloom with vivid gold;

Dead silence, then a little sound,
    The distance chokes the thunder down,
    It shudders faintly in the town.

A fountain plashing in the dark
    Keeps up a mimic dropping strain;
    Ah! God, if it were really rain!

70   *Night and the Pines*

Here in the pine shade is the nest of night,
    Lined deep with shadows, odorous and dim,
And here he stays his sweeping flight,
    Here where the strongest wind is lulled for him,
      He lingers brooding until dawn,
      While all the trembling stars move on and on.

Under the cliff there drops a lonely fall,
    Deep and half heard its thunder lifts and booms;
Afar the loons with eerie call
    Haunt all the bays, and breaking through the glooms
      Upfloats that cry of light despair,
      As if a demon laughed upon the air.

A raven croaks from out his ebon sleep,
    When a brown cone falls near him through the dark;
And when the radiant meteors sweep

95

Afar within the larches wakes the lark;
   The wind moves on the cedar hill,
     Tossing the weird cry of the whip-poor-will.

Sometimes a titan wind, slumbrous and hushed,
   Takes the dark grove within his swinging power;
And like a cradle softly pushed,
   The shade sways slowly for a lulling hour;
     While through the cavern sweeps a cry,
      A Sibyl with her secret prophecy.

When morning lifts its fragile silver dome,
   And the first eagle takes the lonely air,
Up from his dense and sombre home
   The night sweeps out, a tireless wayfarer,
     Leaving within the shadows deep
      The haunting mood and magic of his sleep.

And so we cannot come within this grove,
   But all the quiet dusk remembrance brings
Of ancient sorrow and of hapless love,
   Fate, and the dream of power, and piercing things,
     Traces of mystery and might,
      The passion-sadness of the soul of night.

71   *Night Hymns on Lake Nipigon*

Here in the midnight, where the dark mainland and island
Shadows mingle in shadow deeper, profounder,
Sing we the hymns of the churches, while the dead water
    Whispers before us.

DUNCAN CAMPBELL SCOTT

Thunder is travelling slow on the path of the lightning;
One after one the stars and the beaming planets
Look serene in the lake from the edge of the storm-cloud,
      Then have they vanished.

While our canoe, that floats dumb in the bursting thunder,
Gathers her voice in the quiet and thrills and whispers,
Presses her prow in the star-gleam, and all her ripple
      Lapses in blackness.

Sing we the sacred ancient hymns of the churches,
Chanted first in old-world nooks of the desert,
While in the wild, pellucid Nipigon reaches
      Hunted the savage.

Now have the ages met in the Northern midnight,
And on the lonely, loon-haunted Nipigon reaches
Rises the hymn of triumph and courage and comfort,
      Adeste Fideles.

Tones that were fashioned when the faith brooded in dark-
      ness,
Joined with sonorous vowels in the noble Latin,
Now are married with the long-drawn Ojibwa,
      Uncouth and mournful.

Soft with the silver drip of the regular paddles
Falling in rhythm, timed with the liquid, plangent
Sounds from the blades where the whirlpools break and are
      carried
      Down into darkness;

Each long cadence, flying like a dove from her shelter
Deep in the shadow, wheels for a throbbing moment,
Poises in utterance, returning in circles of silver
      To nest in the silence.

All wild nature stirs with the infinite, tender
Plaint of a bygone age whose soul is eternal,
Bound in the lonely phrases that thrill and falter
      Back into quiet.

Back they falter as the deep storm overtakes them,
Whelms them in splendid hollows of booming thunder,
Wraps them in rain, that, sweeping, breaks and onrushes
      Ringing like cymbals.

72   *At Gull Lake: August, 1810*

    Gull Lake set in the rolling prairie—
    Still there are reeds on the shore,
    As of old the poplars shimmer
    As summer passes;
    Winter freezes the shallow lake to the core;
    Storm passes,
    Heat parches the sedges and grasses,
    Night comes with moon-glimmer,
    Dawn with the morning-star;
    All proceeds in the flow of Time
    As a hundred years ago.

    Then two camps were pitched on the shore,
    The clustered teepees
    Of Tabashaw Chief of the Saulteaux.

And on a knoll tufted with poplars
Two grey tents of a trader—
Nairne of the Orkneys.
Before his tents under the shade of the poplars
Sat Keejigo, third of the wives
Of Tabashaw Chief of the Saulteaux;
Clad in the skins of antelopes
Broidered with porcupine quills
Coloured with vivid dyes,
Vermilion here and there
In the roots of her hair,
A half-moon of powder-blue
On her brow, her cheeks
Scored with light ochre streaks.
Keejigo daughter of Launay
The Normandy hunter
And Oshawan of the Saulteaux,
Troubled by fugitive visions
In the smoke of the camp-fires,
In the close dark of the teepee,
Flutterings of colour
Along the flow of the prairies,
Spangles of flower tints
Caught in the wonder of dawn,
Dreams of sounds unheard—
The echoes of echo,
Star she was named for
Keejigo, star of the morning,
Voices of storm—
Wind-rush and lightning,—
The beauty of terror;
The twilight moon
Coloured like a prairie lily,

DUNCAN CAMPBELL SCOTT

The round moon of pure snow,
The beauty of peace;
Premonitions of love and of beauty
Vague as shadows cast by a shadow.
Now she had found her hero,
And offered her body and spirit
With abject unreasoning passion,
As Earth abandons herself
To the sun and the thrust of the lightning.
Quiet were all the leaves of the poplars,
Breathless the air under their shadow,
As Keejigo spoke of these things to her heart
In the beautiful speech of the Saulteaux.

> *The flower lives on the prairie,*
> *The wind in the sky,*
> *I am here my beloved;*
> *The wind and the flower.*

> *The crane hides in the sand-hills,*
> *Where does the wolverine hide?*
> *I am here my beloved,*
> *Heart's-blood on the feathers,*
> *The foot caught in the trap.*

> *Take the flower in your hand,*
> *The wind in your nostrils;*
> *I am here my beloved;*
> *Release the captive,*
> *Heal the wound under the feathers.*

A storm-cloud was marching
Vast on the prairie,

Scored with livid ropes of hail,
Quick with nervous vines of lightning—
Twice had Nairne turned her away
Afraid of the venom of Tabashaw,
Twice had the Chief fired at his tents
And now when two bullets
Whistled above the encampment
He yelled, 'Drive this bitch to her master.'

Keejigo went down a path by the lake;
Thick at the tangled edges,
The reeds and the sedges
Were grey as ashes
Against the death-black water;
The lightning scored with double flashes
The dark lake-mirror and loud
Came the instant thunder.
Her lips still moved to the words of her music,
'Release the captive,
Heal the wound under the feathers.'

At the top of the bank
The old wives caught her and cast her down
Where Tabashaw crouched by his camp-fire.
He snatched a live brand from the embers,
Seared her cheeks,
Blinded her eyes,
Destroyed her beauty with fire,
Screaming, 'Take that face to your lover.'
Keejigo held her face to the fury
And made no sound.
The old wives dragged her away
And threw her over the bank
Like a dead dog.

Then burst the storm—
The Indians' screams and the howls of the dogs
Lost in the crash of hail
That smashed the sedges and reeds,
Stripped the poplars of leaves,
Tore and blazed onwards,
Wasting itself with riot and tumult—
Supreme in the beauty of terror.

The setting sun struck the retreating cloud
With a rainbow, not an arc but a column
Built with the glory of seven metals;
Beyond in the purple deeps of the vortex
Fell the quivering vines of the lightning.
The wind withdrew the veil from the shrine of the moon,
She rose changing her dusky shade for the glow
Of the prairie lily, till free of all blemish of colour
She came to her zenith without a cloud or a star,
A lovely perfection, snow-pure in the heaven of midnight.
After the beauty of terror the beauty of peace.

But Keejigo came no more to the camps of her people;
Only the midnight moon knew where she felt her way,
Only the leaves of autumn, the snows of winter
Knew where she lay.

73   *A Prairie Water Colour*

Beside the slew the poplars play
In double lines of silver-grey:—
A trembling in the silver trees
A shadow-trembling in the slew.

Standing clear above the hill
The snow-grey clouds are still,
Floating there idle as light;
Beyond, the sky is almost white
Under the pure deep zenith-blue.
Acres of summer-fallow meet
Acres of growing gold-green wheat
That ripen in the heat.
Where a disc-harrow tears the soil,
Up the long slope six horses toil,
The driver, one with the machine;—
The group is dimly seen
For as they go a cloud of dust
Comes like a spirit out of earth
And follows where they go.
Upward they labour, drifting slow,
The disc-rims sparkle through the veil;
Now upon the topmost height
The dust grows pale,
The group springs up in vivid light
And, dipping below the line of sight,
Is lost to view.
Yet still the little cloud is there,
All dusky-luminous in air,
Then thins and settles on the land
And lets the sunlight through.
All is content. The fallow field
Is waiting there till next year's yield
Shall top the rise with ripening grain,
When the green-gold harvest plain
Shall break beneath the harrow.
Still-purple, growing-gold they lie,
The crop and summer fallow. The vast sky

Holds all in one pure round of blue—
And nothing moves except the play
Of silver-grey in the poplar trees
Of shadow in the slew.

74   *En Route*

The train has stopped for no apparent reason
In the wilds;
A frozen lake is level and fretted over
With rippled wind lines;
The sun is burning in the South; the season
Is winter trembling at a touch of spring.
A little hill with birches and a ring
Of cedars—all so still, so pure with snow—
It seems a tiny landscape in the moon.
Long wisps of shadow from the naked birches
Lie on the white in lines of cobweb-grey;
From the cedar roots the snow has shrunk away,
One almost hears it tinkle as it thaws.
Traces there are of wild things in the snow—
Partridge at play, tracks of the foxes' paws
That broke a path to sun them in the trees.
They're going fast where all impressions go
On a frail substance—images like these,
Vagaries the unconscious mind receives
From nowhere, and lets go to nothingness
With the lost flush of last year's autumn leaves.

GONZALVE DESAULNIERS

1863–1934

75   *Le Matin à la Malbaie*

L'aurore a déchiré les ténèbres; le flot
S'émiette en se heurtant aux roches de la grève;
L'air adoucit le chant dolent du matelot,
Il semble que la mer s'éveille d'un long rêve.

Elle monte, gonflant son vaste sein rougi
Par une cendre d'or qu'éparpille la nue
Et s'abat lentement dans le cercle élargi
De la baie où l'amène une force inconnue.

Un goéland s'ébroue et plane par moment
Ou roule dans le creux de ses vagues perfides
Dont la croupe s'irise et dont l'alignement
Offre aux regards charmés de glauques Laurentides.

Émergeant de la coupe énorme de la mer,
Des brouillards, s'élevant sur des ailes d'ouate,
Se raccrochent aux flancs des montagnes de fer
Et couvrent les récifs d'une ombre délicate.

Le vent verse aux sapins l'odeur des goémons
Déchiquetés le long des plages écumantes
Et le golfe berceur promène autour des monts
Le souple enlacement de ses formes mouvantes.

Et tout à coup le jour éclate, l'orient
Déroule son velum de lumière sereine
Et les vapeurs qu'un souffle chasse en défaillant
Font taire sur les eaux le cri de la sirène.

GONZALVE DESAULNIERS

Si quelque blanche barque au loin se courbe encor
Sous l'étreinte subtile et molle de la brise,
Ses filets relevés sèment des gouttes d'or
Sur le bleu de la mer que le calme a surprise.

Le ciel prend peu à peu les teintes des glaciers,
L'azur est blanc, plus blanc qu'un marbre pentélique,
Et rêveur, je regarde expirer à mes pieds
Les houles d'un steamer filant vers l'Atlantique.

LOUIS DANTIN

1865–1945

76 *Noël intime*

DÉCEMBRE 1900

Oh! qu'ils furent heureux, les pâtres de Judée
Éveillés au buccin de l'Ange triomphant,
Et la troupe des Rois par l'étoile guidée
Vers le chaume mystique où s'abritait l'Enfant!

Tous ceux qui, dans la paix de cette nuit agreste,
Trouvèrent le Promis, le Christ enfin venu;
Et ceux même, ignorants de l'Envoyé céleste,
Qui L'avaient repoussé, mais du moins L'avaient vu!

La Mère, s'enivrant d'extase virginale,
Joseph, pour qui tout le mystère enfin a lui,
Et l'étable, et la crèche, et la bise hivernale
Par les vieux ais disjoints se glissant jusqu'à Lui!

LOUIS DANTIN

Tout ce qui Le toucha dans sa chair ou son âme,
Tont ce que son rayon commença d'éblouir,
Princes savants, bergers pieux, Hérode infâme,
Tout ce qui crut en Lui, fût-ce pour le haïr !

Oh ! qu'ils furent heureux. Moi, dans l'ombre muette,
Je m'asseois, pasteur morne et blême de soucis,
Et jamais un archange à ma veille inquiète
Ne vient jeter le *Gloria in Excelsis*.

Je scrute le reflet de toutes les étoiles,
Mage pensif, avec un désir surhumain;
Mais leur front radieux pour moi n'a que des voiles,
Et pas une du doigt ne me montre un chemin.

Et mon âme est la Vierge attendant la promesse,
Mais que ne touche point le souffle de l'Esprit;
Ou le vieillard en pleurs qu'un sombre doute oppresse
Et qui n'a jamais su d'où venait Jésus-Christ.

Je suis l'étable offrant en vain son sol aride
Au Roi toujours lointain et toujours attendu;
Et dans mon cœur voici la crèche, berceau vide,
Où le vent froid gémit comme un espoir perdu.

TOM MacINNES

1867–1951

77   *The Tiger of Desire*

VILLANELLE

Starving, savage, I aspire
    To the red meat of all the World:
I am the Tiger of Desire !

With teeth bared, and claws uncurled,
  By leave o' God I creep to slay
The innocent of all the World.

Out of the yellow, glaring day,
  When I glut my appetite,
To my lair I slink away.

But in the black, returning night
  I leap resistless on my prey,
Mad with agony and fright.

The quick flesh I tear away,
  Writhing till the blood is hurled
On leaf and flower and sodden clay.

My teeth are bared, my claws uncurled,
  Of the red meat I never tire;
In the black jungle of the World
  I am the Tiger of Desire!

CHARLES GILL

1871–1918

Le Cap Trinité

Ce rocher qui de Dieu montre la majesté,
Qui dresse sur le ciel ses trois gradins énormes,
Et verticalement divise en trois ses formes,
Il mérite trois fois son nom de Trinité!

Son flanc vertigineux, creusé de cicatrices,
Et plein d'âpres reliefs qu'effleure le soleil,
Aux grimoires sacrés de l'Égypte est pareil,
Quand l'ombre et la lumière y mêlent leurs caprices.

Les bruns, les gris, les ors, les tendres violets,
A ces signes précis joignent des traits plus vagues
Et le céleste azur y flotte au gré des vagues
Qui dans les plis profonds dardent leurs gais reflets

Est-ce quelque Titan, est-ce plutôt la foudre,
Qui voulut imprimer ici le mot 'toujours'?
Quel sens recèlent donc ces étranges contours?
Pour la postérité quel problème à résoudre!

O cap! en confiant au vertige des cieux
Notre globe éperdu dans la nuit séculaire,
Le Seigneur s'est penché sur ta page de pierre
Digne de relater des faits prodigieux.

Il a mis sur ton front l'obscur secret des causes,
Les lois de la nature et ses frémissements,
Pendant qu'elle assignait leur forme aux éléments
Dans l'infini creuset de ses métamorphoses.

Et scellant à jamais les arrêts du destin
Avec l'ardent burin de la foudre qui gronde,
Il a, dans ton granit, gravé le sort du monde,
En symboles trop grands pour le génie humain,

En signes trop profonds pour que notre œil pénètre
La simple vérité des terrestres secrets,
Pendant que nous osons forger des mots abstraits
Et sonder le mystère insondable de l'être.

La Nature nous parle, et nous l'interrompons!
Aveugles aux rayons de la sainte lumière,
Sourds aux enseignements antiques de la terre,
Nous ne connaissons pas le sol où nous rampons.

CHARLES GILL

Nous n'avons pas assez contemplé les aurores,
Nous n'avons pas assez frémi devant la nuit,
Mornes vivants dont l'âme est en proie aux vains bruits
Des savantes erreurs et des longs mots sonores.

En vain la vérité s'offre à notre compas,
Et la création ouvre pour nous son livre;
Avides des secrets radieux qu'il nous livre,
Nous les cherchons ailleurs, et ne les trouvons pas.

Nous n'avons pas appris le langage des cimes;
Nous ne comprenons pas ce que clament leurs voix,
Quand les cris de l'enfer et du ciel à la fois
Semblent venir à nous dans l'écho des abîmes.

Et l'ange qui régit l'or, le rose et le bleu,
Pour nos yeux sans regard n'écarte pas ses voiles,
Quand le roi des rochers et le roi des étoiles
Nous parlent à midi dans le style de Dieu.

JOHN McCRAE

1872–1918

79   *In Flanders Fields*

In Flanders fields the poppies blow
Between the crosses, row on row,
    That mark our place; and in the sky
    The larks, still bravely singing, fly
Scarce heard amid the guns below.

We are the Dead. Short days ago
We lived, felt dawn, saw sunset glow,
    Loved and were loved, and now we lie
        In Flanders fields.

JOHN McCRAE

Take up our quarrel with the foe:
To you from failing hands we throw
   The torch; be yours to hold it high.
   If ye break faith with us who die
We shall not sleep, though poppies grow
   In Flanders fields.

ALBERT FERLAND

1872–1943

80   *La Patrie au poète*

Poète, mon enfant, tu me chantes en vain,
Je suis la Terre ingrate où rêva Crémazie;
Célèbre si tu veux ma grave poésie,
Mais pour toi, mon enfant, je n'aurai pas de pain !

Pour toi mes paysans ne sèment pas la terre.
Quand tu presses l'Été de blondir leurs moissons,
Généreux, daignent-ils honorer tes chansons ?
Poète, le semeur ne se dit pas ton frère.

Au bercement des vers, Poète, endors ta faim.
Que la gloire du Rêve ennoblisse ta vie,
Proclame qu'elle est belle et grande, ta Patrie,
Mais pour toi, mon enfant, je n'aurai pas de pain !

Rêveur, pourquoi m'aimer comme on aime une femme ?
Tes yeux se sont mouillés d'avoir vu ma beauté;
Pour comprendre ton cœur et vivre ta fierté,
Poète, mon enfant, il me faudrait une âme !

Les noms des fiers Aïeux dont l'honneur et la foi
Font pensif l'Étranger qui traverse mes plaines,
Chante-les, plein d'orgueil, dans tes strophes hautaines;
Poète, ces grands Morts ne revivent qu'en toi.

Va, Barde primitif des vierges Laurentides,
Va-t'en pleurer ton cœur comme un fou dans les bois,
Fidèle au souvenir des héros d'autrefois,
Tandis que l'or vainqueur fait les hommes avides!

Poète, mon enfant, tu me chantes en vain.
Je suis la Terre ingrate où rêva Crémazie;
Célèbre si tu veux ma grave poésie,
Mais pour toi, mon enfant, je n'aurai pas de pain!

81   *Terre nouvelle*

Lorsque le blanc Hiver, aux jours tièdes mêlé,
Recule vers le Nord de montagne en montagne,
La gaîté du semeur envahit la campagne,
Et du sein des greniers renaît l'âme du blé.

Ennui de mars, espoir d'avril, attente et rêve!
C'est, avant les bourgeons et les proches labours,
L'inquiétude exquise et sourde des amours,
C'est dans l'arbre vivant la marche de la sève.

C'est ton œuvre, soleil, créateur des matins,
Semeur de jours, passant du souverain abîme,
Toi qui, majestueux, vas ton chemin sublime,
Jetant un printemps neuf sur nos printemps éteints.

C'est pour t'aimer, soleil, et vivre ta lumière,
Que le semeur ainsi t'accueille à l'horizon,
Que le blé, prisonnier dans sa blanche maison,
Dès les aubes d'avril redemande la terre !

82   *Berceuse âtœna*

    Le vent souffle sur le fleuve
    Youkon, et mon époux poursuit
    le renne sur les monts Koyoukon.
    Xami, Xami, dors mon petit !

       BALLADE DES ÂTŒNAS — ALASKA

En rafales l'Hiver déchaîne
Ses vents hurleurs sur le Youkon,
Et, seul dans la forêt lointaine
Qui longe les monts Koyoukon,
Mon cher époux chasse le renne.

Xami, Xami, dors doucement;
Xami, Xami, dors, mon enfant !

J'ai brisé ma hache de pierre;
Bientôt je n'aurai plus de bois.
Les jours gris traînent leur lumière.
L'arbre se fend sous les cieux froids.
J'ai brisé ma hache de pierre . . .

Xami, Xami, dors doucement;
Xami, Xami, dors, mon enfant !

Ah ! le soleil a fui la terre !
Et nous disons, hommes du Nord,

Que sa chaleur est prisonnière
Dans la loge du grand Castor.
Ah! le soleil a fui la terre!

Xami, Xami, dors doucement;
Xami, Xami, dors, mon enfant!

Depuis longtemps la *cache* est vide.
Mes yeux, tournés vers les buissons,
Ne voient plus les corbeaux avides
Couvrir l'échafaud aux poissons.
Depuis longtemps la *cache* est vide.

Xami, Xami, dors doucement;
Xami, Xami, dors, mon enfant!

Mon petit, j'ai le cœur en peine!
Que fait-il donc si loin de nous,
Kouskokrala, chasseur de rennes?
Ah! qu'il est longtemps, mon époux!...
Mon petit, j'ai le cœur en peine!...

Xami, Xami, dors doucement;
Xami, Xami, dors, mon enfant!

En rafales l'Hiver déchaîne
Ses vents hurleurs sur le Youkon,
Et, seul, dans la forêt lointaine
Qui longe les monts Koyoukon,
Mon cher époux chasse le renne.

Xami, Xami, dors doucement;
Xami, Xami, dors, mon enfant!

1873–1932

83   *The Hanging*

'*It has been decided that the law must be allowed to take its course.*'
DAILY PAPER

THE LAW SPEAKS:

> *I bind the Soul that fathered me;*
> *I am the Law, and resolute*
> *Against the growing of the Soul,*
> *I hang, behead, electrocute.*

I take my course. How fine the day!
And all are here by duty stirred,
Hangman and prisoner, warden and press,
And Jesus with the Holy Word.

I am the Law. May order rule!
My warrant let the warden read,
Then all with proper decency
Will to our lifted stage proceed.

How fine the day! The happy sun
Beams into corridor and square
To cheer our prisoner and bless
The purpose of our altar there.

Our footsteps on the sunny stones
Beat to the pulse of earth and star;
The law that drives yon budding tree
Condemned our prisoner at its bar.

Let Jesus hold his trembling arm
And stand beside him to the end
(He loves these opportunities
To function as experienced friend.)

Now, hangman, use your cunning well,
And hide his face that none may see
The anguish of his tortured soul.
I take my course, let these things be.

Come, Jesus, speak your little prayer
And, when 'Deliver us' is said,
Then, hangman, draw the gliding bolt
And give our brother air to tread.

'Our Father,' sound the gracious words,
'Thy will be done'—and all the rest—
(I hope our poor delivered friend
Had time to note the subtle jest).

He shoots into the opened dark,
His soul is torn through narrow ways.
I take my course. I only see
A straightened rope that trembling sways.

I bind the Soul that fathered me;
I am the Law, and resolute
Against the growing of the Soul,
I hang, behead, electrocute.

THEODORE GOODRIDGE ROBERTS

1877–1953

84   *The Wreckers' Prayer*

Give us a wrack or two, Good Lard,
For winter in Tops'il Tickle bes hard,
Wid grey frost creepin' like mortal sin
And perishin' lack of bread in the bin.

A grand, rich wrack, us do humbly pray,
Busted abroad at the break o' day
An' hove clear in 'crost Tops'il Reef,
Wid victuals an' gear to beguile our grief.

God of reefs an' tides an' sky,
Heed Ye our need an' hark to our cry!
Bread by the bag an' beef by the cask.
Ease for sore bellies bes all we ask.

One grand wrack—or maybe two?—
Wid gear an' victuals to see us through
'Til Spring starts up like the leap of day
An' the fish strike back into Tops'il Bay.

One rich wrack—for Thy hand bes strong!
A barque or a brig from up-along
Bemused by Thy twisty tides, O Lard!
For winter in Tops'il Tickle bes hard.

Loud an' long will us sing Yer praise,
Marciful Fadder, O Ancient of Days,
Master of fog an' tide an' reef!
Heave us a wrack to beguile our grief. *Amen.*

85   *The Blue Heron*

In a green place lanced through
With amber and gold and blue;
A place of water and weeds
And roses pinker than dawn,
And ranks of lush young reeds,

THEODORE GOODRIDGE ROBERTS

And grasses straightly withdrawn
From graven ripples of sands,
The still blue heron stands.

Smoke-blue he is, and grey
As embers of yesterday.
Still he is, as death;
Like stone, or shadow of stone,
Without a pulse or breath,
Motionless and alone
There in the lily stems:
But his eyes are alive like gems.

Still as a shadow; still
Grey feather and yellow bill:
Still as an image made
Of mist and smoke half hid
By windless sunshine and shade,
Save when a yellow lid
Slides and is gone like a breath:
Death-still—and sudden as death.

LUCIEN RAINIER

b. 1877

86   *Somnium*

Parfois, quand le grand sommeil obscurcit ma prunelle,
je vois paraître en moi, songe mystérieux,
l'un après l'autre, en long cortège, mes aïeux,
spectres psalmodiant une plainte éternelle.

LUCIEN RAINIER

Lugubres, n'ayant plus la parure charnelle,
dans le linceul qui tranche en blancheur sur les cieux,
ils vont, funèbrement tranquilles, et mes yeux
regardent défiler leur suite solennelle.

Lorsque le dernier mort à son tour est passé,
je songe que, plus tard, ainsi qu'eux trépassé,
j'aurai l'horrible aspect de leurs vieux os livides . . .

Et je tremble d'avoir, au fond de mon esprit,
vu le destin de l'homme en lettres d'ombre écrit
dans l'effrayante horreur de leurs orbites vides.

ALBERT LOZEAU

1878-1924

87   *Intimité*

En attendant le jour où vous viendrez à moi
Les regards pleins d'amour, de pudeur et de foi,
Je rêve à tous les mots futurs de votre bouche,
Qui sembleront un air de musique qui touche
Et dont je goûterai le charme à vos genoux . . .
Et ce rêve m'est cher comme un baiser de vous !
Votre beauté saura m'être indulgente et bonne,
Et vos lèvres auront le goût des fruits d'automne !
Par les longs soirs d'hiver, sous la lampe qui luit,
Douce, vous resterez près de moi, sans ennui,
Tandis que, feuilletant les pages d'un vieux livre,
Dans les poètes morts je m'écouterai vivre,
Ou que, songeant depuis des heures, revenu
D'un voyage lointain en pays inconnu,

Heureux, j'apercevrai, sereine et chaste ivresse,
A mon côté veillant, la fidèle tendresse !
Et notre amour sera comme un beau jour de mai,
Calme, plein de soleil, joyeux et parfumé !
Et nous vivrons ainsi, dans une paix profonde,
Isolés du vain bruit dont s'étourdit le monde,
Seuls comme deux amants qui n'ont besoin entre eux
Que de se regarder, pour s'aimer, dans les yeux !

88   *Effets de neige et de givre*

I

Les arbres ont l'aspect de blancs marbres qui poussent
Au bord des blancs trottoirs et des toits blancs qui moussent ;
Il neige ! Tout se vêt de divine blancheur.
Pour couvrir le sol noir du vieux monde pécheur,
On dirait que la nue au vent se désagrège
Et tombe par milliers de flocons purs. Il neige !
Les champs, sur qui tout un long jour il a neigé,
Semblent lointainement des lacs de lait figé.
Dans les chemins ouatés où l'air froid souffle, il tinte
Une argentine voix de grelot, vite éteinte.
Et les petits enfants s'exclament, réjouis
Par le poudroiement clair du ciel de mon pays.

II

Un grain de neige fond en larme sur ma vitre.
Je referme mon livre au milieu d'un chapitre,
Pour regarder tomber la neige du ciel blanc,
Et la suivre en son vol tourbillonnant et lent.
Elle est molle, elle est vive, elle est fantasque et folle ;

Elle plane, elle flotte, elle vogue, elle vole;
Elle est frivole et grave; elle a, comme un rimeur
Sensible, de soudains revirements d'humeur,
Selon qu'un petit vent nonchalant se révèle
Ou qu'un souffle nouveau soudain la renouvelle!
Mais tout cela finit, pour elle comme lui,
Par de longs pleurs coulés et par de l'eau qui fuit . . .

III

Ma vitre, ce matin, est toute en feuilles blanches,
En fleurs de givre, en fruits de frimas fins, en branches
D'argent, sur qui des frissons blancs se sont glacés.
Des arbres de vermeil l'un à l'autre enlacés,
Immobiles, ont l'air d'attendre qu'un vent passe
Tranquille, mol et blanc. Calme petit espace
Où tout a le repos profond de l'eau qui dort,
Parce que tout cela gît insensible et mort.
Vision qui fondra dès la première flamme,
Comme le rêve pur des jeunes ans de l'âme;
Espoirs, illusions qu'on regrette tout bas:
Sur la vitre du cœur, frêles fleurs de frimas . . .

IV

Par ces longs soirs d'hiver où, fatigués des livres,
Les yeux suivent l'effet sur la vitre des givres
Dessinant d'un pinceau lent et mystérieux,
Sous l'inspiration des grands vents furieux,
Des jardins, des forêts blanches et toujours calmes,
De fantastiques fleurs et de bizarres palmes, —
Ces soirs-là, comparant l'ombre qui rôde en lui
A la blanche splendeur des choses de la nuit,

Le poète isolé du monde, dans sa chambre,
Rêve à la grande paix des tombes de décembre
Et du linceul d'hermine amoncelé sans bruit
Qui, sous le ciel empli de clair de lune, luit . . .

89   *La Royale Chanson*

Prends ton vieux violon,
Sonne la chanterelle
Et suis ma voix, le long
De la *Chanson pour Elle.*

L'amoureuse n'est plus et le poète est mort;
Mais la chanson d'amour, vivante, chante encor.

La chanson s'alanguit encore de leurs fièvres
En s'exhalant, le soir, aux lents soupirs des lèvres.

Le poète est sous terre et l'amoureuse aussi;
Ils dorment, l'un tout près de l'autre, sans souci.

Des désirs qu'ils n'ont plus la chanson est brûlante;
De leur bonheur passé la chanson seule chante.

Ils sont un peu de cendre au fond de deux cercueils,
Et la chanson exalte encore leur orgueil.

Elle était belle et douce aussi, la Bien-Aimée;
La chanson de son souffle est toute parfumée.

Elle était reine, et lui grand prince ami de l'Art:
La chanson que je chante est du temps de Ronsard.

ALBERT LOZEAU

Sonne la chanterelle
A ton vieux violon,
Et suis ma voix, le long
De la *Chanson pour Elle*.

90   *Épilogue*

J'ai versé tout le sang de mon cœur dans mes vers.
Ma fatigue a laissé souvent la page blanche.
Ma vie intérieure en poème s'épanche
Aux rythmes variés des sentiments divers.

Sur ma profonde nuit mes yeux se sont ouverts;
J'ai dit ce que j'ai vu d'une voix simple et franche.
Si j'ai menti d'un mot douteux, je le retranche:
J'errais en des sentiers de ténèbres couverts.

Et maintenant, Seigneur, de ces heures passées
A traduire mon âme en strophes cadencées,
Me tiendrez-vous rigueur au jour du Jugement?

Ai-je perdu le temps précieux de la vie?
Si je n'ai jamais su vous chanter autrement,
Votre gloire n'a-t-elle été par moi servie?

JOSEPH-ARTHUR LAPOINTE

b. 1878

91   *Les Pauvres*

Ils ne protestent pas, ces tristes chiens battus.
On dit: La pauvreté fait fleurir les vertus.
Et comme ils sont naïfs et bons, ils se résignent.

Ils portent les fardeaux les plus vils, les plus lourds.
On dit: La pauvreté doit travailler toujours.
Et comme ils sont naïfs et bons, ils se résignent.

Ils ont faim, ils ont froid, ils ont le cœur meurtri.
On dit: La pauvreté rend sublime l'esprit.
Et comme ils sont naïfs et bons, ils se résignent.

Enfin, un soir, ils voient la tombe s'entr'ouvrir.
On dit: La pauvreté sait dignement mourir.
Et comme ils sont naïfs et bons, ils se résignent.

ÉMILE NELLIGAN

1879–1941

92   *La Romance du vin*

Tout se mêle en un vif éclat de gaîté verte.
Ô le beau soir de mai! Tous les oiseaux en chœur,
Ainsi que les espoirs naguères à mon cœur,
Modulent leur prélude à ma croisée ouverte.

Ô le beau soir de mai! le joyeux soir de mai!
Un orgue au loin éclate en froides mélopées;
Et les rayons, ainsi que de pourpres épées,
Percent le cœur du jour qui se meurt parfumé.

Je suis gai! je suis gai! Dans le cristal qui chante,
Verse, verse le vin! verse encore et toujours,
Que je puisse oublier la tristesse des jours,
Dans le dédain que j'ai de la foule méchante!

ÉMILE NELLIGAN

Je suis gai ! je suis gai ! Vive le vin et l'Art ! . . .
J'ai le rêve de faire aussi des vers célèbres,
Des vers qui gémiront les musiques funèbres
Des vents d'automne au loin passant dans le brouillard.

C'est le règne du rire amer et de la rage
De se savoir poète et l'objet du mépris,
De se savoir un cœur et de n'être compris
Que par le clair de lune et les grands soirs d'orage

Femmes ! je bois à vous qui riez du chemin
Où l'Idéal m'appelle en ouvrant ses bras roses;
Je bois à vous surtout, hommes aux fronts moroses
Qui dédaignez ma vie et repoussez ma main !

Pendant que tout l'azur s'étoile dans la gloire,
Et qu'un hymne s'entonne au renouveau doré,
Sur le jour expirant je n'ai donc pas pleuré,
Moi qui marche à tâtons dans ma jeunesse noire !

Je suis gai ! je suis gai ! Vive le soir de mai !
Je suis follement gai, sans être pourtant ivre ! . . .
Serait-ce que je suis enfin heureux de vivre;
Enfin mon cœur est-il guéri d'avoir aimé?

Les cloches ont chanté; le vent du soir odore . . .
Et pendant que le vin ruisselle à joyeux flots,
Je suis si gai, si gai, dans mon rire sonore,
Oh ! si gai, que j'ai peur d'éclater en sanglots !

Le Mai d'amour

Voici que verdit le printemps
Où l'heure au cœur sonne vingt ans,
  Larivarite et la la ri;
Voici que j'ai touché l'époque
Où l'on est las d'habits en loque,
Au gentil sieur il faudra ça
   Ça
  La la ri
Jeunes filles de bel humour,
Donnez-nous le mai de l'amour,
  Larivarite et la la ri.

Soyez blonde ou brune ou châtaine,
Ayez les yeux couleur lointaine
  Larivarite et la la ri
Des astres bleus, des perles roses,
Mais surtout, pas de voix moroses,
Belles de liesse, il faudra ça
   Ça
  La la ri
Il faudra battre un cœur de joie
Tout plein de gaîté qui rougeoie,
  Larivarite et la la ri.

Moi, j'ai rêvé de celle-là
Au cœur triste dans le gala,
  Larivarite et la la ri,
Comme l'oiseau d'automne au bois
Ou le rythme du vieux hautbois,
Un cœur triste, il me faudra ça

Ça
La la ri
Triste comme une main d'adieu
Et pur comme les yeux de Dieu,
Larivarite et la la ri.

Voici que vient l'amour de mai,
Vivez-le vite, le cœur gai,
Larivarite et la la ri;
Ils tombent tôt les jours méchants,
Vous cesserez aussi vos chants;
Dans le cercueil il faudra ça
Ça
La la ri
Belles de vingt ans au cœur d'or,
L'amour, sachez-le, tôt s'endort,
Larivarite et la la ri.

94   *Devant deux portraits de ma mère*

Ma mère, que je l'aime en ce portrait ancien,
Peint aux jours glorieux qu'elle était jeune fille,
Le front couleur de lys et le regard qui brille
Comme un éblouissant miroir vénitien !

Ma mère que voici n'est plus du tout la même;
Les rides ont creusé le beau marbre frontal;
Elle a perdu l'éclat du temps sentimental
Où son hymen chanta comme un rose poème.

Aujourd'hui je compare, et j'en suis triste aussi,
Ce front nimbé de joie et ce front de souci,
Soleil d'or, brouillard dense au couchant des années.

Mais, mystère de cœur qui ne peut s'éclairer !
Comment puis-je sourire à ces lèvres fanées ?
Au portrait qui sourit, comment puis-je pleurer ?

95   *Placet*

Reine, acquiescez-vous qu'une boucle déferle
Des lames des cheveux aux lames du ciseau,
Pour que j'y puisse humer un peu de chant d'oiseau,
Un peu de soir d'amour né de vos yeux de perle ?

Au bosquet de mon cœur, en des trilles de merle,
Votre âme a fait chanter sa flûte de roseau.
Reine, acquiescez-vous qu'une boucle déferle
Des lames des cheveux aux lames du ciseau ?

Fleur soyeuse aux parfums de rose, lis ou berle,
Je vous la remettrai, secrète comme un sceau,
Fût-ce en Éden, au jour que nous prendrons vaisseau
Sur la mer idéale où l'ouragan se ferle.

Reine, acquiescez-vous qu'une boucle déferle ?

96   *Les Communiantes*

Calmes, elles s'en vont, défilant aux allées
De la chapelle en fleurs, et je les suis des yeux,
Religieusement joignant mes doigts pieux,
Plein de l'ardent regret des ferveurs en allées.

Voici qu'elles se sont toutes agenouillées
Au mystique repas qui leur descend des cieux,
Devant l'autel piqué de flamboiements joyeux
Et d'une floraison de fleurs immaculées.

Leur séraphique ardeur fut si lente à finir
Que tout à l'heure encore, à les voir revenir
De l'agape céleste au divin réfectoire,

Je crus qu'elles allaient vraiment prendre l'essor,
Comme si, se glissant sous leurs voiles de gloire,
Un ange leur avait posé des ailes d'or.

97 *Le Cloître noir*

Ils défilent au chant étouffé des sandales,
Le chef bas, égrenant de massifs chapelets,
Et le soir qui s'en vient, du sang de ses reflets
Mordore la splendeur funéraire des dalles.

Ils s'effacent soudain, comme en de noirs dédales,
Au fond des corridors pleins de pourpres relais
Où de grands anges peints aux vitraux verdelets
Interdisent l'entrée aux terrestres scandales.

Leur visage est funèbre, et dans leurs yeux sereins
Comme les horizons vastes des cieux marins,
Flambe l'austérité des froides habitudes.

La lumière céleste emplit leur large esprit,
Car l'Espoir triomphant creusa les solitudes
De ces silencieux spectres de Jésus-Christ.

L'Idiote aux cloches

I

Elle a voulu trouver les cloches
Du Jeudi-Saint sur les chemins;
Elle a saigné ses pieds aux roches
A les chercher dans les soirs maints,
　　Ah! lon lan laire,
Elle a meurtri ses pieds aux roches;
On lui disait: 'Fouille tes poches.
— Nenni, sont vers les cieux romains:
Je veux trouver les cloches, cloches,
　　Je veux trouver les cloches
Et je les aurai dans mes mains';
Ah! lon lan laire et lon lan la.

II

Or vers les heures vespérales
Elle allait, solitaire, aux bois.
Elle rêvait des cathédrales
Et des cloches dans les beffrois;
　　Ah! lon lan laire,
Elle rêvait des cathédrales,
Puis tout à coup, en de fous râles
S'élevait tout au loin sa voix:
'Je veux trouver les cloches, cloches,
　　Je veux trouver les cloches
Et je les aurai dans mes mains';
Ah! lon lan laire et lon lan la

III

Une aube triste, aux routes croches,
On la trouva dans un fossé.
Dans la nuit du retour des cloches
L'idiote avait trépassé;
    Ah! lon lan laire,
Dans la nuit du retour des cloches,
A leurs métalliques approches,
Son rêve d'or fut exaucé:
Un ange mit les cloches, cloches,
    Lui mit toutes les cloches,
Là-haut, lui mit toutes aux mains;
Ah! lon lan laire et lon lan la.

99   *Le Vaisseau d'or*

Ce fut un grand Vaisseau taillé dans l'or massif:
Ses mâts touchaient l'azur, sur des mers inconnues;
La Cyprine d'amour, cheveux épars, chairs nues,
S'étalait à sa proue, au soleil excessif.

Mais il vint une nuit frapper le grand écueil
Dans l'Océan trompeur où chantait la Sirène,
Et le naufrage horrible inclina sa carène
Aux profondeurs du Gouffre, immuable cercueil.

Ce fut un Vaisseau d'or, dont les flancs diaphanes
Révélaient des trésors que les marins profanes,
Dégoût, Haine et Névrose, entre eux ont disputés.

Que reste-t-il de lui dans la tempête brève?
Qu'est devenu mon cœur, navire déserté?
Hélas! il a sombré dans l'abîme du Rêve!

I lift the Lord on high,
Under the murmuring hemlock boughs, and see
The small birds of the forest lingering by
And making melody.
These are mine acolytes and these my choir,
And this mine altar in the cool green shade,
Where the wild soft-eyed does draw nigh
Wondering, as in the byre
Of Bethlehem the oxen heard Thy cry
And saw Thee, unafraid.

My boatmen sit apart,
Wolf-eyed, wolf-sinewed, stiller than the trees.
Help me, O Lord, for very slow of heart
And hard of faith are these.
Cruel are they, yet Thy children. Foul are they,
Yet wert Thou born to save them utterly.
Then make me as I pray
Just to their hates, kind to their sorrows, wise
After their speech, and strong before their free
Indomitable eyes.

Do the French lilies reign
Over Mont Royal and Stadacona still?
Up the St. Lawrence comes the spring again,
Crowning each southward hill
And blossoming pool with beauty, while I roam
Far from the perilous folds that are my home,
There where we built St. Ignace for our needs,
Shaped the rough roof tree, turned the first sweet sod,
St. Ignace and St. Louis, little beads
On the rosary of God.

Pines shall Thy pillars be,
Fairer than those Sidonian cedars brought
By Hiram out of Tyre, and each birch-tree
Shines like a holy thought.
But come no worshippers; shall I confess,
St. Francis-like, the birds of the wilderness?
O, with Thy love my lonely head uphold,
A wandering shepherd I, who hath no sheep;
A wandering soul, who hath no scrip, nor gold,
Nor anywhere to sleep.

My hour of rest is done;
On the smooth ripple lifts the long canoe;
The hemlocks murmur sadly as the sun
Slants his dim arrows through.
Whither I go I know not, nor the way,
Dark with strange passions, vexed with heathen charms,
Holding I know not what of life or death;
Only be Thou beside me day by day,
Thy rod my guide and comfort, underneath
Thy everlasting arms.

101   *Resurgam*

I shall say, Lord, 'Is it music, is it morning,
Song that is fresh as sunrise, light that sings?'
When on some hill there breaks the immortal warning
Of half-forgotten springs.

I shall say, Lord, 'I have loved you, not another,
Heard in all quiet your footsteps on my road,
Felt your strong shoulder near me, O my brother,
Lightening the load.'

I shall say, Lord, 'I remembered, working, sleeping,
One face I looked for, one denied and dear.
Now that you come my eyes are blind with weeping,
But you will kiss them clear.'

I shall say, Lord, 'Touch my lips, and so unseal them;
I have learned silence since I lived and died.'
I shall say, Lord, 'Lift my hands, and so reveal them,
Full, satisfied.'

I shall say, Lord, 'We will laugh again to-morrow,
Now we'll be still a little, friend with friend.
Death was the gate and the long way was sorrow.
Love is the end.'

102   *Quiet*

Come not the earliest petal here, but only
Wind, cloud, and star,
Lovely and far,
Make it less lonely.

Few are the feet that seek her here, but sleeping
Thoughts sweet as flowers
Linger for hours,
Things winged, yet weeping.

Here in the immortal empire of the grasses,
Time, like one wrong
Note in a song,
With their bloom, passes.

E. J. PRATT

103   From *The Cachalot*

I

A thousand years now had his breed
Established the mammalian lead;
The founder (in cetacean lore)
Had followed Leif to Labrador;
The eldest-born tracked all the way
Marco Polo to Cathay;
A third had hounded one whole week
The great Columbus to Bahama;
A fourth outstripped to Mozambique
The flying squadron of da Gama;
A fifth had often crossed the wake
Of Cortez, Cavendish and Drake;
The great grandsire—a veteran rover—
Had entered once the strait of Dover,
In a naval fight, and with his hump
Had stove a bottom of Van Tromp;
The grandsire at Trafalgar swam
At the *Redoubtable* and caught her,
With all the tonnage of his ram,
Deadly between the wind and water;
And his granddam herself was known
As fighter and as navigator,
The mightiest mammal in the zone
From Baffin Bay to the Equator.
From such a line of conjugate sires
Issued his blood, his lumbar fires,
And from such dams imperial-loined
His Taurian timbers had been joined,
And when his time had come to hasten

Forth from his deep sub-mammary basin,
Out on the ocean tracts, his mama
Had, in a North Saghalien gale,
Launched him, a five-ton healthy male,
Between Hong Kong and Yokohama.
Now after ninety moons of days,
Sheltered by the mammoth fin,
He took on adolescent ways
And learned the habits of his kin;
Ransacked the seas and found his mate,
Established his dynastic name,
Reared up his youngsters, and became
The most dynamic vertebrate
(According to his Royal Dame)
From Tonga to the Hudson Strait.
And from the start, by fast degrees,
He won in all hostilities;
Sighted a hammerhead and followed him,
Ripped him from jaw to ventral, swallowed him;
Pursued a shovelnose and mangled him;
Twisted a broadbill's neck and strangled him;
Conquered a rorqual in full sight
Of a score of youthful bulls who spurred
Him to the contest, and the fight
Won him the mastery of the herd.

Another ninety moons and Time
Had cast a marvel from his hand,
Unmatched on either sea or land—
A sperm whale in the pitch of prime.
A hundred feet or thereabout
He measured from the tail to snout,
And every foot of that would run

From fifteen hundred to a ton.
But huge as was his tail or fin,
His bulk of forehead, or his hoists
And slow subsidences of jaw,
He was more wonderful within.
His iron ribs and spinal joists
Enclosed the sepulchre of a maw.
The bellows of his lungs might sail
A herring skiff—such was the gale
Along the wind-pipe; and so large
The lymph-flow of his active liver,
One might believe a fair-sized barge
Could navigate along the river;
And the islands of his pancreas
Were so tremendous that between 'em
A punt would sink; while a cart might pass
His bile-duct to the duodenum
Without a peristaltic quiver.
And cataracts of red blood stormed
His heart, while lower down was formed
That fearful labyrinthine coil
Filled with the musk of ambergris;
And there were reservoirs of oil
And spermaceti; and renal juices
That poured in torrents without cease
Throughout his grand canals and sluices.
And hid in his arterial flow
Were flames and currents set aglow
By the wild pulses of the chase
With fighters of the Saxon race.
A tincture of an iron grain
Had dyed his blood a darker stain;
Upon his coat of toughest rubber

A dozen cicatrices showed
The place as many barbs were stowed,
Twisted and buried in his blubber,
The mute reminders of the hours
Of combat when the irate whale
Unlimbered all his massive powers
Of head-ram and of caudal flail,
Littering the waters with the chips
Of whale-boats and vainglorious ships.

II

Where Cape Delgado strikes the sea,
A cliff ran outward slantingly
A mile along a tossing edge
Of water towards a coral ledge,
Making a sheer and downward climb
Of twenty fathoms where it ended,
Forming a jutty scaur suspended
Over a cave of murk and slime.
A dull reptilian silence hung
About the walls, and fungus clung
To knots of rock, and over boles
Of lime and basalt poisonous weed
Grew rampant, covering the holes
Where crayfish and sea-urchins breed.
The upper movement of the seas
Across the reefs could not be heard;
The nether tides but faintly stirred
Sea-nettles and anemones.
A thick festoon of lichens crawled
From crag to crag, and under it
Half-hidden in a noisome pit

Of bones and shells a kraken sprawled.
Moveless, he seemed, as a boulder set
In pitch, and dead within his lair,
Except for a transfixing stare
From lidless eyes of burnished jet,
And a hard spasm now and then
Within his viscous centre, when
His scabrous feelers intertwined
Would stir, vibrate, and then unwind
Their ligatures with easy strength
To tap the gloom, a cable length;
And finding no life that might touch
The mortal radius of their clutch,
Slowly relax, and shorten up
Each tensile tip, each suction cup,
And coil again around the head
Of the mollusc on its miry bed,
Like a litter of pythons settling there
To shutter the Gorgonian stare.

But soon the squid's antennæ caught
A murmur that the waters brought—
No febrile stirring as might spring
From a puny barracuda lunging
At a tuna's leap, some minor thing,
A tarpon or a dolphin plunging—
But a deep consonant that rides
Below the measured beat of tides
With that vast, undulating rhythm
A sounding sperm whale carries with him.
The kraken felt that as the flow
Beat on his lair with plangent power,

It was the challenge of his foe,
The prelude to a fatal hour;
Nor was there given him more than time,
From that first instinct of alarm,
To ground himself in deeper slime,
And raise up each enormous arm
Above him, when, unmeasured, full
On the revolving ramparts, broke
The hideous rupture of a stroke
From the forehead of the bull.
And when they interlocked, that night—
Cetacean and cephalopod—
No Titan with Olympian god
Had ever waged a fiercer fight;
Tail and skull and teeth and maw
Met sinew, cartilage, and claw,
Within those self-engendered tides,
Where the Acherontic flood
Of sepia, mingling with the blood
Of whale, befouled Delgado's sides.
And when the cachalot out-wore
The squid's tenacious clasp, he tore
From frame and socket, shred by shred,
Each gristled, writhing tentacle,
And with serrated mandible
Sawed cleanly through the bulbous head;
Then gorged upon the fibrous jelly
Until, finding that six tons lay
Like Vulcan's anvil in his belly,
He left a thousand sharks his prey,
And with his flukes, slow-labouring, rose
To a calm surface where he shot
A roaring geyser, steaming hot,

From the blast-pipe of his nose.
One hour he rested, in the gloom
Of the after-midnight; his great back
Prone with the tide and, in the loom
Of the Afric coast, merged with the black
Of the water; till a rose shaft, sent
From Madagascar far away,
Etched a ripple, eloquent
Of a freshening wind and a fair day.

Flushed with the triumph of the fight,
He felt his now unchallenged right
To take by demonstrated merit
What he by birth-line did inherit—
The lordship of each bull and dam
That in mammalian water swam,
As Maharajah of the seas
From Rio to the Celebes.
And nobly did the splendid brute
Leap to his laurels, execute
His lineal functions as he sped
Towards the Equator northwards, dead
Against the current and the breeze;
Over his back the running seas
Cascaded, while the morning sun,
Rising in gold and beryl, spun
Over the cachalot's streaming gloss,
And from the foam, a fiery floss
Of multitudinous fashionings,
And dipping downward from the blue,
The sea-gulls from Comoro flew,
And brushed him with their silver wings;

Then at the tropic hour of noon
He slackened down; a drowsy spell
Was creeping over him, and soon
He fell asleep upon the swell. . . .

104   From *Brébeuf and his Brethren*

[*The Martyrdom of Brébeuf and
Lalemant, 16 March 1649*]

Less than two hours it took the Iroquois
To capture, sack and garrison St. Ignace,
And start then for St. Louis. The alarm
Sounded, five hundred of the natives fled
To the mother fort only to be pursued
And massacred in the snow. The eighty braves
That manned the stockades perished at the breaches;
And what was seen by Ragueneau and the guard
Was smoke from the massed fire of cabin bark.

Brébeuf and Lalemant were not numbered
In the five hundred of the fugitives.
They had remained, infusing nerve and will
In the defenders, rushing through the cabins
Baptizing and absolving those who were
Too old, too young, too sick to join the flight.
And when, resistance crushed, the Iroquois
Took all they had not slain back to St. Ignace,
The vanguard of the prisoners were the priests.
Three miles from town to town over the snow,
Naked, laden with pillage from the lodges,
The captives filed like wounded beasts of burden,
Three hours on the march, and those that fell
Or slowed their steps were killed.

E. J. PRATT

Three days before
Brébeuf had celebrated his last mass.
And he had known it was to be the last.
There was prophetic meaning as he took
The cord and tied the alb around his waist,
Attached the maniple to his left arm
And drew the seamless purple chasuble
With the large cross over his head and shoulders,
Draping his body: every vestment held
An immediate holy symbol as he whispered—
'*Upon my head the helmet of Salvation.*
So purify my heart and make me white;
With this cincture of purity gird me,
O Lord.

May I deserve this maniple
Or sorrow and of penance.

Unto me
Restore the stole of immortality.
My yoke is sweet, my burden light.

Grant that
I may so bear it as to win Thy grace.'

Entering, he knelt before as rude an altar
As ever was reared within a sanctuary,
But hallowed as that chancel where the notes
Of Palestrina's score had often pealed
The *Assumpta est Maria* through Saint Peter's.
For, covered in the centre of the table,
Recessed and sealed, a hollowed stone contained
A relic of a charred or broken body
Which perhaps a thousand years ago or more
Was offered as a sacrifice to Him
Whose crucifix stood there between the candles.

And on the morrow would this prayer be answered:—
'Eternal Father, I unite myself
With the affections and the purposes
Of Our Lady of Sorrows on Calvary.
And now I offer Thee the sacrifice
Which Thy Beloved Son made of Himself
Upon the Cross and now renews on this,
His holy altar . . .

> *Graciously receive*
My life for His life as he gave His life
For mine . . .

> *This is my body.*
> > *In like manner . . .*
Take ye and drink—the chalice of my blood.'

No doubt in the mind of Brébeuf that this was the last
Journey—three miles over the snow. He knew
That the margins as thin as they were by which he escaped
From death through the eighteen years of his mission toil
Did not belong to this chapter: not by his pen
Would this be told. He knew his place in the line,
For the blaze of the trail that was cut on the bark by Jogues
Shone still. He had heard the story as told by writ
And word of survivors—of how a captive slave
Of the hunters, the skin of his thighs cracked with the frost,
He would steal from the tents to the birches, make a rough
    cross
From two branches, set it in snow and on the peel
Inscribe his vows and dedicate to the Name
In 'litanies of love' what fragments were left
From the wrack of his flesh; of his escape from the tribes;
Of his journey to France where he knocked at the door of
    the College

Of Rennes, was gathered in as a mendicant friar,
Nameless, unknown, till he gave for proof to the priest
His scarred credentials of faith, the nail-less hands
And withered arms—the signs of the Mohawk fury.
Nor yet was the story finished—he had come again
Back to his mission to get the second death.
And the comrades of Jogues—Goupil, Eustache and Couture,
Had been stripped and made to run the double files
And take the blows—one hundred clubs to each line—
And this as the prelude to torture, leisured, minute,
Where thorns on the quick, scallop shells to the joints
        of the thumbs,
Provided the sport for children and squaws till the end.
And adding salt to the blood of Brébeuf was the thought
Of Daniel—was it months or a week ago?
So far, so near, it seemed in time, so close
In leagues—just over there to the south it was
He faced the arrows and died in front of his church.

But winding into the greater artery
Of thought that bore upon the coming passion
Were little tributaries of wayward wish
And reminiscence. Paris with its vespers
Was folded in the mind of Lalemant,
And the soft Gothic lights and traceries
Were shading down the ridges of his vows.
But two years past at Bourges he had walked the cloisters,
Companioned by Saint Augustine and Francis,
And wrapped in quiet holy mists. Brébeuf,
His mind a moment throwing back the curtain
Of eighteen years, could see the orchard lands,
The *cidreries*, the peasants at the Fairs,
The undulating miles of wheat and barley,

Gardens and pastures rolling like a sea
From Lisieux to Le Havre. Just now the surf
Was pounding on the limestone Norman beaches
And on the reefs of Calvados. Had dawn
This very day not flung her surplices
Around the headlands and with golden fire
Consumed the silken argosies that made
For Rouen from the estuary of the Seine?
A moment only for that veil to lift—
A moment only for those bells to die
That rang their matins at Condé-sur-Vire.

By noon St. Ignace! The arrival there
The signal for the battle-cries of triumph,
The gauntlet of the clubs. The stakes were set
And the ordeal of Jogues was re-enacted
Upon the priests—even with wilder fury,
For here at last was trapped their greatest victim,
Echon. The Iroquois had waited long
For this event. Their hatred for the Hurons
Fused with their hatred for the French and priests
Was to be vented on this sacrifice,
And to that camp had come apostate Hurons,
United with their foes in common hate
To settle up their reckoning with *Echon*.

.   .   .

Now three o'clock, and capping the height of the passion,
Confusing the sacraments under the pines of the forest,
Under the incense of balsam, under the smoke
Of the pitch, was offered the rite of the font. On the head,
The breast, the loins and the legs, the boiling water!
While the mocking paraphrase of the symbols was hurled

At their faces like shards of flint from the arrow heads—
'We baptize thee with water . . .

That thou mayest be led
To Heaven . . .

To that end we do anoint thee.
We treat thee as a friend: we are the cause
Of thy happiness; we are thy priests; the more
Thou sufferest, the more thy God will reward thee,
So give us thanks for our kind offices.'

The fury of taunt was followed by fury of blow.
Why did not the flesh of Brébeuf cringe to the scourge,
Respond to the heat, for rarely the Iroquois found
A victim that would not cry out in such pain—yet here
The fire was on the wrong fuel. Whenever he spoke,
It was to rally the soul of his friend whose turn
Was to come through the night while the eyes were uplifted
     in prayer,
Imploring the Lady of Sorrows, the mother of Christ,
As pain brimmed over the cup and the will was called
To stand the test of the coals. And sometimes the speech
Of Brébeuf struck out, thundering reproof to his foes,
Half-rebuke, half-defiance, giving them roar for roar.
Was it because the chancel became the arena,
Brébeuf a lion at bay, not a lamb on the altar,
As if the might of a Roman were joined to the cause
Of Judaea? Speech they could stop for they girdled his lips,
But never a moan could they get. Where was the source
Of his strength, the home of his courage that topped the best
Of their braves and even out-fabled the lore of their legends?
In the bunch of his shoulders which often had carried a load
Extorting the envy of guides at an Ottawa portage?
The heat of the hatchets was finding a path to that source.

In the thews of his thighs which had mastered the trails of the
    Neutrals?
They would gash and beribbon those muscles. Was it the
    blood?
They would draw it fresh from its fountain. Was it the heart?
They dug for it, fought for the scraps in the way of the wolves.
But not in these was the valour or stamina lodged;
Nor in the symbol of Richelieu's robes or the seals
Of Mazarin's charters, nor in the stir of the *lilies*
Upon the Imperial folds; nor yet in the words
Loyola wrote on a table of lava-stone
In the cave of Manresa—not in these the source—
But in the sound of invisible trumpets blowing
Around two slabs of board, right-angled, hammered
By Roman nails and hung on a Jewish hill.

105   *The Truant*

'What have you there?' the great Panjandrum said
To the Master of the Revels who had led
A bucking truant with a stiff backbone
Close to the foot of the Almighty's throne.

'Right Reverend, most adored,
And forcibly acknowledged Lord
By the keen logic of your two-edged sword!
This creature has presumed to classify
Himself—a biped, rational, six feet high
And two feet wide; weighs fourteen stone;
Is guilty of a multitude of sins.
He has abjured his choric origins,
And like an undomesticated slattern,

Walks with tangential step unknown
Within the weave of the atomic pattern.
He has developed concepts, grins
Obscenely at your Royal bulletins,
Possesses what he calls a will
Which challenges your power to kill.'

'What is his pedigree?'

'The base is guaranteed, your Majesty—
Calcium, carbon, phosphorus, vapour
And other fundamentals spun
From the umbilicus of the sun,
And yet he says he will not caper
Around your throne, nor toe the rules
For the ballet of the fiery molecules.'

'His concepts and denials—scrap them, burn them—
To the chemists with them promptly.'
                                        'Sire,
The stuff is not amenable to fire.
Nothing but their own kind can overturn them.
The chemists have sent back the same old story—
"With our extreme gelatinous apology,
We beg to inform your Imperial Majesty,
Unto whom be dominion and power and glory,
There still remains that strange precipitate
Which has the quality to resist
Our oldest and most trusted catalyst.
It is a substance we cannot cremate
By temperatures known to our Laboratory."'

And the great Panjandrum's face grew dark—
'I'll put those chemists to their annual purge,

And I myself shall be the thaumaturge
To find the nature of this fellow's spark.
Come, bring him nearer by yon halter rope:
I'll analyse him with the cosmoscope.'

Pulled forward with his neck awry,
The little fellow six feet short,
Aware he was about to die,
Committed grave contempt of court
By answering with a flinchless stare
The Awful Presence seated there.

The ALL HIGH swore until his face was black.
He called him a coprophagite,
A genus *homo*, egomaniac,
Third cousin to the family of worms,
A sporozoan from the ooze of night,
Spawn of a spavined troglodyte:
He swore by all the catalogue of terms
Known since the slang of carboniferous Time.
He said that he could trace him back
To pollywogs and earwigs in the slime.
And in his shrillest tenor he began
Reciting his indictment of the man,
Until he closed upon this capital crime—
'You are accused of singing out of key,
(A foul unmitigated dissonance)
Of shuffling in the measures of the dance,
Then walking out with that defiant, free
Toss of your head, banging the doors,
Leaving a stench upon the jacinth floors.
You have fallen like a curse
On the mechanics of my Universe.

'Herewith I measure out your penalty—
Hearken while you hear, look while you see:
I send you now upon your homeward route
Where you shall find
Humiliation for your pride of mind.
I shall make deaf the ear, and dim the eye,
Put palsy in your touch, make mute
Your speech, intoxicate your cells and dry
Your blood and marrow, shoot
Arthritic needles through your cartilage,
And having parched you with old age,
I'll pass you wormwise through the mire:
And when your rebel will
Is mouldered, all desire
Shrivelled, all your concepts broken,
Backward in dust I'll blow you till
You join my spiral festival of fire.
Go, Master of the Revels—I have spoken.'

And the little genus *homo*, six feet high,
Standing erect, countered with this reply—
'You dumb insouciant invertebrate,
You rule a lower than a feudal state—
A realm of flunkey decimals that run,
Return; return and run; again return,
Each group around its little sun,
And every sun a satellite.
There they go by day and night,
Nothing to do but run and burn,
Taking turn and turn about,
Light-year in and light-year out,
Dancing, dancing in quadrillions,
Never leaving their pavilions.

'Your astronomical conceit
Of bulk and power is anserine.
Your ignorance so thick,
You did not know your own arithmetic.
We flung the graphs about your flying feet.
We measured your diameter—
Merely a line
Of zeros prefaced by an integer.
Before we came
You had no name.
You did not know direction or your pace;
We taught you all you ever knew
Of motion, time and space.
We healed you of your vertigo
And put you in our kindergarten show,
Perambulated you through prisms, drew
Your mileage through the Milky Way,
Lassoed your comets when they ran astray,
Yoked Leo, Taurus, and your team of Bears
To pull our kiddy cars of inverse squares.

'Boast not about your harmony,
Your perfect curves, your rings
Of *pure and endless light*—'Twas we
Who pinned upon your Seraphim their wings,
And when your brassy heavens rang
With joy that morning while the planets sang
Their choruses of archangelic lore,
'Twas we who ordered the notes upon their score
Out of our winds and strings.
Yes! all your shapely forms
Are ours—parabolas of silver light,
Those blueprints of your spiral stairs

From nadir depth to zenith height,
Coronas, rainbows after storms,
Auroras on your eastern tapestries
And constellations over western seas.

'And when, one day, grown conscious of your age,
While pondering an eolith,
We turned a human page
And blotted out a cosmic myth
With all its baby symbols to explain
The sunlight in Apollo's eyes,
Our rising pulses and the birth of pain,
Fear, and that fern-and-fungus breath
Stalking our nostrils to our caves of death—
That day we learned how to anatomize
Your body, calibrate your size
And set a mirror up before your face
To show you what you really were—a rain
Of dull Lucretian atoms crowding space,
A series of concentric waves which any fool
Might make by dropping stones within a pool,
Or an exploding bomb forever in flight
Bursting like hell through Chaos and Old Night.

'You oldest of the hierarchs
Composed of electronic sparks,
We grant you speed,
We grant you power, and fire
That ends in ash, but we concede
To you no pain nor joy nor love nor hate,
No final tableau of desire,
No causes won or lost, no free
Adventure at the outposts—only

The degradation of your energy
When at some late
Slow number of your dance your sergeant-major Fate
Will catch you blind and groping and will send
You reeling on that long and lonely
Lockstep of your wave-lengths towards your end.

'We who have met
With stubborn calm the dawn's hot fusillades;
Who have seen the forehead sweat
Under the tug of pulleys on the joints,
Under the liquidating tally
Of the cat-and-truncheon bastinades;
Who have taught our souls to rally
To mountain horns and the sea's rockets
When the needle ran demented through the points;
We who have learned to clench
Our fists and raise our lightless sockets
To morning skies after the midnight raids,
Yet cocked our ears to bugles on the barricades,
And in cathedral rubble found a way to quench
A dying thirst within a Galilean valley—
No! by the Rood, we will not join your ballet.'

E. J. PRATT

From *Towards the Last Spike*

(*i*)

The Gathering

'*Oats—a grain which in England is generally given to horses,
but in Scotland supports the people.*'—DR. SAMUEL JOHNSON.
'*True, but where will you find such horses, where such men?*'
—LORD ELIBANK'S REPLY AS RECORDED BY SIR WALTER SCOTT.

Oatmeal was in their blood and in their names.
Thrift was the title of their catechism.
It governed all things but their mess of porridge
Which, when it struck the hydrochloric acid
With treacle and skim-milk, became a mash.
Entering the duodenum, it broke up
Into amino acids: then the liver
Took on its natural job as carpenter:
Foreheads grew into cliffs, jaws into juts.
The meal, so changed, engaged the follicles:
Eyebrows came out as gorse, the beards as thistles,
And the chest-hair the fell of Grampian rams.
It stretched and vulcanized the human span:
Nonagenarians worked and thrived upon it.
Out of such chemistry run through by genes,
The food released its fearsome racial products:—
The power to strike a bargain like a foe,
To win an argument upon a burr,
Invest the language with a Bannockburn,
Culloden or the warnings of Lochiel,
Weave loyalties and rivalries in tartans,
Present for the amazement of the world
Kilts and the civilized barbaric Fling,
And pipes which, when they acted on the mash,
Fermented lullabies to *Scots wha hae*.

Their names were like a battle-muster—Angus
(He of the Shops) and Fleming (of the Transit),
Hector (of the *Kicking Horse*), Dawson,
'Cromarty' Ross, and Beatty (Ulster Scot),
Bruce, Allan, Galt and Douglas, and the 'twa'—
Stephen (Craigellachie)[1] and Smith (Strathcona)—
Who would one day climb from their Gaelic hide-outs,
Take off their plaids and wrap them round the mountains.
And then the everlasting tread of the Macs,
Vanguard, centre and rear, their roving eyes
On summits, rivers, contracts, beaver, ledgers;
Their ears cocked to the skirl of Sir John A.,
The general of the patronymic march.

107   *(ii)*

[*The Precambrian Shield*]

On the North Shore a reptile lay asleep—
A hybrid that the myths might have conceived,
But not delivered, as progenitor
Of crawling, gliding things upon the earth.
She lay snug in the folds of a huge boa
Whose tail had covered Labrador and swished
Atlantic tides, whose body coiled itself
Around the Hudson Bay, then curled up north
Through Manitoba and Saskatchewan
To Great Slave Lake. In continental reach
The neck went past the Great Bear Lake until

---

1 'Stand Fast, Craigellachie', the war-cry of the Clan Grant, named
after a rock in the Spey Valley, and used as a cable message from
Stephen in London to the Directors in Montreal.

Its head was hidden in the Arctic Seas.
This folded reptile was asleep or dead:
So motionless, she seemed stone dead—just seemed:
She was too old for death, too old for life,
For as if jealous of all living forms
She had lain there before bivalves began
To catacomb their shells on western mountains.
Somewhere within this life-death zone she sprawled,
Torpid upon a rock-and-mineral mattress.
Ice-ages had passed by and over her,
But these, for all their motion, had but sheared
Her spotty carboniferous hair or made
Her ridges stand out like the spikes of molochs.
Her back grown stronger every million years,
She had shed water by the longer rivers
To Hudson Bay and by the shorter streams
To the great basins to the south, had filled
Them up, would keep them filled until the end
Of Time.
              Was this the thing Van Horne set out
To conquer?

108   *Silences*

There is no silence upon the earth or under the earth like the
    silence under the sea;
No cries announcing birth,
No sounds declaring death.
There is silence when the milt is laid on the spawn in the weeds
    and fungus of the rock-clefts;
And silence in the growth and struggle for life.
The bonitoes pounce upon the mackerel,

And are themselves caught by the barracudas,
The sharks kill the barracudas
And the great molluscs rend the sharks,
And all noiselessly—
Though swift be the action and final the conflict,
The drama is silent.

There is no fury upon the earth like the fury under the sea.
For growl and cough and snarl are the tokens of spendthrifts
    who know not the ultimate economy of rage.
Moreover, the pace of the blood is too fast.
But under the waves the blood is sluggard and has the same
    temperature as that of the sea.

There is something pre-reptilian about a silent kill.

Two men may end their hostilities just with their battle-cries.
'The devil take you,' says one.
'I'll see you in hell first,' says the other.
And these introductory salutes followed by a hail of gutturals
    and sibilants are often the beginning of friendship, for
    who would not prefer to be lustily damned than to be
    half-heartedly blessed?
No one need fear oaths that are properly enunciated, for they
    belong to the inheritance of just men made perfect, and,
    for all we know, of such may be the Kingdom of Heaven.
But let silent hate be put away for it feeds upon the heart of
    the hater.
Today I watched two pairs of eyes. One pair was black and
    the other grey. And while the owners thereof, for the
    space of five seconds, walked past each other, the grey
    snapped at the black and the black riddled the grey.
One looked to say—'The cat,'
And the other—'The cur.'

But no words were spoken;
Not so much as a hiss or a murmur came through the perfect
    enamel of the teeth; not so much as a gesture of enmity.
If the right upper lip curled over the canine, it went un-
    noticed.
The lashes veiled the eyes not for an instant in the passing.
And as between the two in respect to candour of intention or
    eternity of wish, there was no choice, for the stare was
    mutual and absolute.
A word would have dulled the exquisite edge of the feeling,
An oath would have flawed the crystallization of the hate.
For only such culture could grow in a climate of silence,—
Away back back before the emergence of fur or feather, back
    to the unvocal sea and down deep where the darkness spills
    its wash on the threshold of light, where the lids never
    close upon the eyes, where the inhabitants slay in silence
    and are as silently slain.

RENÉ CHOPIN

1885–1953

109   *Paysages polaires*

Le firmament arctique étoile sa coupole,
Le vent glacé des nuits halène irrégulier
Et fait étinceler tous les astres du Pôle,
Le Cygne crucial, la Chèvre, le Bélier . . .

Rideau de gaze en sa transparence hyaline,
Les écharpes de l'air flottent dans les lointains.
Comme un disque argenté, la Lune cristalline
Plonge dans l'Océan ses deux grands yeux éteints.

RENÉ CHOPIN

Telle que nous la montre, étrange architecture
De neige et de glaçons étagés par degrés,
Sur la page de pulpe ou sur la couverture,
Le dessin suggestif des livres illustrés,

Géante elle apparaît, manoir ou cathédrale,
La banquise polaire avec grottes à jour,
Comme un magique écran de clarté sépulcrale
Où l'on voit s'ériger les créneaux d'une tour.

Elle a porche sur mer à sa vaste muraille,
Avec, en escaliers, de larges monceaux vifs
Où nul pas ne se pose, et que la lame taille,
Et qui sont, émergés, de somptueux récifs.

Édifice branlant d'assises colossales
Aux colonnes d'azur, aux piliers anguleux,
J'y vois des corridors et de profondes salles
Où pendent par milliers cristaux et lustres bleus.

Trésors inexplorés de fausses pierreries,
Aiguilles et joyaux, métal immaculé,
Parmi leur amas clair les marines féeries
Jadis ont déposé la coupe de Thulé.

.   .   .

Là, bien loin, du côté des étoiles polaires,
Se dresse l'enfer froid des hauts caps convulsifs.
Et je crois voir les flottilles crépusculaires
Errantes sur le globe aux âges primitifs.

Monts à pic titubant sur une mer étale,
Cascades d'argent pur dont le saut fait un lac;
Dolmens bruts avec leurs tables horizontales,
Menhirs et tumuli, vastes champs de Carnac.

RENÉ CHOPIN

Par bandes les ours blancs seront expiatoires;
L'écume aux dents, lascifs, ils bâilleront d'ennui
Tandis qu'à l'horizon, au ras des promontoires
Brillera, globe d'or, le soleil de minuit.

.   .   .

Les fiers Aventuriers, captifs de la banquise,
En leurs tombeaux de glace à jamais exilés,
Avaient rêvé que leur gloire s'immortalise:
Le Pôle comme un Sphinx demeure inviolé.

Sur une île neigeuse, avouant la défaite,
Et l'amertume au cœur, sans vivres, sans espoir,
Ils gravèrent leurs noms, homicide conquête,
Et tristes, résignés, moururent dans le soir.

Les voiles luxueux d'aurores magnétiques,
Déroulant sur le gouffre immense du Chaos
Leurs franges de couleurs aux éclairs prismatiques,
Ont enchanté la fin tragique des Héros.

Leur sang se congela, plus de feux dans les tentes . . .
En un songe livide ont-ils revu là-bas,
Par delà la mer sourde et les glaces flottantes,
Le clocher du village où l'on sonne les glas,

Et, regrets superflus germés dans les Érèbes,
La vigne ensoleillée au pan du toit natal,
Le miracle, à l'été fertile, de la glèbe,
Avec le cendrier, l'âtre familial?

110 *Épigramme contre moi*

Vous m'avez épinglé dans votre anthologie
Comme un insecte rare, un brillant papillon;
Je me vois, à l'honneur de l'entomologie,
Mon docte Maître, orner votre collection.

Sur mon aile chacun jugera si la goutte
D'émail qui l'agrémente a perdu son éclat,
Si cette poudre exquisement qui la veloute
Sous le coup d'éventail des heures s'envola.

Chacun mesurera la longueur de mon aile.
Je suis étiqueté, classé, catalogué.
Lecteur, admire-moi si je te semble un aigle.
Si je suis un nabot tu pourras me narguer.

Je brille tel un astre — il me faut bien le croire —
'De moyenne grandeur'; car vous aurez voulu
Vous faire le gardien de ma durable gloire
Aussi longtemps que votre ouvrage sera lu.

Pour soi-même souvent l'on a des complaisances.
Mais comment d'un regard calme et judicieux,
Qui veut être étranger, se lire avec aisance
Entre les grands élus et les morts sourcilleux?

Ce qu'il en est de la fantasque renommée!
La noble chose, et qui vous sauve du néant!
L'avenir oubliera ma belle âme embaumée
De poète ancien, épineux et né en . . .

RENÉ CHOPIN

Un soir, lorsque du Temps auront fui les décades,
Un vieux bibliomane, un savant avisé
Dont on aime à flatter l'innocente toquade,
En m'exhumant, voudra me conférencier.

Ce méconnu . . . (dira sa bouche doctrinale)
De nombreuses erreurs son œuvre se chargea . . .
Parmi les 'poetae minores', je signale . . .
Que dira-t-il? Au fait, je me sens 'feu' déjà.

GUY DELAHAYE

b. 188

III   *Air de glas*

Coups d'ailes que donne le métal
A la prière de ceux qui pleurent,
Les bourdons frappent d'un son bruta

Les airs se brisant comme un cristal;
Puis, tel le souffle de ceux qui meurent,
Pures de la pureté d'antan,

Les ondulations, en montant,
Se raidissent, retombent, s'effleurent,
Et bientôt s'endorment en chantant.

112   *Moine*

Ployé sous l'univers et son Dieu,
Le front grand comme l'intelligence;
L'œil doux et voilé comme un adieu;

Rayonnant de son corps odieux,
Magnifique dans son indigence,
Et maître de tout sans liberté,

Il va, consumé de Vérité,
D'Idéal, d'Amour ou d'Indulgence,
Il va son vol à l'Éternité.

113 *Amour*

Éternité qui n'a qu'un sourire,
Minute qui n'a qu'un souvenir,
Marque sur l'airain, trait sur la cire;

Abîme où le contenant s'attire
Dans le contenu pour se l'unir,
Où le cœur disparaît et se brûle;

Aurore, Soleil et Crépuscule;
Le Passé, le Présent, l'Avenir;
Toujours devant Jamais qui recule.

PAUL MORIN

1889-1963

114 *A ceux de mon pays*

Et si je n'ai pas dit la terre maternelle,
        Si je n'ai pas chanté
Les faits d'armes qui sont la couronne éternelle
        De sa grave beauté,

Ce n'est pas que mon cœur ait négligé de rendre
        Hommage à son pays,
Ou que, muet aux voix qu'un autre sait entendre,
        Il ne l'ait pas compris;

Mais la flûte sonore est plus douce à ma bouche
        Que le fier olifant,
Et je voulais louer la fleur après la souche,
        La mère avant l'enfant.

N'ayant pour seul flambeau qu'une trop neuve lampe,
        Les héros et les dieux
N'étant bien célébrés que l'argent à la tempe
        Et les larmes aux yeux,

J'attends d'etre mûri par la bonne souffrance
        Pour, un jour, marier
Les mots canadiens aux rythmes de la France
        Et l'érable au laurier.

115   *Harmonie pour un soir d'Italie*

Nuit de Ravenne ou nuit de Parme,
Je me souviens d'un soir si pur
(Plus diaphane que l'azur
Et plus transparent qu'une larme),

D'un soir si pur, qu'une chanson,
Traversant l'air calme, fut telle
Qu'une harmonieuse dentelle
Faite d'un rire et d'un frisson.

PAUL MORIN

Aux ailes d'une vocalise
La voix adorable monta
Des jardins de la Steccata,
Ce fut d'une tristesse exquise . . .

Ou me trompe-je? Était-ce au chœur
De Notre-Dame-Ravennate
Que jaillissait cette cantate
Vers les sept rubis de son cœur?

Qu'importe? Amoureuse ou brutale,
D'une cellule ou d'un balcon,
Plainte d'ardeur ou d'abandon
Dans la nuit trop sentimentale,

Qu'importe? Une femme chantait
— Jeune ou vieille, nonne ou gredine,
Ariette, hymne, ou cavatine —
Son chaud, voluptueux secret.

Et, déjouant les portes closes
Qui muraient ma sévère humeur,
Ce cri fit fleurir dans mon cœur
Des larmes, du rire, et des roses.

On aurait dit le tendre vol
D'une colombe paresseuse,
La lente, lointaine berceuse
D'une fontaine en porcelaine,
Ou bien l'âme d'un rossignol
Soupirant au croissant sa peine.

.   .   .

PAUL MORIN

Ce trille de pâtre amoureux,
Fraîche arabesque capriote,
Devrait-il alanguir sa note
Jusque dans mon exil frileux?

Me faudra-t-il entendre, arpège,
Le preste cristal de ta voix
Sous mon banal et morne toit
Qui plie et gémit sous la neige?

Chez l'amant des filles du Rhin,
Ah, pourquoi faut-il que revienne,
Jaune guitare italienne,
Ton mol et sensuel refrain?

Et puisque je me barricade
Avec Parsifal et Klingsor
Dans ma rude ville du Nord . . .
Qu'y viens-tu faire, sérénade?

. . .

Nuits douces comme des baisers,
Jardins brûlants comme des lèvres,
Il ne me reste de vos fièvres
Que des regrets inapaisés;

Et je t'ajoute, angoisse vaine,
A mon innombrable désir,
Ô cruel, ô beau souvenir
D'un soir de Parme . . . ou de Ravenne.

Harmonie pour un soir grec

Heure pourpre où fleurit un blanc vol de mouettes,
Et toi dont je rêvais quand je lisais Byron,
Parfumé de laurier, de miel, de violettes,
Vent de Missolonghi qui promets à mon front
        La fraîcheur des nuits violettes . . .

Vous ayant désirés si fortement, avec
Toute la fièvre de ma chaude adolescence,
Dans l'odeur, sensuelle et vive, du varech,
Ce soir, je vous possède enfin, brève puissance
        Du noble crépuscule grec !

Comme un lierre, Itiès embrasse les collines
Parmi les oliviers au feuillage changeant;
Des tartanes et des felouques levantines
Heurtent au môle, ourlé de coquilles d'argent,
        Leurs flancs trop lourds d'herbes marines.

Au loin, sur les monts roux, encore soleilleux,
La tour d'une forteresse vénitienne,
Sépulcre triomphal d'un doge audacieux,
Clame inlassablement sa puissance ancienne
        A l'impassible azur des cieux.

Miroitant à mes pieds, la mer Ionienne
(Telle, aux jours fabuleux de l'intrépide Argo,
Sa voix berçait les pleurs d'Andromaque et d'Hélène . . .)
Scande de ses flots bleus les rythmes inégaux
        D'une éternelle ode païenne.

Du rivage sonore et d'écume argenté
Jusqu'à l'horizon rose, où fuit la voile oblique,
Monte traîtreusement du sein d'Aphroditè
Le frisson précurseur, ardent, et magnifique,
  De la nocturne volupté;

Et sur la grève, assis autour d'un feu de joie,
Graves et contemplant les étincelles d'or,
Des pêcheurs, aux profils cruels d'oiseaux de proie,
Chantent l'Amour, la Guerre, et la Gloire, et la Mort,
  Comme aux jours illustres de Troie.

117   *Le Paon royal*

Quelque vieux jardinier, à l'âme orientale,
Donna le nom sonore et fier de paon royal
A l'œillet odorant, dont chaque lourd pétale
S'irise de velours, de flamme et de métal.

Or, je connais l'ardent et mauve héliotrope
Dont l'arome fougueux fait défaillir les sens
Des chauds sérails d'Asie aux doux jardins d'Europe,
Les roses de Mossoul et les jasmins persans,

Les soucis d'or, qu'avait à son front Orcavelle
La nuit qu'elle mourut d'entendre un rossignol,
L'écarlate aloès, que sur sa caravelle
Don Pizarre apporta vers le ciel espagnol,

Le lys tigré de vert qui croît dans Samarcande,
Le chrysanthème roux, l'hélianthe de feu,
L'hyacinthe étoilant les prés blonds de Hollande,
La tulipe de jaspe et l'hortensia bleu . . .

Moi j'aime surtout voir étinceler dans l'ombre
La coupe transparente en fragile cristal
Où fleurit, violent, voluptueux et sombre,
Sur sa tige d'émail, le pourpre paon royal.

118 *La Rose au jardin smyrniote*

Lorsque je serai vieux, lorsque la gloire humaine
Aura cessé de plaire à mon cœur assagi,
Lorsque je sentirai, de semaine en semaine,
Plus proche le néant d'où mon être a surgi;

Quand le jour triomphal et la nuit transparente
Alterneront leur cours sans éblouir mes yeux;
Alors, ayant fermé mon âme indifférente
Au tumulte incessant d'un orgueil soucieux,

J'irai, sans un regret et sans tourner la tête,
Dans l'ombre du torride et de l'âpre Orient
Attendre que la mort indulgente soit prête
A frapper mon corps las, captif, et patient.

Ô profonde, amoureuse paix orientale
Des cyprès ombrageant un sépulcre exigu,
Vous me garderez mieux que la terre natale
Sous l'érable neigeux et le sapin aigu !

Puisqu'il n'est de si frêle et fine broderie,
De si léger, si vif, et lumineux matin,
Qu'un platane dressé sur un ciel de Syrie,
Qu'une aube ensoleillant un clair port levantin,

PAUL MORIN

J'aurai cette maison, si longtemps désirée,
Pour son silence où glisse une odeur de jasmin,
Pour ses murs où s'enlace une vigne dorée,
Et sa fontaine pure, et son étroit jardin . . .

C'est là que je lirai, dès l'aube douce et verte,
Les poèmes d'Hafiz et le grave Koran,
Un cèdre allongera jusqu'à ma porte ouverte
Son feuillage verni, touffu, sombre, odorant.

Puisqu'il n'est pas d'endroit qu'une ville d'Asie
Ne surpasse en mystère, en calme, en volupté,
J'y connaîtrai la chaude et tendre frénésie
D'un chant de rossignol, dans le soir turc, — l'été.

Le temps effeuillera ses changeantes guirlandes
De l'aurore nacrée au crépuscule bleu,
Dans le sonore azur bruiront les sarabandes
Des guêpes d'émeraude et des frelons de feu;

Couleur d'ambre et de miel, mille flèches laquées
Siffleront à midi sur les vergers voisins,
J'écouterai jaillir au faîte des mosquées
L'aérien appel que font les muezzins;

Le couchant, saturé d'essences et d'aromes,
Couvrira d'un manteau de pourpre et de parfums
Et les marchés fiévreux et les paisibles dômes
Sous lesquels on coucha les califes défunts . . .

Et je verrai, plus tard, à l'heure où la pensée
Danse, plus ondoyante et vive qu'un jet d'eau,
Comme une lampe d'or, la lune balancée
Sur les toits blancs de Smyrne et de Cordelio.

Mais ni la vasque rose où mes paons viendront boire
Le cristal émaillé de leurs propres reflets,
Ni la pâle, limpide, et délicate moire
Que l'été trame au long des muets minarets,

Ni la voûte d'argent où plane l'astre courbe,
Ne pourront vous chasser, vivace souvenir
Du Passé tour à tour délicieux et fourbe
Et de ce bel émoi que j'aurai voulu fuir . . .

Car, pour exaspérer ma subtile souffrance
Par le rappel toujours présent des jours meilleurs
Je veux, dans un jardin que le croissant nuance,
Qu'éblouissante et noble entre toutes les fleurs,

S'effeuille sur ma tombe une rose de France.

KENNETH LESLIE

b. 1892

119　　*'The silver herring throbbed thick
in my seine'*

The silver herring throbbed thick in my seine,
silver of life, life's silver sheen of glory;
my hands, cut with the cold, hurt with the pain
of hauling the net, pulled the heavy dory,
heavy with life, low in the water, deep
plunged to the gunwale's lips in the stress of rowing,
the pulse of rowing that puts the world to sleep,
world within world endlessly ebbing, flowing.

At length you stood on the landing and you cried,
with quick low cries you timed me stroke on stroke
as I steadily won my way with the fulling tide
and crossed the threshold where the last wave broke
and coasted over the step of water and threw
straight through the air my mooring line to you.

120 *'My love is sleeping'*

My love is sleeping; but her body seems
awake within itself, secure from ills
of consciousness; her veins are buried streams,
her flanks are ghostly vales, her breasts are hills
of some far planet finding its sure way
beyond the orbit of this night of fears,
beyond the burnished darkness of this day;
my love is sleeping out of reach of tears.
How can her limbs dance motionless, what makes
her lips curve smiling to a crescent moon,
what does her hand reach out for, what dawn breaks
beneath her eyelids, to her ears what tune?
I shall not sleep, nor seek that yonder land
where her hand yearns, but not to touch my hand.

121 *'From soil somehow the poet's word'*

From soil somehow the poet's word
and from that word the spreading tree
where swells all fruit, sings every bird,
whose strong trunk is philosophy.

whose branches thrust in legal maze,
whose leaves are myriad windows green
sifting the one to many ways,
tinting the unseen to the seen.
Your teachers list the birds and fruit,
the trunk and branches of the tree;
but they forget about the root,
because the root they cannot see.
Yet have the roots a ray to find
their road between the stones and clay;
like Raftery, the singing blind,
better than day they know the day.

ARTHUR S. BOURINOT

b. 1893

122   *Under the Pines*

All is still
Under the Pines,
All is still.
Still as the heart of Eve
When fear first came
And the flush
Of shame
Mantled her cheek
And the sword of flame
Flashed
In the garden of the Lord.
All is still
Under the Pines,
All is still.

123   *The Diver*

I would like to dive
Down
Into this still pool
Where the rocks at the bottom are safely deep,

Into the green
Of the water seen from within,
A strange light
Streaming past my eyes—

Things hostile,
You cannot stay here, they seem to say;
The rocks, slime-covered, the undulating
Fronds of weeds—

And drift slowly
Among the cooler zones;
Then, upward turning,
Break from the green glimmer

Into the light,
White and ordinary of the day,
And the mild air,
With the breeze and the comfortable shore.

124   *The Creek*

The creek, shining,
out of the deep woods
comes with the rippling of
water over the pebbly bottom,

moving between
banks crowded with raspberry
bushes, the ripe red
berries in their short season

to deepen slowly
among tall pines, athletes in
the wind, then the swampy
ground low-lying and damp

where sunlight strikes
glints on the gliding surface
of the clear cold
creek winding towards the shore

of the lake, blue,
not far through reeds and rushes,
where with a plunge, a small
waterfall, it disappears

among the waves
hastening from far to meet
the stranger, the stream issuing
from depths of green unknown.

125   *The Snake Trying*

The snake trying
to escape the pursuing stick,
with sudden curvings of thin
long body. How beautiful

and graceful are his shapes!
He glides through the water away
from the stroke. O let him go
over the water

into the reeds to hide
without hurt. Small and green
he is harmless even to children.
Along the sand

he lay until observed
and chased away, and now
he vanishes in the ripples
among the green slim reeds.

126   *Pine Gum*

The white gum showing
in the gloom
along the massive
trunk of a great
pine-tree standing
on the hill
with a deep bed
of needles below;—

scarcely a breeze
along the hill;
scarcely a current
of moving air

to make the pine's
old melody,
for it is evening;
the air has ceased

its daily stirring;
the light grows dimmer
in the deep shadow
of the pine,
but ever appears
through the darkness
the ghostly glimmering
of the gum.

127   *If Ice*

                    If
ice shall melt   if
thinly the fresh
cold clear   water
running   shall make
grooves in the sides
of the ice;
if life return

                after death,
or depart not at death,
then shall buds
burst into   may-
leafing, the blooms of may
appear like stars
on the brown dry

                forest-bed.

RAYMOND KNISTER

1899–1932

128   *The Hawk*

Across the bristled and sallow fields,
The speckled stubble of cut clover,
Wades your shadow.

Or against a grimy and tattered
Sky
You plunge.

Or you shear a swath
From trembling tiny forests
With the steel of your wings—

Or make a row of waves
By the heat of your flight
Along the soundless horizon.

129   From *A Row of Stalls*

Nell

Nellie Rakerfield
Came from an estate in Scotland,
Two years old, and won a championship.
It was not her fault that her foals
Were few, and mostly died or were runted.
She worked every day when she raised them,
Never was tired of dragging her
Nineteen hundred pounds
About the farm and the roads, with
Great loads behind it.

She never kicked, bit, nor crowded
In the stall,
Was always ready at a chirp
And seemed to have forgotten delicate care.

But the day they hitched her
To the corpse of her six-months-old colt,
She tried to run away, half way to the bush.
She never seemed quite so willing, afterward.
But the colt was too heavy.

130 *Feed*

For Danny whistling slowly
'Down in Tennessee'
A fat white shoat by the trough
Lifts his snout a moment to hear,
Among the guzzling and slavering comrades,
Squeezing and forcing:
And begins to feed again.
Whenever a certain note comes
He will raise his jaws
His unturning eyes,
Then lean again to scoop up the swill.

131 *The Plowman*

All day I follow
Watching the swift dark furrow
That curls away before me,
And care not for skies or upturned flowers,

And at the end of the field
Look backward
Ever with discontent.

A stone, a root, a strayed thought
Has warped the line of that furrow—
And urge my horses round again.

Sometimes even before the row is finished
I must look backward;
To find, when I come to the end
That there I swerved.

Unappeased I leave the field,
Expectant, return.

The horses are very patient.
When I tell myself
This time
The ultimate unflawed turning
Is before my share,
They must give up their rest.

Someday, someday, be sure,
I shall turn the furrow of all my hopes
But I shall not, doing it, look backward.

132   *Change*

I shall not wonder more, then,
But I shall know.

Leaves change, and birds, flowers,
And after years are still the same.

The sea's breast heaves in sighs to the moon,
But they are moon and sea forever.

As in other times the trees stand tense and lonely,
And spread a hollow moan of other times.

You will be you yourself,
I'll find you more, not else,
For vintage of the woeful years.

The sea breathes, or broods, or loudens,
Is bright or is mist and the end of the world;
And the sea is constant to change.

I shall not wonder more, then,
But I shall know.

F. R. SCOTT

b. 1899

133   *Laurentian Shield*

Hidden in wonder and snow, or sudden with summer,
This land stares at the sun in a huge silence
Endlessly repeating something we cannot hear.
Inarticulate, arctic,
Not written on by history, empty as paper,
It leans away from the world with songs in its lakes
Older than love, and lost in the miles.

This waiting is wanting.
It will choose its language
When it has chosen its technic,
A tongue to shape the vowels of its productivity.

A language of flesh and of roses.

182

Now there are pre-words,
Cabin syllables,
Nouns of settlement
Slowly forming, with steel syntax,
The long sentence of its exploitation.

The first cry was the hunter, hungry for fur,
And the digger for gold, nomad, no-man, a particle;
Then the bold commands of monopoly, big with machines,
Carving its kingdoms out of the public wealth;
And now the drone of the plane, scouting the ice,
Fills all the emptiness with neighbourhood
And links our future over the vanished pole.

But a deeper note is sounding, heard in the mines,
The scattered camps and the mills, a language of life,
And what will be written in the full culture of occupation
Will come, presently, tomorrow,
From millions whose hands can turn this rock into children.

134   *Lakeshore*

The lake is sharp along the shore
Trimming the bevelled edge of land
To level curves; the fretted sand
Goes slanting down through liquid air
Till stones below shift here and there
Floating upon their broken sky
All netted by the prism wave
And rippled where the currents are.

F. R. SCOTT

I stare through windows at this cave
Where fish, like planes, slow-motioned, fly.
Poised in a still of gravity
The narrow minnow, flicking fin,
Hangs in a paler, ochre sun,
His doorways open everywhere.

And I am a tall frond that waves
Its head below its rooted feet
Seeking the light that leads it down
To forest floors beyond its reach
Vivid with gloom and Beebe dreams.

The water's deepest colonnades
Contract the blood, and to this home
That stirs the dark amphibian
With me the naked swimmers come
Drawn to their prehistoric womb.

They too are liquid as they fall
Like tumbled water loosed above
Until they lie, diagonal,
Within the cool and sheltered grove
Stroked by the fingertips of love.

Silent, our sport is drowned in fact
Too virginal for speech or sound
And each is personal and laned
Along his private aqueduct.

Too soon the tether of the lungs
Is taut and straining, and we rise
Upon our undeveloped wings

Toward the prison of our ground
A secret anguish in our thighs
And mermaids in our memories.

This is our talent, to have grown
Upright in posture, false-erect,
A landed gentry, circumspect,
Tied to a horizontal soil
The floor and ceiling of the soul;
Striving, with cold and fishy care
To make an ocean of the air.

Sometimes, upon a crowded street,
I feel the sudden rain come down
And in the old, magnetic sound
I hear the opening of a gate
That loosens all the seven seas.
Watching the whole creation drown
I muse, alone, on Ararat.

135 *Bangkok*

Deep in the brown bosom
Where all the temples rose
I wandered in a land
That I had never owned
With millions all around.

I had been here before
But never to this place
Which seemed so nearly home
Yet was so far away
I was not here at all.

There was a central mound
That took away my breath
So steep it was and round
So sudden by my side
So Asia all beyond.

And when I came inside
I had to walk barefoot
For this was holy ground
Where I was being taught
To worship on a mat.

A great white wind arose
And shakes of temple bells
Descended from the eaves
To make this gold and brown
One continent of love.

And only my own lack
Of love within the core
Sealed up my temple door
Made it too hard to break
And forced me to turn back.

136 *Bonne Entente*

The advantages of living with two cultures
Strike one at every turn,
Especially when one finds a notice in an office building:
'This elevator will not run on Ascension Day;'

Or reads in the *Montreal Star:*
'Tomorrow being the feast of the Immaculate Conception,
There will be no collection of garbage in the city';
Or sees on the restaurant menu the bilingual dish:

DEEP APPLE PIE

TARTE AUX POMMES PROFONDES

137   *Will to Win*

    Your tall French legs, my V for victory,
    My sign and symphony, Eroica,
    Uphold me in these days of my occupation
    And stir my underground resistance.

    Crushed by the insidious infiltration of routine
    I was wholly overrun and quite cut off.
    The secret agents of my daily detail
    Had my capital city under their rule and thumb.

    Only a handful of me escaped to the hillside,
    Your side, my sweet and holy inside,
    And cowering there for a moment I drew breath,
    Grew solid as trees, took root in a fertile soil.

    Here, by my hidden fires, drop your supplies—
    Love, insight, sensibility, and myth—
    Thousands of fragments rally to my cause.
    I ride like Joan to conquer my whole man.

138 *The Canadian Authors Meet*

Expansive puppets percolate self-unction
Beneath a portrait of the Prince of Wales.
Miss Crotchet's muse has somehow failed to function,
Yet she's a poetess. Beaming, she sails

From group to chattering group, with such a dear
Victorian saintliness, as is her fashion,
Greeting the other unknowns with a cheer—
Virgins of sixty who still write of passion.

The air is heavy with 'Canadian' topics.
And Carman, Lampman, Roberts, Campbell, Scott
Are measured for their faith and philanthropics,
Their zeal for God and King, their earnest thought.

The cakes are sweet, but sweeter is the feeling
That one is mixing with the *literati*;
It warms the old and melts the most congealing.
Really, it is a most delightful party.

Shall we go round the mulberry bush, or shall
We gather at the river, or shall we
Appoint a poet laureate this Fall,
Or shall we have another cup of tea?

O Canada, O Canada, Oh can
A day go by without new authors springing
To paint the native maple, and to plan
More ways to set the selfsame welkin ringing?

b. 1900

139   *Egg-and-Dart*

This never-ended searching for the eyes
Wherein the unasked question's answer lies;
This beating, beating, beating of the heart
Because a contour seems to fit the part;
The long, drear moment of the look that spoils
The little bud of hope; the word that soils
The pact immaculate, so newly born;
The noisy silence of the old self-scorn;
These, and the sudden leaving in the lurch;
Then the droll recommencement of the search.

140   *Peacock and Nightingale*

Look at the eyes look from my tail!
What other eyes could look so well?
A peacock asks a nightingale.

And how my feathers twist the sun!
Confess that no one, no, no one
Has ever seen such colour spun.

Who would not fall in ecstasy
Before the gemmed enamelry
Of ruby-topaz-sapphire me?

When my proud tail parades its fan,
You, little bird, are merely an
Anachronism in its van.

Let me advise that you be wise,
Avoid the vision of my eyes.
And then the nightingale replies.

141   *Train Window*

The dark green truck on the cement platform
is explicit as a paradigm.
Its wheels are four black cast-iron starfish.
Its body, a massive tray of planking,
ends in two close-set dark green uprights
crossed with three straight cross-pieces, one
looped with a white spiral of hose.

The truck holds eleven cakes of ice,
each cake a different size and shape.
Some look as though a weight had hit them.
One, solid glass, has a core of sugar.
They lean, a transitory Icehenge,
in a moor of imitation snow
from the hatchet's bright wet-sided steel.

Five galvanized pails, mottled, as if
of stiffened frosted caracul, three
with crescent lids and elbowed spouts,
loom in the ice, their half-hoop handles
linking that frozen elocution
to the running chalk-talk of powder-red
box-cars beyond, while our train waits here.

The Statue

142

A small boy has thrown a stone at a statue,
And a man who threatened has told a policeman so.
Down the pathway they rustle in a row,
The boy, the man, the policeman. If you watch you

Will see the alley of trees join in the chase
And the flower-beds stiffly make after the boy,
The fountains brandish their cudgels in his way
And the sky drop a blue netting in his face.

Only the statue unmoved in its moving stillness
Holds the park as before the deed was done
On a stone axis round which the trio whirls.

Stone that endured the chisel's cutting chillness
Is tolerant of the stone at its foot of stone
And the pigeon sitting awry on its carved curls.

Turning

143

This winter's morning, turning the other way
I thought of the wood I had faced the moment before,
Crystal arches leaping a crystal floor
Where like brown ghosts of fish the oak-leaves lay.

The view ahead was no view to be spurned,
A plain of whiteness with one raven elm
Lifting the tent of winter on its helm,
The white tent of the sky. Again I turned

And as I turned the sun came out, the sky
Fell down into the wood among the snow
Till snow and sky and sun began to flow
Into an animation like a sea:

Through purple waves brown fishes swam in shoals
Or pondered in blue depths of russet glass,
The trees were azure fountains in a race
To graze the sky or melt into its pools,

And as I looked, remembering the plain
Behind me, the black elm, the white tent,
I marvelled what a single turn had sent
And wondered now whether to turn again.

ALAIN GRANDBOIS

b. 1900

144   *Fermons l'armoire*

Fermons l'armoire aux sortilèges
Il est trop tard pour tous les jeux
Mes mains ne sont plus libres
Et ne peuvent plus viser droit au cœur
Le monde que j'avais créé
Possédait sa propre clarté
Mais de ce soleil
Mes yeux sont aveuglés
Mon univers sera englouti avec moi
Je m'enfoncerai dans les cavernes profondes
La nuit m'habitera et ses pièges tragiques

ALAIN GRANDBOIS

Les voix d'à côté ne me parviendront plus
Je posséderai la surdité du minéral
Tout sera glacé
Et même mon doute

Je sais qu'il est trop tard
Déjà la colline engloutit le jour
Déjà je marque l'heure de mon fantôme
Mais ces crépuscules dorés je les vois encore se penchant sur
     des douceurs de lilas
Je vois ces adorables voiles nocturnes trouées d'étoiles
Je vois ces rivages aux rives inviolées
J'ai trop aimé le regard extraordinairement fixe de l'amour
     pour ne pas regretter l'amour
J'ai trop paré mes femmes d'auréoles sans rivales
J'ai trop cultivé de trop miraculeux jardins

Mais une fois j'ai vu les trois cyprès parfaits
Devant la blancheur du logis
J'ai vu et je me tais
Et ma détresse est sans égale

Tout cela est trop tard
Fermons l'armoire aux poisons
Et ces lampes qui brûlent dans le vide comme des fées mortes
Rien ne remuera plus dans l'ombre
Les nuits n'entraîneront plus les cloches du matin
Les mains immaculées ne se lèveront plus au seuil de la maison

Mais toi ô toi je t'ai pourtant vue marcher sur la mer avec ta
     chevelure pleine d'étincelles
Tu marchais toute droite avec ton blanc visage levé

Tu marchais avec tout l'horizon comme une coupole autour
    de toi
Tu marchais et tu repoussais lentement la prodigieuse frontière
    des vagues
Avec tes deux mains devant toi comme les deux colombes de
    l'arche
Et tu nous portais au rendez-vous de l'archange
Et tu étais pure et triste et belle avec un sourire de cœur
    désemparé

Et les prophètes couchaient leur grand silence sur la jalousie
    des eaux
Et il ne restait plus que le grand calme fraternel des sept mers
Comme le plus mortel tombeau

145   *Rivages de l'homme*

Longues trop longues ténèbres voraces
Voûtes exagérément profondes
Ô cercles trop parfaits
Qu'une seule colonne
Nous soit enfin donnée
Qui ne jaillisse pas du miracle
Qui pour une seule fois
Surgisse de la sourde terre
De la mer et du ciel
Et de deux belles mains fortes
D'homme de fièvre trop franche
De son long voyage insolite
A travers l'incantation du temps

ALAIN GRANDBOIS

Parmi son pitoyable périple
Parmi les mirages de sa vie
Parmi les grottes prochaines de sa mort
Cette frêle colonne d'allégresse
Polie par des mains pures
Sans brûler de ses fautes
Sans retour sur le passé
Qu'elle lui soit enfin donnée

Les cris n'importent pas
Ni le secours du poing
Contre le rouet du deuil
Ni le regard angoissé
Des femmes trop tôt négligées
Nourrissant la revendication
D'un autre bonheur illusoire
Ô corps délivrés sans traces

Mais si pour une seule fois
Sans le fléchissement du geste
Sans les ruses pathétiques
Sans ce poison des routes
Depuis longtemps parcourues
Sans la glace des villes noires
Qui n'en finissent jamais plus
Sous la pluie le vent
Balayant les rivages de l'homme

Dans le ravage le naufrage de sa nuit
Dans ce trop vif battement de son artère
Dans la forêt de son éternité
Si pour une seule fois

S'élevait cette colonne libératrice
Comme un immense geyser de feu
Trouant notre nuit foudroyée

Nous exigerions cependant encore
Avec la plus véhémente maladresse
Avec nos bouches marquées d'anonymat
Le dur œil juste de Dieu

146   *Demain seulement*

Long murmure étonnant ô pluie
Ô solitude
Ô faiblesse des doigts
Tremblants de désarroi
Chemins irréductibles
Mobilité de l'eau
Ma vie m'échappe
Ma vie nourrit
Autour de moi
Dix mille vies
Ô beaux soirs d'or

Il y aura demain mon éternelle nuit
La dure et seule nudité de mes os
Ma surdité mes yeux aveugles
Les îles de mes archipels
Seront profondément englouties

L'aube immense
M'enveloppe comme la mer
Le corps du plongeur

196

Cruelle et dangereuse sécurité
Je suis comme tapi au flanc de ma mère
Dans la chaleur magique
D'avant la délivrance du jour

Ma mort je la repousse jusqu'à demain
Je la repousse et je la refuse et je la nie
Dans la plus haute clameur
Avec les grands gestes inutiles
De l'écroulement de mon monde

Car je n'ai pas encore épuisé
La merveille étonnante des heures
Je n'ai pas suffisamment pénétré
Le cœur terrible et pourpre
Des crépuscules interdits
Des musiques ignorées
Me sont encore défendues

Je n'ai pas encore entendu
Chaque rumeur grelottante
Des villes d'ombre de neige et de rêve
Je n'ai pas encore vu
Tous les visages changeants
Tous les visages fuyants
Tous les hommes bouleversés
Et ceux qui marchent à pas feutrés
Comme autour de chambres vides
Vers les carrefours de la terre

Je n'ai rien vu
Je n'ai rien goûté

Je n'ai rien souffert
Et soudain l'âge bondit sur moi comme une panthère noire

Mais je trouverai demain ces perles
Qu'elle apporte au creux rose
De sa main mouillée
Je trouverai ce diamant
De son sourire absent
L'étoile mauve de son sein
La nuit prolongée
Par l'ombre émouvante
De sa toison ténébreuse

Ah je naviguerai demain
Sur ces bateaux perdus
Larguant leurs voiles rouges
Pour des mers inconsidérées
Avec elle au bronze de mon bras droit
Avec elle comme le coffret des bijoux redoutables

Je vaincrai demain
La nuit et la pluie
Car la mort
N'est qu'une toute petite chose glacée
Qui n'a aucune sorte d'importance
Je lui tendrai demain
Mais demain seulement
Demain
Mes mains pleines
D'une extraordinaire douceur

b. 1901

147   *Je suis un fils déchu*

Je suis un fils déchu de race surhumaine,
Race de violents, de forts, de hasardeux,
Et j'ai le mal du pays neuf, que je tiens d'eux,
Quand viennent les jours gris que septembre ramène.

Tout le passé brutal de ces coureurs des bois:
Chasseurs, trappeurs, scieurs de long, flotteurs de cages,
Marchands aventuriers ou travailleurs à gages,
M'ordonne d'émigrer par en haut pour cinq mois.

Et je rêve d'aller comme allaient les ancêtres;
J'entends pleurer en moi les grands espaces blancs,
Qu'ils parcouraient, nimbés de souffles d'ouragans,
Et j'abhorre comme eux la contrainte des maîtres.

Quand s'abattait sur eux l'orage des fléaux,
Ils maudissaient le val, ils maudissaient la plaine,
Ils maudissaient les loups qui les privaient de laine.
Leurs malédictions engourdissaient leurs maux.

Mais quand le souvenir de l'épouse lointaine
Secouait brusquement les sites devant eux,
Du revers de leur manche, ils s'essuyaient les yeux
Et leur bouche entonnait: 'A la claire fontaine'. . .

Ils l'ont si bien redite aux échos des forêts,
Cette chanson naïve où le rossignol chante,
Sur la plus haute branche, une chanson touchante,
Qu'elle se mêle à mes pensers les plus secrets:

Si je courbe le dos sous d'invisibles charges,
Dans l'âcre brouhaha de départs oppressants,
Et si, devant l'obstacle ou le lien, je sens
Le frisson batailleur qui crispait leurs poings larges;

Si d'eux, qui n'ont jamais connu le désespoir,
Qui sont morts en rêvant d'asservir la nature,
Je tiens ce maladif instinct de l'aventure,
Dont je suis quelquefois tout envoûté, le soir;

Par nos ans sans vigueur, je suis comme le hêtre
Dont la sève a tari sans qu'il soit dépouillé,
Et c'est de désirs morts que je suis enfeuillé,
Quand je rêve d'aller comme allait mon ancêtre;

Mais les mots indistincts que profère ma voix
Sont encore: un rosier, une source, un branchage,
Un chêne, un rossignol parmi le clair feuillage,
Et comme au temps de mon aïeul, coureur des bois,

Ma joie ou ma douleur chante le paysage.

148   *Le Dérochage*

Sur la lividité de l'aube printanière
Qu'assombrissent la pluie imminente et l'embrun,
Les forêts de sapin se découpent en brun,
Continuant l'argile ouverte de la terre.

Malgré l'humidité qui moisit l'atmosphère,
Les hommes au travail déjà s'en vont—à jeun,
Car il faut profiter du moment opportun
Pour dérocher les champs neufs qu'encombre la pierre.

Sur un fond-plat traîné par de lourds percherons,
Ils jettent les cailloux découverts des sillons,
Et vont, cassés aux reins, les pieds massifs de glaise;

Quelquefois, l'un d'entre eux, lâchant son faix visqueux,
Comme un ressort brisé jaillit de sa mortaise,
Dresse en arc ogival son torse musculeux.

149   *La Boucherie*

Pressentant que sur lui plane l'heure fatale,
L'Yorkshire, dont le groin se retrousse en sabot,
Évite le garçon d'un brusque soubresaut,
Et piétine énervé le pesat de sa stalle.

Il éternue un grognement parmi la bale,
Quand un câble brûlant se serre sur sa peau.
Ses oreilles, qu'il courbe en cuillères à pot,
Surplombent ses yeux bruns où la frayeur s'étale.

On le traîne au grand jour de soleil ébloui;
Et le porc sent le sol se dérober sous lui,
Lorsque la lame au cœur lui pénètre: il s'affaisse

Puis se dresse, et son rauque appel, alors qu'il meurt,
Répand sur la campagne une telle tristesse
Qu'un hurlement de chien se mêle à sa clameur.

150　　　　*La Modiste*

La modiste, mademoiselle Véronique,
Impeccable et rigide en sa jupe à bouillon,
Tantôt la main au rein, tantôt la main au front,
Geint et se plaint sans fin de son corps dyspepsique.

Et c'est ainsi depuis vingt ans, et c'est ainsi que
Le village oublia d'elle jusqu'à son nom:
Le squelette à migraine (ainsi la nomma-t-on)
Attend de s'y guérir d'une attaque phtisique.

L'étalage est orné d'un éternel turban
Qui repose avec art sur lé de velours blanc.
Mais la cliente est rare et la vieille regrette

La grande ville et le bon temps — qui fut si beau !
Où ses doigts enlaçaient sur le même chapeau
Le casoar avec le ménure et l'aigrette.

151　　　　*'City-Hotel'*

'Nous n'irons plus voir nos blondes.'

Le sac au dos, vêtus d'un rouge mackinaw,
Le jarret musculeux étranglé dans la botte,
Les *shantymen* partants s'offrent une ribote
Avant d'aller passer l'hiver à Malvina.

Dans le bar, aux vitraux orange et pimbina,
Un rayon de soleil oblique, qui clignote,
Dore les appui-corps nickelés, où s'accote,
En pleurant, un gaillard que le gin chagrina.

Les vieux ont le ton haut et le rire sonore,
Et chantent des refrains grassouillets de folklore;
Mais un nouveau, trouvant ce bruit intimidant,

S'imagine le camp isolé des Van Dyke,
Et sirote un *demi-schooner* en regardant
Les danseuses sourire aux affiches de laque.

L. A. MACKAY

b. 1901

152   *Admonition for Spring*

Look away now from the high lonesome hills
So hard on the hard sky since the swift shower;
See where among the restless daffodils
The hyacinth sets his melancholy tower.

Draw in your heart from vain adventurings;
Float slowly, swimmer, slowly drawing breath.
See, in this wild green foam of growing things
The heavy hyacinth remembering death.

153   *Nunc scio, quid sit amor*

I know him now, not now to know demanding.
No goddess-mother bore a child so grim,
So only terrible, though he were standing
Swordless, among the sworded Seraphim.

The hard rock was his mother; he retains
Only her kind, nor answers any sire.
His hand is the black basalt, and his veins
Are rocky veins, ablaze with gold and fire.

154   From *The Ill-Tempered Lover*

I wish my tongue were a quiver the size of a huge cask
Packed and crammed with long black venomous rankling
  darts.
I'd fling you more full of them, and joy in the task,
Than ever Sebastian was, or Caesar, with thirty-three swords
  in his heart.

I'd make a porcupine out of you, or a pin-cushion, say;
The shafts should stand so thick you'd look like a headless hen
Hung up by the heels, with the long bare red neck stretching,
  curving, and dripping away
From the soiled floppy ball of ruffled feathers standing on end.

You should bristle like those cylindrical brushes they use to
  scrub out bottles,
Not even to reach the kindly earth with the soles of your
  prickled feet.
And I would stand by and watch you wriggle and writhe,
  gurgling through the barbs in your throttle
Like a woolly caterpillar pinned on its back—man, that would
  be sweet!

L. A. MACKAY

155 *Battle Hymn of the Spanish Rebellion*

The Church's one foundation
   Is now the Moslem sword,
In meek collaboration
   With flame, and axe, and cord;
While overhead are floating,
   Deep-winged with holy love,
The battle-planes of Wotan,
   The bombing-planes of Jove.

ROY DANIELLS

b. 1902

156 *Farewell to Winnipeg*

I

Farewell to Winnipeg, the snow-bright city
Set in the prairie distance without bound
Profound and fathomless, encompassed round
By the wind-haunted country and wide winter.

Farewell to Winnipeg, the sun-bright city
Lapped in light summer leaves by turning waters,
Lost in a level land of endless acres,
Found in the endless memories of my heart.

As the pale face of some remembered darling
Calm under floods and bound about the brows
With dream-refracted light no daytime knows
Moves the mute soul to desperate hope and fearing,

So I remember you, the brightening city
Of snows and summer storms and shining days;
So shall my mind recall you in amazement,
Dazed with the past, its wonder and its pity.

While the clouds mass in storm, turn and repass,
What forms are these that hourly hover over,
Cover the city and again discover
Dim faces while the night winds westward press?

While the skies cloud, repass again and mass,
What forms, what faces, voices in the wind?
Crying from the farthest darkness of my mind
Even as the westward winds cry in the grass.

While the winds rise, while the clouds westward move,
What tumults mourn aloud, what portents form
In storm of memories and murmur of doom
In ireful skies where over the city heave,

Hover, form and reform the shock troops
And the armour of the storm. O city unsung,
They ring your triumph; with prophetic tongue
They tell your destiny and imminent doom.

II

City of portents and of silences,
Here in the heart of the world your word beats strong
With a tale of old unrest, a tale of wrong,
Portending change and strange injustices.

For this great vision haunts me early and late,
The fiery face of Riel turning again,
Reining his horse a moment, into the rain
Galloping. We with Wolseley cross the gate,

Now by the vortex of the searching snow
That shrinks the last leaf in its cataract,
By the edged deadly ice that burns like fact
Not to be argued with—now let us know

What was the meaning. Under the moving sky
Let us reply to Riel, he whose tongue
Asks (while the storm yet chants its threatening song),
Whose eye, inquiring, puts the insistent, Why?

What shall we answer, what shall ever be said
To him? the rebel, withstander of our ways
Not his, for we had come new tracks to blaze.
His neck is broken, his spoken defiance dead.

His was the heavy word that stopped Scott's mouth,
His the allies that slaughtered mother and child,
His the great heart that beat at last too wild;
He made the Ottawa a deepening gulf.

Alien to me his race and his religion—
Yet while the storm mounts, while clouds westward fly
Swift as the swift spirit of Shelley in the sky,
Still haunts that face the airy, fiery region.

He is with the defeated, with the dead;
He set his foot down on the surveyor's chain
Challenging empire, challenging law, in vain.
It is the others we honour, who succeed.

III

Soon our turn will come, when by northern ice
Over the wide white causeway their armour moves:
When the swift craft conspiracy so loves
Darts on us, when the guided missile flies

ROY DANIELLS

Soundless—when the ensuing roar
Falls on stopped ears, when our laborious walls
Rise like lightning in the summer squalls
And over our ruin the cold starlight pours.

Soon, soon, for the hurrying beat of the dove
Leaves, and not like Noah's to return.
Soon, for the augurs cry and the portents warn
And who shall meet strong hate with tender love?

No more shall distance sentinel us, no more
Come warning of a conqueror's far tread;
One step shall part the living from the dead,
Heard overhead or unheard the rotor's roar.

And when all hope dies in the hurricane,
The northern storm or hot blast from the south,
When the strong hand strikes freedom on the mouth
And a great age of darkness falls again,

Remember Riel in Regina falling forlorn,
Old faiths and empires gone down in the dark;
Foster within your breast the living spark
That here the flame of freedom spring reborn.

       .   .   .

O much enduring unenduring city,
In the ring of time set like a faceted stone,
On whom the blinding drops of summer shone
Or the white fortune of the winter's entry—

Even of the unsung city let us tell
The story and her ancient tale of wrong,
Her strength and splendour when her heart beat strong,
For even as I in going bid farewell

To the place my heart remembers, now the storm
Presses about her, cloud battalions crowd
In portent over, wild winds shout aloud,
And mimic armies have begun to form.

A. J. M. SMITH

b. 1902

157   *Like an Old Proud King in a*
Parable

A bitter king in anger to be gone
From fawning courtier and doting queen
Flung hollow sceptre and gilt crown away,
And breaking bound of all his counties green
He made a meadow in the northern stone
And breathed a palace of inviolable air
To cage a heart that carolled like a swan,
And slept alone, immaculate and gay,
With only his pride for a paramour.

O who is that bitter king? It is not I.

Let me, I beseech thee, Father, die
From this fat royal life, and lie
As naked as a bridegroom by his bride,
And let that girl be the cold goddess Pride.

And I will sing to the barren rock
Your difficult, lonely music, heart,
Like an old proud king in a parable.

158   *The Plot Against Proteus*

This is a theme for muted coronets
To dangle from debilitated heads
Of navigation, kings, or riverbeds
That rot or rise what time the seamew sets
Her course by stars among the smoky tides
Entangled. Old saltencrusted Proteus treads
Once more the watery shore that water weds
While rocking fathom bell rings round and rides.

Now when the blind king of the water thinks
The sharp hail of the salt out of his eyes
To abdicate, run thou, O Prince, and fall
Upon him. This cracked walrus skin that stinks
Of the rank sweat of a mermaid's thighs
Cast off, and nab him; when you have him, call.

159   *Ode*

ON THE DEATH OF WILLIAM BUTLER YEATS

An old thorn tree in a stony place
Where the mountain stream has run dry,
Torn in the black wind under the race
Of the icicle-sharp kaleidoscopic white sky,
   Bursts into sudden flower.

Under the central dome of winter and night
A wild swan spreads his fanatic wing.
Ancestralled energy of blood and power
Beats in his sinewy breast. And now the ravening
Soul, fulfilled, his first-last hour
   Upon him, chooses to exult.

Over the edge of shivering Europe,
Over the chalk front of Kent, over Eire,
Dwarfing the crawling waves' amoral savagery,
Daring the hiding clouds' rhetorical tumult,
   The white swan plummets the mountain top.

The stream has suddenly pushed the papery leaves!
It digs a rustling channel of clear water
On the scarred flank of Ben Bulben.
The twisted tree is incandescent with flowers.
The swan leaps singing into the cold air:
   This is a glory not for an hour.

   Over the Galway shore
   The white bird is flying
   Forever, and crying
   To the tumultuous throng
Of the sky his cold and passionate song.

160   *To Henry Vaughan*

Homesick? and yet your country walks
Were heaven'd for you. Such bright stalks
Of grasses! such pure Green! such blue
Clear skies! such light! such silver dew!—
On each brief bud and shining twig
White pregnant jewels, each one big
With meaning, rich pearls cast before
Not swine but men, who toss or snore.
   Thou didst not so: thou wert awake;
And stirring forth before the break
Of day, thou wouldst enquire

A. J. M. SMITH

If, with the Cock, no angel choir
Meant to announce th'eternal Day;
If, in the sun's first quick'ning ray
Thou might'st observe the flaming hair
Of thy wish'd Lord, thy Bridegroom dear.
    Yet when the Constellations fine
Stand where the sun before did shine,
You may not in your good-night pray'r
Ask day more holy, heav'n more near:
Earth's angels, these tall feathery trees,
Sang in thy loved one's praise; thy bees
Gather'd his Honey; one small bird
In three clear notes his Name preferr'd.
    Celestial strings might not surpass
Thy morning breezes in long grass;
The slow rain from the laden tree,
Dropping from heaven, brought to thee
Sounds of the purest harmony,
Setting thy caged soul free to fly,
Borne on the breath of fruits and flow'rs
Sweeten'd and made fresh in silver show'rs.
    And add to these thy bubbling rills;
Soft winds; the intricate rich trills
Of happy larks that climb the air
Like a broad golden winding Stair
To Heaven, singing as they climb,
Lifting the rapt soul out of Time
Into a long Eternity
Where Heaven is now, and still to be.
    Yet art thou Homesick! to be gone
From all this brave Distraction
Wouldst seal thine ear, nail down thine eye;
To be one perfect Member, die;

And anxious to exchange in death
Thy foul, for thy Lord's precious, breath,
Thou art content to beg a pall,
Glad to be Nothing, to be All.

161   *The Archer*

Bend back thy bow, O Archer, till the string
Is level with thine ear, thy body taut,
Its nature art, thyself thy statue wrought
Of marble blood, thy weapon the poised wing
Of coiled and aquiline Fate. Then, loosening, fling
The hissing arrow like a burning thought
Into the empty sky that smokes as the hot
Shaft plunges to the bullseye's quenching ring.

So for a moment, motionless, serene,
Fixed between time and time, I aim and wait;
Nothing remains for breath now but to waive
His prior claim and let the barb fly clean
Into the heart of what I know and hate—
That central black, the ringed and targeted grave.

162   *My Death*

'I carry my death within me.'
Who was it said that?—Saint-Denys-Garneau?
It's true. Everyone—free
Or enslaved, Christian or Jew,
Coloured or white, believer or
Sceptic or the indifferent worldling—
Knows death, at least as metaphor.

213

But this says more. My death is a thing—
Physical, solid, sensuous, a seed
Lodged like Original Sin
In the essence of being, a need
Also, a felt want within.

It lies dormant at first—
Lazy, a little romantic
In childhood, later a thirst
For what is no longer exotic.
It lives on its own phlegm,
And grows stronger as I grow stronger,
As a flower grows with its stem.

I am the food of its hunger.
It enlivens my darkness,
Progressively illuminating
What I know for the first time, yes,
Is what I've been always wanting.

SIMONE ROUTIER

b. 1903

163   *J'aime*

J'aime, et la beauté du soir chante en moi;
Soyeux mes pas vont sur les fleurs heureuses;
Leurs petites chairs se brisent d'émoi:
Toutes je les sens fléchir — amoureuses.

J'aime, et le couchant soudain embrasé,
Sur ses lourds parfums, sur ses fauves teintes,
Refermant son long rideau damassé
M'enveloppe de ses moites étreintes.

J'aime, et le ciel pur m'ouvre son trésor.
Tout m'est enivrant et doux de la terre.
J'aime. Qui? — Mon cœur ne sait pas encor.
J'aime, et sur la nuit mon bras se resserre.

164 *Simple désir de femme*

Oui,
Ami,
C'est un rêve
Que je tiens d'Ève.
Il vient me tenter,
Saurai-je résister?
Ton sourire fin exprime
Ce soir, oh! tout un monde intime,
Et tes yeux, citernes de reflets,
Ont cet art précieux d'être indiscrets.
Mais voici: je voudrais ouvrir ta cervelle
Pour voir mieux, de plus près, tout ce qui gite en elle.

165 *La Mer*

*Ne craignez pas, pécheurs, c'est peu de dire que vous êtes attendus,
il y a pour vous comme une préférence.*

A. D. SERTILLANGES, O.P.

Ah cette extravagante prise de possession de la
  plage franche, rêche et altérée; de cette plage où
  il faut courir pour ne faire que marcher!
Ce n'est que sur la dernière dune, aux confins de la
  tentation, à l'orée de la grâce, qu'il faut t'y étendre.

Là que la fraîcheur de quelque lame plus hardie te
      secouant les épaules, te baisant au visage, du rire
      blanc de sa mousse,
Tandis que son ressac vivement ramène à la raison le
      sable sous toi, te gagne au jeu viril du pardon et du
      repentir.

Car c'est sur la dernière dune que la mer te donne
      rendez-vous, pour d'abord te plus décemment vêtir
      de la mousseline de son écume
Et te tonifier de son haleine iodée avant de t'enve-
      lopper, de te porter et, du troisième coup de son
      ressac, t'engloutir,
T'engloutir à sa possession profonde, te ravir à son
      incessante extase; car sur terre et au ciel, il n'y a
      qu'un amour,
Le même, et qui prend tout, corps et âme, et dont ce
      que t'offre la plage des hommes—le plaisir—
      n'est que l'infâme parodie.

166   *Le Divin Anéantissement*

*Cette assomption de la chair en l'unité de Dieu
concerne chacun de nous.*
                  A. D. SERTILLANGES, O.P.

La mer qui berce, chante et endort,
L'Église qui écoute, pardonne et absout.
La mer berçante qui porte la barque et ramène le pêcheur,
La mer qui chante et rend la terre au marin,
La mer qui endort l'exilé et dilate le cœur
En mal de plongeurs la mer ne se lasse jamais de bercer.
En mal d'âme l'Église ne se lasse jamais de prêcher.

SIMONE ROUTIER

Une prière excite une autre prière,
Une lame épaule une autre lame
Et l'écume qui sur la plage
T'apprend la saveur de la mer
A mis des années à t'en préparer le sel.

Entre dans la mer et laisse-toi couper les jambes.
Dans la vague qui porte on n'a que faire des chevilles.
Coupe les amarres des attaches charnelles.
L'Église te prend dans ses bras
Et le corps ne peut appartenir à deux étreintes.

Le coquillage à ton oreille a porté toute la mer.
Le prédicateur t'a conté l'Évangile.
Mais quel infime secret, dans un seul coquillage
L'immense mer a-t-elle pu emprisonner?
Qu'est à l'homme la douceur du plus poignant Évangile
En regard de tout l'amour de son Auteur même, en lui?

Confonds-toi à la mer: elle se confondra à toi.
Ses trésors, un à un, jour après jour,
D'un coquillage, d'une vague, d'une marée à l'autre,
D'une grâce à l'autre tous elle te les confiera dès ici-bas.
Ne discute et ne pêche plus sur la plage.
Donne-toi; fais confiance à l'eau.

L'Église n'est point une doctrine, c'est une tendresse.
La mer n'est point un abîme, c'est un refuge.
Combien léger ton cœur dans la poitrine de l'Église,

Combien libre le poids de ton corps dans l'eau,
Dans l'eau salée de la mer qui porte,
Qui soulève, assainit, dégage et assouplit.

Romps les amarres, jette-toi à Dieu.
Ne supporte plus le soleil qu'à travers l'eau,
La tentation qu'à travers la grâce;
Ne remets plus au sablier du temps le sable,
Bois au sable noyé l'éternité.

Dans la résille d'or que la crête multiple des vagues,
A marée basse, forme sur ce sable,
Tends pour toi au fond de la mer,
Laisse-toi prendre, c'est le filet du Divin Pêcheur,
Le filet des troisièmes conversions.

Seul l'œil t'y peut croire prisonnière,
C'est là que tu conquiers la vraie liberté,
L'exaltante liberté, dans la lumière, des Enfants de Dieu.

Abandonne-toi à la mer,
Laisse-la te sculpter à son image,
Te polir de son éternelle patience.

Laisse la grâce t'envelopper, te pénétrer de toutes parts
Et tu oublieras les contours de ton corps,
Tu trouveras enfin ceux de ton âme,
Infinie à la mesure de la mer, infinie à la mesure de Dieu.

Pour oublier la ville, ne va plus au village,
Pour oublier le village, égare ici tes sandales

Et pour renoncer aux sandales, laisse-toi scier les chevilles.
Laisse-moi, dit la mer, t'enlever à la terre,
Laisse-moi t'apprendre le véritable abandon et la joie,
Laisse-moi t'apprendre l'extase infinie, mon Divin
    anéantissement.

EARLE BIRNEY

b. 1904

167   *Slug in Woods*

For eyes he waves greentipped
taut horns of slime. They dipped,
hours back, across a reef,
a salmonberry leaf.
Then strained to grope past fin
of spruce. Now eyes suck in
as through the hemlock butts
of his day's ledge there cuts
a vixen chipmunk. Stilled
is he—green mucus chilled,
or blotched and soapy stone,
pinguid in moss, alone.
Hours on, he will resume
his silver scrawl, illume
his palimpsest, emboss
his diver's line across
that waving green illim-
itable seafloor. Slim
young jay his sudden shark;
the wrecks he skirts are dark

and fungussed firlogs, whom
spirea sprays emplume,
encoral. Dew his shell,
while mounting boles foretell
of isles in dappled air
fathoms above his care.
Azygous muted life,
himself his viscid wife,
foodward he noses cold beneath his sea.
So spends a summer's jasper century.

168 *Mappemounde*

No not this old whalehall can whelm us,
shiptamed, gullgraced, soft to our glidings.
Harrows that mere more that squares our map.
See in its north where scribe has marked *mermen*,
shore-sneakers who croon, to the seafarer's girl,
next year's gleewords. East and west *nadders*,
flamefanged baletwisters; their breath dries up tears,
chars in the breast-hoard the dear face-charm.
Southward *Cetegrande*, that sly beast who sucks in
with whirlwind also the wanderer's pledges.
That sea is hight Time, it hems heart's landtrace.
Men say the redeless, reaching its bounds,
topple in maelstrom, tread back never.
Adread in that mere we drift toward map's end.

EARLE BIRNEY

The Road to Nijmegen

December, my dear, on the road to Nijmegen,
between the stones and the bitter skies was your face.

At first only the gatherings of graves
along the lank canals, each with a frosted
billy-tin for motto; the bones of tanks
beside the stoven bridges; old men in the mist
knifing chips from a boulevard of stumps;
or women riding into the wind on the rims of their cycles,
like tattered sailboats tossing over the cobbles.

These at first, and the fangs of homes, but more
The clusters of children, like flies, at the back of messhuts,
or groping in gravel for knobs of coal,
their legs standing like dead stems out of their clogs.
Numbed on the long road to mangled Nijmegen,
I thought that only the living of others assures us;
we remember the gentle and true as trees walking,
as the men and women whose breath is a garment about us;
that we who are stretched now in this tomb of time
may remount like Lazarus into the light of kindness
by a hold in the hands of the kind.

And so in the sleet as we neared Nijmegen,
searching my heart for the hope of our minds,
for the proof in the flesh of the words we wish,
for laughter outrising at last the rockets,
I saw the rainbow answer of you,
of you and your seed who, peopling the earth, would distil
our not impossible dreamed horizon,
and who, moving within the nightmare Now,

give us what creed we have for our daily crimes,
for this road that arrives at no future,
for this guilt
in the griefs of the old and the graves of the young.

170   From *Damnation of Vancouver*
          [*Speech of the Salish Chief*]

Where once we hunted, white men have built many long-
     houses,
but they are uneasy as mice within them.
They have made slaves of waterfalls
and magic from the invisible dust of rocks
and are stronger than grizzlies—
but their slaves bully them,
and they are chickadees in council.
Some of you say: give them time, they will grow wise and
     find peace.
Others say: the sun slides into the saltwater;
they must follow the Indian into the trail of darkness.

Before the tall ships tossed their shining tools
to us, my uncle was our carpenter.
With saw of flame he laid the great cedars low,
split the sweet-smelling planks with adze of slate,
bowed them his way with steam and thong,
shaped the long wind-silvered house
where fifty of my kin and I lived warm as bear and lusty.
He made it tight against the rain's long fingers,
yet panelled to let in the red-faced sun.

EARLE BIRNEY

He hollowed the great canoes we rode the gulf in safe as gulls.
My uncle knew the high song of the cedar tree;
he had a Guarding Power with Brother Wood.

The tides bore in unasked our kelp-float flagons;
our wood-drills gave us fire, earth and stones our ovens.
Red roots and yellow reeds entwined themselves within
our women's hands, coiled to those baskets dancing
with the grey wave's pattern or the wings
of dragonflies you keep in the great cities now
within glass boxes. Now they are art, white man's tabu,
but once they held sweet water.

The wild lilies grew their pungent bulbs unprompted,
the vines unfurled their green shoots for the plucking.
The children dried our currants from the saskatoon,
made cakes of blackberry, jam from the lush salal.
My father and I were hunters for the longhouse.
He taught me to bend a yew-bow, with snakeskin tape it taut,
whittle arrows wind-light from the cedar,
feathered and jasper-tipped.
At night we would return with deer from the mountains
or ducks glistening from the still shore-coves.
Sometimes, gliding hushed on the sea,
I would raise my lance, my slate blade shining,
hurl it home into a fat black porpoise;
or with my horned harpoon hook Brother Seal.
Then all the longhouse would make music,
there would be roasting of the spicey fern-roots,
there would be sweet small plums,
the shell-spoons would dip and glitter from the carved feasting
    bowls.

There were bright days when all my village paddled,
racing the wolfhead canoes to a rippled beach.
The heady seasmell rose from glowing stone-pits;
then we held crab- and clam-feast,
lay in talk till the beachfires came alight
in the seas of the sky.

Salmon was bread.
When in the Tide of Thimbleberries the first silverback
threshed in our dip-nets, my father's drum
called all the village.
The red flesh flaked steaming from the ceremonial spit.
My father gave thanks to the Salmon Power,
and everyone tasted bird-like. Then we young men
ran to the water with trolls and seine-nets.
The bows of our canoes returning were flecked like mica.
With flying fingers the women split the shiny ones,
hung them on cunning cedar racks;
our friends, the air and the sun,
sealed the good oils for the winter storing.
Salmon was bread.
But my brothers could fashion bone-hooks
strong as the wolverine's jaw to gaff the great river-sturgeon.
Every year came the cod and the sea-trout to their hands,
their nets boiled with shoals of the candlefish.
It was not till your time, sir,
I saw a Salish go hungry.

There was something, I do not know,
a way of life that died for yours to live.
We gambled like fool-hens but we did not steal.
My father spoke to the people always what was true.
When there was quarrel, he made us speak it out in reason,

or wrestle weaponless on the clean sand.
We kept no longhouse for warriors, we held not state on
    others.
Each in his village had his work, and all made certain all
    were fed.

It is true the Kwakiutls would come like sea-wolves
riding their war-canoes, raiding for slaves,
and we could resist only as wrens flying.
My grandmother fell by the woods' edge
as she ran from their arrows.

The Kwakiutls were warriors and were quickly gone;
they went looking for braves more worthy to conquer.
With the long years they dwindled.
It was our people who grew like the grey geese.
When we paddled to others it was only to visit;
our young men lived to be old.

Each summer the salmon came, the deer were plump in the
    river groves.

Sometimes a young man would be many months in the woods
    thinking, alone as a heron,
and learning the powers of the creatures.
I lay and watched the little grey doctor, the lizard;
I studied the spirit of bear; I came by their songs.
When I was chief I carved Brother Bear on my houseposts,
took the red earths and the white and painted his strength.

It is true we saw marvels in each life,
and wished to learn the eagle's dignity, the beaver's wisdom.
It is true my village held no ceremonies of blood-drinking,
and we did not think of Jehovah.
These, and Hell, the white man brought us.

EARLE BIRNEY

Once our kindred gathered from many villages.
Like dolphin they came arching over the waves.
My father stood tall on the house-roof, called each by name,
threw down a soft cloak of marten and mink,
white rug of the wild goat's wool,
or shaggy leggings of bearskin,
tossed down for the catching red capes of the cedar bark,
blankets woven with the woodpecker's colours,
tanned shoes of deerhide, and root-mats
brown as the last cloud in the sun's downgoing.
The men made jokes, there was squirrel-laughter of women,
we boys ran races over the hot sea-sand.
After, by the full tide's brim,
the Dance.
My father put on the great-eyed mask of his Power;
with his secret kelp-whistle he talked owl-talk as he swayed.
My uncle held his drum close to a tidepool,
rubbed the skin cunningly with his hands,
made the downy whoosh of the owl's wings in the night air.
There was one who drew frog-talk from cockle-shells
hidden in the pool of his fingers.
The old men sang of wise chiefs that had been, and their
        spirits,
the songs dying slowly as wind, then swelling
as the board-drums beat tremolos, as the carved rattles clacked,
as the shell hoops spoke to the ritual sticks.
Once there was a silence; no one stirred; I heard my heart
        beat.
Then, like an arrow's thud, one beat of a drum, one . . .
another . . . another . . . a fourth—
and suddenly all the drums were thunder
and everyone leaped singing and surging in the last dance. . . .
That was my first potlatch. . . .

In those times we drank only our sounds and thoughts,
giving unhurt to those who gave.
When your fathers took our food and left us little coins,
when they took our songs and left us little hymns,
the music and the potlatch stopped.

Comfort was in the dogwool shirt of my youth,
the tassels of flying squirrel
tailing like smoke from my shoulders,
not the trader's cast-offs in my aging.
Comfort was the winter's bear-haunches safe in the rafters,
when as a child I darted laughing under the reed hangings,
with a little fist of hazelnuts clutched from the cedar chest.
Comfort was waking beside my wife
on our bed of musk-sweet rushes.

Before even the Captain's cloud-canoe, before I was chief,
the Sechelts held a great gift-giving on the tiderim.
Something, flung gleaming through the air, fell in the water.
I dived; my fingers clutched a gun, a flintlock.
Spaniards had made it;
the Nootkas gave its height in otter skins.
Now it was mine; I shot the deer my arrows fainted to reach.
With other years came other traders
and stronger fire unsealed from iron tube and bottle;
I gave my only son the flintlock.
He walked into the whisky-house they built in our village;
He drank its madness;
he killed his cousin, my brother's heir.
The white men choked my son with a rope.
From that day my life was a walking backwards.

What trails we would have stumbled on alone none now will
    know.
In a moon of heat the tall priest came;
with his magic twig of fire he lit the dried grass
and spoke in the raven's voice of Hell,
unrolled a painting bright as the sundown,
showed us our dead in Hell's flame.
In fear we let the little wisps of our marvels
lose themselves in the black cloud of his god.
And ever the whites came crowding our shoreline
like summer smelts, and the deer fled.
My grandsons, my hunters, went to grease logs for the skid-
    ders;
one died under a felled tree,
the other black and gasping with smallpox.

I had yet two daughters; their eyes were chaste.
To one a sailor gave rum, and a glass necklace,
and the secret rot of his thighs; she died barren and young.
The other went to a trader, to be his woman;
when he had turned her away,
before she spat out her lungs with his plague,
she bore him my only grand-daughter.
In my old age the child grew tall, fair as a waterfall.
The factor married her; he made her give up our people.
There are white chiefs now in Vancouver who carry her
    blood,
but it is a long time now and they do not know,
or they are ashamed.
These are all my descendants. . . .

When the measles passed from my village, ten of us lived
to bury our ninety, and I, their Chief, was blind.

We left the longhouses for the burning,
the burial grove and the carvings to loggers.
They sent me over the Sound to sit
dark and alone by the smokehouse fire of my cousins.
One night I felt with shuffling feet the beach-path.
I walked into the saltwater,
I walked down to the home of the Seal Brother. . . .

171   *Bushed*

He invented a rainbow but lightning struck it
shattered it into the lake-lap of a mountain
so big his mind slowed when he looked at it

Yet he built a shack on the shore
learned to roast porcupine belly and
wore the quills on his hatband

At first he was out with the dawn
whether it yellowed bright as wood-columbine
or was only a fuzzed moth in a flannel of storm
But he found the mountain was clearly alive
sent messages whizzing down every hot morning
boomed proclamations at noon and spread out
a white guard of goat
before falling asleep on its feet at sundown

When he tried his eyes on the lake, ospreys
would fall like valkyries
choosing the cut-throat
He took then to waiting
till the night smoke rose from the boil of the sunset

But the moon carved unknown totems
out of the lakeshore
owls in the beardusky woods derided him
moosehorned cedars circled his swamps and tossed
their antlers up to the stars
Then he knew though the mountain slept, the winds
were shaping its peak to an arrowhead
poised

But by now he could only
bar himself in and wait
for the great flint to come singing into his heart

FLORIS CLARK McLAREN

b. 1904

172   *No More the Slow Stream*

No more the slow stream spreading clear in sunlight
Lacing the swamp with intricate shining channels
Patterned by wind and the dipping tall marsh grasses:

No more the mica glint in the sliding water
The bright-winged flies and the muskrat gone like a shadow
No more the curved trout breaking concentric silver:

Now the basalt cliffs and the yellow foam in the eddies
Now the strong brown water boiling deeply from under
Now the log abutment left where the bridge has fallen:

O the slow stream lovely, lovely no more in sunlight:
The flotsam of quiet lives turned over and over,
The dark destructive flood; and the plan the promise
Spun in the current, swept toward no visible ocean.

FLORIS CLARK McLAREN

Visit by Water

We came by boat in the late arctic twilight
To the abandoned town
In the sharp triangular grass at the river mouth
Where the glacier silt fans into the bay.

Cautiously from the slime-encrusted wharf
We found our way
By no path over the tide-flats to the crazy doorstep,
The grey rooms tilted open to the sky.

These were our rooms, accustomed as our hands and features;
Now we try
Each in his separate loneliness to reawaken
The familiar ghosts. And sadly fail.

Only from the trees on the tide-marked cliff the pair of eagles,
Mated how long!
Fierce in their soaring and loving, willing us fiercely out of
        their valley,
Observe the curving wake of our boat on the slate bay.

ALFRED GOLDSWORTHY BAILEY

b. 1905

174   *Colonial Set*

That wolf, shivering by the palisade,
nosed the footprints of a hard winter,
grew thin.
The Indians are fighting drunk.
The Frenchmen keep the squaws.

231

'How I long to be
in Normandy.
The carriages are waiting at the door.
The ladies lie in laces at the fête,
Festin à tout manger[1]
to gobble up
the choicest viands of the *cuisinier*,'
the water murmured,
beating its breasts shapelessly on the shore.

A cold agony kept pace with the storm,
keeping the temper of the waves leashed,
towering with destination in the northeast,
beating away warm
blood from the heart's core,
checking the arteries,
clogging the burden of the veins,
congealing stagnant lusts in an inland pool.
Animalculae shrivel and die in their sacks.
The beaver cowers in his dam. The caribou
snorts frostily.
Hoofs clatter on the ice-pack.
The rampikes of the forest
attain a brittle silence.

175 *Miramichi Lightning*

The sachem voices cloven out of the hills
spat teeth in the sea like nails
before the spruce were combed to soughing peace.

---

[1] Term used by the Jesuits with reference to the 'eat-all' feasts as
practised by the Hurons in the seventeenth century.

They said a goliath alphabet at once
and stopped to listen to their drumming ears
repeat the chorus round a funeral mountain.

Hurdling a hump of whales they juddered east,
and there were horse-faced leaders whipped the breath
from bodies panting on the intervales.

The lights were planets going out for good
as the rancour of a cloud broke off and fell
into the back of town and foundered there.

176   *Algonkian Burial*

Comes the time
I was suddenly aware of the difference.
And by and by the flesh fell away from the bones
and the joints clinked as the wind passed.
There was little left me of the quality of water.

I looked not out of place propped among the birch trees
with my pipe and tobacco and my cold supper beside me.
I could not help feeling
proud of the regularity of my ribs
and my soldierly erectness as I lay at attention
while the morning sun flickered in the hollow sockets of my
    eyes.

ROBERT CHOQUETTE

b. 1905

177　　　　　*Vivre et créer*

Ah! le mal de créer obsède ma jeunesse!
Je voudrais me refaire, afin d'être plus fort
Et meilleur et plus pur, et pour que je renaisse
Et que je vive encor lorsque je serai mort!

Vivre! baigner mon cœur dans l'aurore ineffable!
Chanter la mer profonde et les arbres épais
Jusqu'à ce que la voix de mon corps périssable
Fasse un hymne d'amour qui ne mourra jamais!

Vivre! faire éclater les chaînons de la chaîne!
D'un grand coup d'aile, atteindre au flamboiement de Dieu,
Y ravir l'étincelle et faire une œuvre humaine
Qui soit presque divine et pareille au ciel bleu!

Oh! l'infini du ciel m'étreint. Mon cœur avide
Tel l'éponge des mers se gonfle et se remplit.
Mais ma bouche qui s'ouvre est comme un antre vide
Où la morne impuissance habite et fait son lit;

Et ma langue se meut comme l'algue marine
Que retient par les pieds le rocher triomphant;
Et quand mon cœur gonflé se heurte à ma poitrine
Ma langue balbutie un murmure d'enfant.

Eh bien! je boirai tant les souffles d'aventure,
Je ferai tant chanter dans mes jeunes poumons
La respiration de la forte nature,
Que ma voix bondira sur le sommet des monts.

Choses du monde! O clapotis glouton des vagues;
Irascible soleil, étoiles d'argent pur
Aux doigts fins des bouleaux brillant comme des bagues;
Vents des plaines, glaciers étincelants d'azur;

Rocs que la mer assiège ainsi que des tourelles;
Frais calice où s'engouffre un oiseau-mouche; ô bruit
Métallique et vibrant des brusques sauterelles;
Parfums, aube aux pieds courts que le soleil poursuit;

Nature aux grands yeux verts, créatrice éternelle
Qui tiens l'humanité dans le creux de ta main,
Fais que dans ta lumière immense et maternelle
Bondisse immensément mon faible cœur humain!

Prends ma jeunesse, Terre ineffable et sauvage,
Aïeule au front sans âge et toujours renaissant!
Verse-moi ta fraîcheur comme un divin breuvage!
Ô mère, fais mon corps musculeux et puissant!

Prends-moi, prends-moi, nature aux mamelles fécondes!
Chante-moi ta berceuse, et donne la vigueur
À ton petit d'hier qui veut créer des mondes
Et qui tombe à genoux sous le poids de son cœur!

From *Suite marine*

178   *Les Mers tropicales*

(*i*)

Je marche près de toi parmi le bleu silence
Du midi tropical un comme un marbre grec
Et chantant de beaux vers héroïques, avec
Des rimes de métal, de hardis fers de lance.

235

Je marche. Mais, bientôt, avec tant d'insolence
Me raille la cigale au haut du dattier sec!
L'alouette de mer, un cri plaintif au bec,
Incline l'aile au gré d'une telle indolence!

Et ce frangipanier dont l'haleine de miel
Guiderait une abeille aveugle! Sous ton ciel,
Incomparable éden, ô golfe du Mexique,

On ne sait qu'être nu, de corps et de raison,
Non comme un dieu sculpté dans le marbre classique,
Mais comme un dieu sylvain couché sur le gazon.

179   (*ii*)

Dans la visqueuse nuit de la mer — où soudain
Ce buisson mort s'éveille pieuvre! — l'huître morne
Dort d'un repos si lourd qu'on dirait une borne
Au milieu des bouquets du monstrueux jardin.

Mais le ver est entré, parasite anodin,
Monstre microscopique à tête de licorne.
La victime s'alarme et se défend: elle orne
Son ciel intérieur au cœur incarnadin

D'une perle. Tel l'homme. Amour, deuil, perfidie,
Surgisse la douleur dans son âme engourdie,
Il sanglote, il dévore un poing désespéré.

Puis un jour, ô merveille, il se sent libéré,
Car le cri de l'instinct s'est vu transfiguré,
Dans l'esprit créateur, en une mélodie!

180   (*iii*)

Face à face, sans âge et toujours rajeunis,
Deux abîmes: la Mer qui fut jadis fournaise,
La Nuit céruléenne aux arceaux infinis.

Ici règne éternel le temps de la Genèse,
Quand Jéhovah, planant sur les flots esseulés,
Gardait encore en lui le verbe de semence.

L'abîme de douceur, l'autre d'horreur, mêlés
L'un à l'autre, à jamais, en une étreinte immense,
Échangent des mots d'ombre et des mots étoilés.

Je suis l'éternité qui toujours recommence,
Qui ne change jamais et change à tout instant
Et, sans jamais mourir, se recrée elle-même:

La Mer! Je suis la Nuit, abîme palpitant
Mais éternel à la façon du théorème,
À la façon du cercle, immuable, constant.

Mes astres, entraînés par une loi suprême,
S'équilibrent si bien que j'ai l'illusion
De l'immobilité dans l'âge et dans l'espace.

Je suis la Mer, la mer riche à profusion
De fleurs et d'animaux dont chacun se déplace
D'après l'obscur vouloir de son impulsion.

Je donne forme à la hideur comme à la grâce;
Je risque, en modelant ces animaux, ces fleurs,
Des figures dont Dieu lui-même s'émerveille.

ROBERT CHOQUETTE

Je suis la Nuit, creuset où fondent les couleurs
Et les reliefs du monde ! Et le monde s'éveille
A son rêve, plus haut que la joie et les pleurs.

Je chante, mais mon chant n'est pas fait pour l'oreille,
Ô mes doux carillons qui sonnez pour les yeux,
Étoiles de cristal au plus pur du silence !

Je suis la Mer, je suis l'orgue prodigieux
Aux mille voix intarissables, d'où s'élance
Un hymne tel qu'il fait trembler la nef des cieux,

Un chant qui dit l'horreur, la peur, la violence
Nécessaires, le meurtre implacable et joyeux
Au gouffre de la faim que rien ne rassasie.

Je suis la Nuit, la Nuit dont les doigts emperlés
Portent l'étincelante et sombre Poésie !
Je suis la Mer . . . Ainsi, l'un à l'autre mêlés,

Abîme de douceur, gouffre de frénésie,
Ils disent des mots d'ombre et des mots étoilés,
Le gouffre de la Mer, glaciale fournaise,

L'abîme de la Nuit aux infinis arceaux,
Tels encore aujourd'hui qu'au temps de la Genèse,
Quand Jéhovah flottait sur la face des eaux.

b. 1905

181 *Au pays de Québec*

MÉDITATION PATRIOTIQUE

Ô mon pauvre pays,
Où rien ne change jamais,
Changer pourtant, c'est vivre, ô mon pays !
Et, toi, immobile, fixe, tel un œil de verre dans la tête de
      Robot.
Toi, immuable, avec ton estomac gavé de viandes
Et de promesses.
Toi que l'on souille, sur qui l'on bave une sanie impure.
Oh ! ce filet glaireux sur ta face de Titan !
Tu n'as donc plus de sursauts.
Quand nos pères, sous la chevelure intacte des forêts vierges,
S'en allaient, 'portageant' leurs canots, jouant leur chevelure,
Quand nos pères partaient pour ne plus revenir, —
Et leurs veuves prenaient à deux mains, par les mancherons,
      la charrue, —
Quand nos pères n'étaient morts qu'une fois,
Avant l'oubli . . .
Les grands, les très grands n'engendrent point de rejetons à
      leur taille.
Je croule vers le néant. Moi aussi, je suis le fils indigne de ceux
      qui ont écrit une épopée avec leur sang.
Ils ne savaient point signer.
Et nous ne pouvons plus même créer avec les mots.
Dire que j'ai peut-être du sang de Frontenac dans mes veines
      étroites,
Et que mon front pâle pourrait être la chair de Madeleine.
Quand une race est tarie, elle donne des politiciens.

       .   .   .

Toute cette prose m'assassine. A boire !
C'est une apparition tricolore. Tous les héros,

La robe blanche de Jeanne Mance,
Les habits bleus de la Monongahela,
Et le front pourpre du grand vaincu, Montcalm, avec ce
    coquelicot, là, sur la poitrine . . .
Ils y sont tous, comme au temps de la légende,
Comme au temps de l'Histoire.
De la main, ils font signe: 'Cherche, disent-ils, retrouve le
    filon!'
Et me voici rêvant d'alchimies laborieuses, de transfusions
Idéales.
Oh! laver notre sang maigre dans le leur,
Rouge, riche, du sang de buffle et du sang d'orignal,
Du sang qui ne coule pas, qui caille sur la main.
Dans mon rêve confus, c'est tout un fleuve qui se bouscule
De ce sang d'une réincarnation possible.
Et c'est une fantasmagorie: le sang de ceux de 1660, le sang
    de 1760, le sang
De 1837.
J'en bois, j'en bois. Où suis-je? A mort!

.   .   .

C'était une plaine immense et verte,
Où le soleil buvait les roses.
Et soudain ce fut le cap Éternité.
Rocher indomptable, inviolé et face aux vents,
Aux vents du nord, ces grands oiseaux polaires,
Ceux que d'Iberville a vaincus sur le Pélican;
Aux vents du sud-est qui miaulent comme des chats sauvages:
    les rafales d'Acadie,
Quand le soir tombe sur Port-Royal.
Et le vieux cap les a maudits dans la tempête.
Soudain la forêt s'est dressée. C'était de l'ouest, c'étaient des
    râles,
C'était la voix de Louis Riel.

Et voici qu'une autre voix, que d'autres voix, que mille voix
    m'ont assailli.
Tous à la fois, ils m'ont parlé; les morts m'ont dit:
'Qu'ils nous crachent au visage,
Qu'ils nous oublient, qu'ils nous maudissent,
Qu'ils nous renient, qu'ils nous ignorent,
Mais qu'ils tiennent!'
Voilà ce que mes pères ont dit à mes fils!

      .   .   .

Et le poète est descendu du Sinaï.
Il n'a gardé que la substance,
Que le métal coagulé.
Les temps ne sont pas encore venus.   1939

182   *Le Chant de l'exilé*

Mon malheur est trop grand pour tenir en ce monde,
Il doit gésir quelque part dans une éternité.
Ma damnation est sur place et mon crime est d'être né,
Mais je ne veux pas mourir; j'aime voir le soleil quelquefois
    sur la Seine reluire.
Mon cœur est transpercé de glaives infinis.
J'ai perdu tout mon sang sur des routes de feu,
La glace est en moi-même à demeure,
Mon enfer est glacial. Je me meurs congelé.
J'ai tout perdu ce qu'on peut perdre en cette vie
Et j'attends sans hâte et sans joie
Le jour où je coulerai comme un clou
A pic, au fond des mers, un soir, sans aucun bruit.
Je ne sais même plus formuler ma formule
Spéciale de damnation terrestre.

J'ai perdu jusqu'au rythme
Qui me permit jadis de chasser mes épouvantes
En cadence.
Je chante sans chanter, je me livre au hasard.
J'ai fini d'être beau, j'ai fini de crâner.
Je fus presque un poète et presque un philosophe.
Je souffrais de trop de presque.
Je fus presque un homme.
Je suis presque un mort.

A moi les sursauts du cadavre
Et les affres de la pourriture apprise
Au contact des vers de la vie !
Que j'aime ceux des tombeaux,
Comme ils sont propres et nets et luisants,
Comme ils font bien ce qu'ils savent faire.
Tandis que les autres, ceux qu'on appelle hommes et femmes,
Comme ils vous mordent lâchement au talon
Quand d'être trop absent à cette vie précise
Ils vous soupçonnent,
Quand ils ont enfin compris que vous aviez un certain don
        pour l'inutile,
Un certain amour de l'absolu,
Une certaine soif de l'infini,
Ce qu'ils s'acharnent sur vous désemparé et petit
D'avoir tâché d'être grand.
On est frileux toute sa vie et malade,
On est un nourrisson sans mamelle accueillante,
On est un enfant douloureux, abandonné
Sur le Nil de la destinée,
Quand on a cru qu'il fallait jouer le jeu,
Se donner au monde, être bon, croire aux êtres,
Quand on n'a appris, pendant trente années,

Avec application, malgré ses poussées de haine et ses goûts de
    mépris,
Qu'on n'a appris qu'à aimer.
Alors on s'est mis à cette tâche d'aimer,
Un peu au hasard, sans discernement.
On a aimé tous ceux qui se sont trouvés sur la route.
On voyait là un devoir, une grande tâche.
Une grandeur.
Puis, on se sentait bon: ça faisait chaud au cœur.
On a aimé des enfants qui, devenus des hommes, vous ont
    renié.
On a aimé des hommes qui, devenus des vieillards, vous ont
    haï pour votre jeunesse miraculeusement sauvée.
On a aimé des femmes qui vous ont méprisé parce que vous
    les aviez traitées comme des reines.
On a aimé des vieillards, qui ont eu le temps encore de vous
    vomir dans les râles de leur agonie,
Parce que vous persistiez à demeurer jeune odieusement.
On a aimé Dieu avec désespoir, avec horreur, parce qu'aimer
    Dieu, c'est renoncer un peu à soi,
Et on a senti un jour Dieu se retirer pour ne jamais revenir
    peut-être.
On a été humble jusqu'à l'orgueil de s'anéantir,
On a été chaste jusqu'à cesser de se sentir un homme,
On a été pitoyable jusqu'à s'ôter le pain de la bouche pour le
    jeter aux pourceaux,
On a été juste jusqu'à être loyal avec ses ennemis.
On a été un idiot sublime.

Et voici qu'un bon matin on se réveille, porc parmi les porcs,
Avec tous ces instincts qu'on déplorait chez les autres
Et qu'on a cru refoulés en soi,
Avec tous ces instincts luisants comme des fauves léchés,

Déchaînés et dévorants.

On s'était cru béni, on n'était que plus sûrement maudit que
les autres.

Et ce qu'on a vu surtout, ce sont les regards de joie de tous,

Des enfants, des hommes, des femmes et des vieillards,

De tous ceux en somme qu'on avait aimés,

Pour lesquels on s'était débité

Comme une bûche à brûler dans l'âtre de toutes les bien-
faisances,

Et qui sont heureux de se rendre compte qu'un homme n'est
qu'un homme,

Et qu'ils n'ont pas à rougir plus souvent qu'à leur tour.

Croulons enfin, colonne,

Mur, écroulons-nous.

Cessons d'être l'opprobre de nos frères,

Et de leur faire honte d'avoir été bon.

Devenons ce tigre impardonné,

Soyons le fouet impitoyable emporté par une main sans but

Vers des itinéraires sans pardons.

Claquez donc, fouet de ma vengeance,

Et meurtrissez-moi, haire de ma haine !

Cette humanité tant de foi maudite,

Maudissons-la encore un peu pour la forme

Et pour que Dieu n'ait pas été le seul à se repentir de la
naissance de l'homme !

CHARLES BRUCE

b. 1906

183   *Words are Never Enough*

These are the fellows who smell of salt to the prairie,
Keep the back country informed of crumbling swell
That buckles the international course off Halifax
After a night of wind:

Angus Walters and Ben Pine, carrying on for Tommy
    Himmelman and Marty Welch,
Heading up the tough men who get into the news,
Heading up the hard men of Lunenburg and Gloucester,
Keeping the cities bordered with grass and grain
Forever mindful that something wet and salt
Creeps and loafs and marches round the continent,
Careless of time, careless of change, obeying the moon.

Listen to little Angus, squinting at the *Bluenose*:
'The timber that'll beat her still grows in the woods.'
Yes, these are the fellows who remind you again of the sea.

But one town, or two,
Are never enough to keep the salt in the blood.

I haven't seen Queensport Light over the loom of Ragged
    Head in years,
And never a smell of rollers coming up the bay from Canso.
No one ever heard of Queensport outside of a bait report;
No one ever saw the name of Ragged Head anywhere.

Off that obscure beach Will Bruce and George McMaster
Set their herring nets, and went farther out for mackerel.
The mackerel never ran, but in July

245

Fat herring tangled in wet twine were silver-thick,
And the flat low in the water as we hauled around
To head back for the huts;
In full daylight now,
After the grey dusk of a windless morning,
After the bay, gently stirring in half darkness,
Tipped down again to blush at the sun's rim.

Cleaning fish is a job you would baulk at;
But nothing is mean with gulls hovering down,
Sun brighter than life on glistening eelgrass,
The bay crawling again in a quickening southwest wind.

There was always time, after the wash-barrels were empty,
After hand-barrows were lugged up the beach to the hut,
And herring lay behind hand-wrought staves, clean with salt,

Time to lie on warm stone and listen,
While the sting went out of crooked fingers and thighs ceased
     to ache;
Time to hear men's voices, coming quietly through a coloured
     cloth of sound
Woven in the slap of water on fluent gravel.

Their talk was slow and quiet, of fish and men
And fields back on the hill with fences down,
Hay to be made through long hot days with never a splash on
     the oilskins,
Or the lift of water awake under half-inch pine.

The mackerel never ran; and if the herring
Had been only a story, a legend for midnight telling,
These would have launched their flats and tended the empty
     nets.

CHARLES BRUCE

I know it now, remembering now the calm;
Remembering now the lowering care that lifted
From a face turned to the wind off Ragged Head.

These are the fellows who keep the salt in the blood.
Knowing it fresh in themselves, needful as hope,
They give to the cities bordered with woods and grass
A few homesick men, walking an alien street;
A few women, remembering misty stars
And the long grumbling sigh of the bay at night.

Words are never enough; these are aware
Somewhere deep in the soundless well of knowing
That sea, in the flesh and nerves and the puzzling mind
Of children born to the long grip of its tide,
Must always wash the land's remotest heart.
These are the fellows who keep the salt in the blood.

LEO KENNEDY

b. 1907

184   *Epithalamium*

This body of my mother, pierced by me,
In grim fulfilment of our destiny,
Now dry and quiet as her fallow womb
Is laid beside the shell of that bridegroom
My father, who with eyes towards the wall
Sleeps evenly; his dust stirs not at all,
No syllable of greeting curls his lips,
As to that shrunken side his leman slips.

Lo! these are two of unabated worth
Who in the shallow bridal bed of earth
Find youth's fecundity, and of their swift
Comminglement of bone and sinew, lift
—A lover's seasonable gift to blood
Made bitter by a parchéd widowhood—
This bloom of tansy from the fertile ground:
My sister, heralded by no moan, no sound.

185   *Words for a Resurrection*

Each pale Christ stirring underground
Splits the brown casket of its root,
Wherefrom the rousing soil upthrusts
A narrow, pointed shoot,

And bones long quiet under frost
Rejoice as bells precipitate
The loud, ecstatic sundering,
The hour inviolate.

This Man of April walks again—
Such marvel does the time allow—
With laughter in His blesséd bones,
And lilies on His brow.

1909–1957

186   *Salmon Drowns Eagle*

The golden eagle swooped out of the sky
And flew back with a salmon in her claws,
Well-caught herself, till she could light near by
On her own rock. Meantime she heard loud caws.
So freighted, she could not fly fast nor far;
Nor, by God, could she let that salmon go.
Hoarse scavengers approached over the bar,
The one thing that fierce eagle hated: crow.
Now there was her rock, to stamp her prey loose,
And crows grabbing chunks of wild flesh away.
There is no argument with crows, nor truce,
The eagle said, heading across the bay!
The sea is wide, black and tempestuous,
But let me disintegrate to a hook
Before I share with the incestuous
Daughters of some ineligible rook!
Oh, she'd have made the land easy enough,
But the fish was heavy and pulled her down.
When she lit on the bay to rest, that tough
Salmon turned and threshed in a way not shown
In the books. Twisting over and over,
Pulling the eagle under the water,
Till she would fly off, angry; moreover,
She was tired out. The salmon fought her:
And next time she lit pulled her down under.
She never came up again. . . . It appears,
In the mundial popular thunder,
Any moral to this dins in drowned ears.

187 *In Memoriam*

INGVALD BJORNDAL AND HIS COMRADE

(Translation of a letter written somewhere in the North Atlantic and sent to the Government of Canada by Inspector Ovide Hubert of Cap-aux-Meules, Magdalen Islands. The letter was written in Norwegian and had been found in a bottle by the sea near l'Étang du Nord by Hubert Duclos, a fisherman, on 25 November 1940. The letter was addressed to Lovise Stigen, Kalandeendet [?] Fana.)

While we sail and laugh, joke and fight, comes death
And it is the end. A man toils on board;
His life drifts away like a puff of breath;
Who will know his dreams now when the sea roared?
I loved you, my dear, but now I am dead,
So take somebody else and forget me.
My brothers, I was foolish, as you said:
So are most who place their fate in the sea.
Many tears have you shed for me in vain.
Take my pay, Mother, Father, I have come
A long way to die in the blood and rain.
Buy me some earth in the graveyard at home.
Goodbye. Please remember me with these words
To the green meadows and the blue fjords.

188 *Lupus in Fabula*

Those animals that follow us in dream,
And mean I know not what! But what of those
That hunt us, snuff, stalk us out in life, close
In upon it, belly-down, haunt our scheme

Of building, with shapes of delirium,
Symbols of death, heraldic, and shadows
Glowering?—Just before we left Tlampam
Our cats lay quivering under the maguey;
A meaning had slunk, and now died, with them.
The boy slung them half stiff down the ravine,
Which now we entered, and whose name is hell.
But still our last night had its animal:
The puppy, in the cabaret, obscene,
Looping-the-loop, and dirtying the floor,
And fastening itself to that horror
Of our last night: and the very last day
While I sat bowed, frozen over mescal,
They dragged two shrieking fawns through the hotel
And slit their throats, behind the barroom door. . . .

189   *'Cain shall not slay Abel today on*
our good ground'

Cain shall not slay Abel today on our good ground,
Nor Adam stagger on our shrouded moon,
Nor Ishmael lie stiff in 28th Street,
With a New Bedford harpoon in his brain,
His right lung in a Hoboken garboon.
For this is the long day when the lost are found,
And those, parted by tragedy, meet
With spring-sweet joy. And those who longest should have
    met
Are safe in each other's arms not too late.
Today the forsaken one of the fold is brought home,
And the great cold, in the street of the vulture, are warm,
The numbed albatross is sheltered from the storm,

The tortured shall no longer know alarm
For all in wilderness are free from harm:
Age dreaming on youth, youth dreaming on age, shall not be
    found,
While good Loki chases dragons underground.
Life hears our prayer for the lonely trimmer on watch,
Or shuddering, at one bell, on the wet hatch,
At evening, for the floating sailor by the far coast,
The impaled soldier in the shell-hole or the hail,
The crew of the doomed barque sweeping into the sunset
With black sails; for mothers in anguish and unrest
And each of all the oppressed, a compassionate ghost
Will recommend the Pentecost.
Ah, poets of God's mercy, harbingers of the gale,
Now I say the lamb is brought home, and Gogol
Wraps a warm overcoat about him. . . .
Our city of dreadful night will blossom into a sea-morning!
Only bear with us, bear with my song,
For at dawn is the reckoning and the last night is long.

A. M. KLEIN

b. 1909

190   *Bestiary*

> God breathe a blessing on
> His small bones, every one!
> The little lad, who stalks
> The bible's plains and rocks
> To hunt in grammar'd woods
> Strange litters and wild broods;

A. M. KLEIN

The little lad who seeks
Beast-muzzles and bird-beaks
In cave and den and crypt,
In copse of holy script;
The little lad who looks
For quarry in holy books.

Before his eyes is born
The elusive unicorn;
There, scampering, arrive
The golden mice, the five;
Also, in antic shape,
Gay peacock and glum ape.
He hears a snort of wrath:
The fiery behemoth;
And then on biblic breeze
The crocodile's sneeze.
He sees the lion eat
Straw, and from the teat
Of tigress a young lamb
Suckling, like whelp nigh dam.

Hard by, as fleet as wind
They pass, the roe and hind,
Bravely, and with no risk,
He holds the basilisk,
Pygarg and cockatrice.
And there, most forest-wise
Among the bestiaries,
The little hunter eyes
Him crawling at his leisure:
The beast Nebuchadnezzar.

191   *Heirloom*

My father bequeathed me no wide estates;
No keys and ledgers were my heritage;
Only some holy books with *yahrzeit* dates
Writ mournfully upon a blank front page—

Books of the Baal Shem Tov, and of his wonders;
Pamphlets anent the devil and his crew;
Prayers against road demons, witches, thunders;
And sundry other tomes for a good Jew.

Beautiful: though no pictures on them, save
The Scorpion crawling on a printed track;
The Virgin floating on a scriptural wave,
Square letters twinkling in the Zodiac.

The snuff left on this page, now brown and old,
The tallow stains of midnight liturgy—
These are my coat of arms, and these unfold
My noble lineage, my proud ancestry!

And my tears, too, have stained this heirloomed ground,
When reading in these treatises some weird
Miracle, I turned a leaf and found
A white hair fallen from my father's beard.

192   *The Still Small Voice*

The candles splutter; and the kettle hums;
The heirloomed clock enumerates the tribes,
Upon the wine-stained table-cloth lie crumbs
Of matzoh whose wide scattering describes

Jews driven in far lands upon this earth.
The kettle hums; the candles splutter; and
Winds whispering from shutters tell re-birth
Of beauty rising in an eastern land,
Of paschal sheep driven in cloudy droves;
Of almond-blossoms colouring the breeze;
Of vineyards upon verdant terraces;
Of golden globes in orient orange-groves.
And those assembled at the table dream
Of small schemes that an April wind doth scheme,
And cry from out the sleep assailing them:
Jerusalem, next year! Next year, Jerusalem!

193   *Indian Reservation: Caughnawaga*

Where are the braves, the faces like autumn fruit,
who stared at the child from the coloured frontispiece?
And the monosyllabic chief who spoke with his throat?
Where are the tribes, the feathered bestiaries?—
Rank Aesop's animals erect and red,
with fur on their names to make all live things kin—
Chief Running Deer, Black Bear, Old Buffalo Head?

Childhood, that wished me Indian, hoped that
one afterschool I'd leave the classroom chalk,
the varnish smell, the watered dust of the street,
to join the clean outdoors and the Iroquois track.
Childhood; but always,—as on a calendar,—
there stood that chief, with arms akimbo, waiting
the runaway mascot paddling to his shore.

With what strange moccasin stealth that scene is changed !
With French names, without paint, in overalls,
their bronze, like their nobility expunged,—
the men. Beneath their alimentary shawls
sit like black tents their squaws; while for the tourist's
brown pennies scattered at the old church door,
the ragged papooses jump, and bite the dust.

Their past is sold in a shop: the beaded shoes,
the sweetgrass basket, the curio Indian,
burnt wood and gaudy cloth and inch-canoes—
trophies and scalpings for a traveller's den.
Sometimes, it's true, they dance, but for a bribe;
after a deal don the bedraggled feather
and welcome a white mayor to the tribe.

This is a grassy ghetto, and no home.
And these are fauna in a museum kept.
The better hunters have prevailed. The game,
losing its blood, now makes these grounds its crypt.
The animals pale, the shine of the fur is lost,
bleached are their living bones. About them watch
as through a mist, the pious prosperous ghosts.

194   *The Sugaring*

FOR GUY SYLVESTRE

Starved, scarred, lenten, amidst ash of air,
roped and rough-shirted, the maples in the unsheltered grove
after their fasts and freezings stir.
Ah, winter for each one,
each gospel tree, each saint of the calendar,

256

has been a penance, a purchase: the nails of ice!
wind's scourge! the rooted cross!
Nor are they done with the still stances of love,
the fiery subzeros of sacrifice.

For standing amidst the thorns of their own bones,
eased by the tombs' coolth of resurrection time,—
the pardon, the purgatorial groans
almost at bitter end,
but not at end—the carving auger runs
spiral the round stigmata through each limb!
The saints bleed down their sides!
And look! men catch this juice of their agonized prime
to boil in kettles the sap of seraphim!

O, out of this calvary Canadian comes bliss,
savour and saving images of holy things,
a sugared metamorphosis!
Ichor of dulcitude
shaping sweet relics, crystalled spotlessness!
And the pious pour into the honeyed dies
the sacred hearts, the crowns,
thanking those saints for syrops of their dying
and blessing the sweetness of their sacrifice.

195   *Quebec Liquor Commission Store*

Nonetheless Ali Baba had no richer cave,
nor lamps more sensitive Aladdin's thumb
than this cave, and these lamps which, at the touch,
evoke the growing slave,
and change the rag-poor world to purple-rich.

'O Vizier, wrapped in all knowledge and experience,
bring me, bring me in a flower of air,
the scent of the world's motion, the pollen, the fire,
the fumes, of magnificence!'
'Your servant, my Lord, has done according to your desire!

'And brought you also the pleasures of the skin about the
    round,
the sycophancy of glass, the palm's cool courtier,
and the feel of straw, all rough and rustical,
by some king's daughter donned;
and for your royal eyes, your Ishmael
with rub and abracadabra and obeisance brings
these forms and shapes, that harem opulence
that my Lord dotes on; and, of the same scope
their voices, like happenings
on cushions behind curtains, like whispers at the thrilled ear's
    lobe.'

'Well done! thou gurgling knave, and above all, well done,
in the conjuring of those mischievous genii
who nip at the paps of palate, hop on the tongue,
in the throat make merry and fun!
Lithe, they go tumbling in the paunch's nets! And rung
by rung, disporting, they climb into the brain's bazaar!
Wonderful are their tricks and somersaults,
such ingenuities as do make a king forget
the troubles that there are
even for kings, the rag-poor past, the purple that may set.'

A. M. KLEIN

Political Meeting

FOR CAMILLIEN HOUDE

On the school platform, draping the folding seats,
they wait the chairman's praise and glass of water.
Upon the wall the agonized **Y** initials their faith.

Here all are laic; the skirted brothers have gone.
Still, their equivocal absence is felt, like a breeze
that gives curtains the sounds of surplices.

The hall is yellow with light, and jocular;
suddenly some one lets loose upon the air
the ritual bird which the crowd in snares of singing

catches and plucks, throat, wings, and little limbs.
Fall the feathers of sound, like *alouette's*.
The chairman, now, is charming, full of asides and wit,

building his orators, and chipping off
the heckling gargoyles popping in the hall.
(Outside, in the dark, the street is body-tall,

flowered with faces intent on the scarecrow thing
that shouts to thousands the echoing
of their own wishes.) The Orator has risen!

Worshipped and loved, their favourite visitor,
a country uncle with sunflower seeds in his pockets,
full of wonderful moods, tricks, imitative talk,

he is their idol: like themselves, not handsome,
not snobbish, not of the *Grande Allée! Un homme!*
Intimate, informal, he makes bear's compliments

to the ladies; is gallant; and grins;
goes for the balloon, his opposition, with pins;
jokes also on himself, speaks of himself

in the third person, slings slang, and winks with folklore;
and knows now that he has them, kith and kin.
Calmly, therefore, he begins to speak of war,

praises the virtue of being *Canadien*,
of being at peace, of faith, of family,
and suddenly his other voice: *Where are your sons?*

He is tearful, choking tears; but not he
would blame the clever English; in their place
he'd do the same; maybe.

Where *are* your sons?
                              The whole street wears one face,
shadowed and grim; and in the darkness rises
the body-odour of race.

197   *Montreal*

                              I

        O city metropole, isle riverain!
        Your ancient pavages and sainted routes
        Traverse my spirit's conjured avenues!
        Splendor erablic of your promenades
        Foliates there, and there your maisonry
        Of pendent balcon and escalier'd march,
        Unique midst English habitat,
        Is vivid Normandy!

    260

II

You populate the pupils of my eyes:
Thus, does the Indian, plumèd, furtivate
Still through your painted autumns, Ville-Marie!
Though palisades have passed, though calumet
With tabac of your peace enfumes the air,
Still do I spy the phantom, aquiline,
Genuflect, moccasin'd, behind
His statue in the square!

III

Thus, costumed images before me pass,
Haunting your archives architectural:
Coureur de bois, in posts where pelts were portaged;
Seigneur within his candled manoir; Scot
Ambulant through his bank, pillar'd and vast.
Within your chapels, voyaged mariners
Still pray, and personage departed,
All present from your past!

IV

Grand port of navigations, multiple
The lexicons uncargo'd at your quays,
Sonnant though strange to me; but chiefest, I,
Auditor of your music, cherish the
Joined double-melodied vocabulaire
Where English vocable and roll Ecossic,
Mollified by the parle of French
Bilinguefact your air!

v

Such your suaver voice, hushed Hochelaga!
But for me also sound your potencies,
Fortissimos of sirens fluvial,
Bruit of manufactory, and thunder
From foundry issuant, all puissant tone
Implenishing your hebdomad; and then
Sanct silence, and your argent belfries
Clamant in orison!

vi

You are a part of me, O all your quartiers—
And of dire pauvrete and of richesse—
To finished time my homage loyal claim;
You are locale of infancy, milieu
Vital of institutes that formed my fate;
And you above the city, scintillant,
Mount Royal, are my spirit's mother,
Almative, poitrinate!

vii

Never do I sojourn in alien place
But I do languish for your scenes and sounds,
City of reverie, nostalgic isle,
Pendant most brilliant on Laurentian cord!
The coigns of your boulevards—my signiory—
Your suburbs are my exile's verdure fresh,
Your parks, your fountain'd parks—
Pasture of memory!

A. M. KLEIN

City, O city, you are vision'd as
A parchemin roll of saecular exploit
Inked with the script of eterne souvenir!
You are in sound, chanson and instrument!
Mental, you rest forever edified
With tower and dome; and in these beating valves,
Here in these beating valves, you will
For all my mortal time reside!

JOHN GLASSCO

b. 1909

198   *Deserted Buildings Under Shefford*
            Mountain

These native angles of decay
   In sheds and barns whose broken wings
Lie here half fallen in the way
Of headstones amid uncut hay—
   Why do I love you, ragged things?

What grace, unknown to any art,
   What beauty frailer than a mood
Awake in me their counterpart?
What correspondence of a heart
   That loves the failing attitude?

Here where I grasp the certain fate
   Of all man's work in wood and stone,
And con the lesson of the straight
That shall be crooked soon or late
   And crumble into forms alone,

JOHN GLASSCO

Some troubled joy that's half despair
   Ascends within me like a breath:
I see these silent ruins wear
The speaking look, the sleeping air,
   Of features newly cast in death,

Dead faces where we strive to see
   The signature of something tossed
Between design and destiny,
Between God and absurdity,
   Till, harrowing up a new-made ghost,

We half embrace the wavering form,
   And half conceive the wandering sense
Of some imagined part kept warm
And salvaged from the passing storm
   Of time's insulting accidents.

So I, assailed by the blind love
   That meets me in this silent place,
Lift open arms: Is it enough
That restless things can cease to move
   And leave a ruin wreathed in grace,

Or is this wreck of strut and span
   No more than solace for the creed
Of progress and its emmet plan,
Dark houses that are void of man,
   Dull meadows that have gone to seed?

JOHN GLASSCO

Stud Groom

Your boy's-ambition was to be a Horseman,
Some day to hear tell or overhear your name
Linked with that word. This was the foreseen
Reward for the five years in the dealer's stable,
For strewing your childhood nightly under his horses' feet
And bearing it out at sun-up on a shovel,

When you met all claims with waiver and deferment,
And learned the habit of not coming to grips
With any unhaltered thing that's not dependent
On a boy's will like a pious man on God's,
Till language lapsed back into clucks and chirps,
Hisses and heeyahs, steady-babes, be-goods.

And now it has all come true! and the mountains spill
Your world of cousins, a chorus of witnesses:
Lost Nation, Bolton Centre and Pigeon Hill
Acclaim you who combine, deny and defer
With straps and stalls the heats and the rampancies,
And the act that's blessed with a bucket of cold water.

There stands the World, in the attitude of approval,
Hands in its pockets, hat over its eyes,
Ignorant, cunning, suave and noncommittal,
The ape of knowledge. . . . Say, through what injustice
Has it gained the bounty, by what crazy process
Those eyes fell heir to your vision of success?

For the goal has changed.—It's rather to have made
Of the welcoming music of nickers and whinnies
At feeding time, the brightness of an eye

Fixed on a bucket, the fine restraint of a hoof
Raised and held in a poised meaningless menace,
To have made, of these, assurances of love,

And of the denial of all loving contact
When the ears flatten, the eye rolls white,
The whirring alarm that keeps the dream intact
For poet and pervert too, whose spasm or nightmare
Makes, with the same clean decision of a bite,
Divorce between possession and desire.

For 'one woman leads to another, like one war
Leads to another', and the fever has no end
Till passion turns—from the bright or bloody star,
From the bitter triumph over a stranger's body,
To something between a deity and a friend,
To a service halting between cult and hobby,

And nothing is left for the family or the nation
But a genial curse, and silence. It may be
You are the type of figures long out of fashion,
The Unknown Soldier and the Forgotten Man,
Whom the rest might envy, now, their anonymity
And the fact they were at least left alone;

And who might have said, like you, to a pair
Of nags looking over a sagging roadside fence,
Good morning, girls! O greeting washed in air,
O simple insistence to affirm the Horse,
While the Loans and bomb-loads are hitting new highs
And youth is deducted at the source.

For 'Horseman, what of the future?' is a question
Without a meaning: there is always another race,

Another show, the unquenchable expectation
Of ribbons, the easy applause like a summer storm
And the thrill, like love, of being in first place
For an instant that lasts forever, and does no harm

Except to the altar-fated passion it robs,
The children it cheats of their uniforms and wars,
And the fathomless future of the underdog
It negates—shrugs off like the fate of a foundered mare—
As it sparks the impenetrable lives, like yours
Whose year revolves around the county fair.

200   *The Burden of Junk*

April again, and its message unvaried, the same old impromptu
Dinned in our ears by the tireless dispassionate chortling of
        Nature,
Sunlight on grey land, the grey of the past like a landscape
        around us
Caught in its moment of nakedness also, a pitiful prospect
Bared to the cognitive cruelty shining upon it: O season,
Season that leads me again, like this road going over the moun-
        tain,
Past the old landmarks and ruins, the holdfasts of hope and
        ambition,—

Why is the light doubly hard on the desolate places? why even
Hardest of all on the tumbledown cabin of Corby the Trader?
See, with its tarpaper hanging in tatters, the doorstep awash
        in a
Puddle of cow-piss and kindling-chips, ringed with the mud
        of a fenceless

Yardful of rusty and broken machinery, washstands and
 bedsteads,
Bodies of buggies and berlots, the back seats of autos, bundles
 of
Chicken-wire, leaves of old wagon-springs and miscellaneous
 wheels. . . . But

There is Corby himself in the mud and the sunshine, in front
 of the
Lean-to cowshed, examining something that looks like a side-
 board,
Bidding me stop and admire, and possibly make him an offer:
'Swapped the old three-teated cow for a genuine walnut
 harmonium!
Look, ain't a scratch or a brack in it anywhere—pedals and
 stopples
Work just as good as a fellow could ask for! Over to Broome
 they
Say they used to cost four hundred dollars apiece from the
 factory. . . .'

Here is the happy engrosser of objects, the absolute type of
All who engage in the business of buying and shifting, the man
 who
Turns a putative profit into an immediate pleasure,
Simply by adding a zero to his account with a self-owned
Bank of Junk, and creates a beautiful mood of achievement
Out of nothing at all! Ah, here is the lord of the cipher,
This is the Man of the Springtime, the avatar of Lyaeus!

We should be trading indeed, if we could, I think as I leave
 him.
Mine is a burden of lumber that ought to be left with him
 also:

JOHN GLASSCO

This is where it belongs, with the wheels and the beds and
the organ,
With all the personal trash that the spirit acquires and aban-
dons,
Things that have made the heart warm and bewildered the
senses with beauty
Long ago,—but that weakened and crumbled away with
the passion
Born of their brightness, the loves that a dreary process of
dumping
Leaves at last on a hillside to rot away with the seasons.

RALPH GUSTAFSON

b. 1909

201   *On the* Struma *Massacre*[1]

Now as these slaughtered seven hundreds hear
The vulgar sennet of thine angel sound,
Grant, in thy love, that they may see that ground
Whose promised acres holy footsteps bear.
For they of only this made credulous prayer—
Even for whom thy Son the tempest bound
And waters walked O not those same where, drowned,
Driven by plausible tongues and mute despair,
These faithful roll! No not as they, with board
And spike, who took Thy sweetness then, do we—

[1] The S.S. *Struma*, with 769 Jewish refugees from fascist Rumania,
was denied passage through the Bosphorus because the British govern-
ment had not issued passports for Palestine. Sent out to sea with no
pilot and no destination, she ran into a mine and sank 25 February
1942. There was one survivor.

Studied in ignorance, and knowing Thee.
For Thine archaic crown of thorns and cord,
Statistics are become Thine agony,
The ocean designate, Gabbatha, Lord.

202   *S.S.R.*, *Lost at Sea*—The Times

What heave of grapnels will resurrect the fabric
Of him, oceans drag, whereof he died,
Drowning sheer fathoms down, liquid to grab on—
Sucked by the liner, violence in her side?
Of no more sorrow than a mottled Grief
In marble. There fantastic in the murk,
Where saltwhite solitary forests leaf,
He swings: the dark anonymously works.
For who shall count the countless hands and limbs
In ditch and wall and wave, dead, dead
In Europe: touch with anguished name and claim
And actual tear, what must be generally said?
O let the heart's tough riggings salvage him,
Only whose lengths can grapple with these dead.

203   *The Fish*

It was cause for laughter of a special brand.
The thumb thus, in the O of the gaping perch,
His silver well within the other hand
Tensioned aptly to absorb the lurch,
The while the pink gills shutter on the air,
Index-finger fulcrum, pressure of
The thumb so snaps the narrow gristle there,

The cord at the throat—frenulum of love
If sense allow egregious simile
That likens killing perch to violent sex.
Admitted, a better method than to see
A dry *percida* for an hour flex.
Reluctance was cause for laughter as I say,
That doing it, the boy should look away.

204   *The Meaning*

So I, who love, with all this outward
Now have done, upon each sense
Has purpose inned, the five are sermoned,
Meaning is a prevalence

Not in churches only. There was
A time the world was otherwise,
Sensation had and finished with
And got again nor flesh a guise

That Plato wore. Against the tongue
The tastes of wheat and words were never
Then a scripture; ice was zero;
I did not tremble loving her

Who now, the fool of intellect,
Am hoist with wisdom. Tutelar,
I contemplate a doorknob, prove,
Proclaim like any thunderer.

No sooner love than hell and heaven
Batter at the pagan sense:

My coatsleeve grazes fire; snow,
My elbow jostles permanence;

Within my waiting skull terror
Hunches in a wainscot's mouse;
Where the oak is, the woodbird heedless
Hammers at my final house.

205   *At the Ocean's Verge*

I should pray but my soul is stopt.
This is a bombast world: fig-trees,
Snow, macacos, ocean's hurl
And surf and surge, on applebough
As crag whose cave holds kraken or
With comb of coral mermaid cuddles.
All's mad majesty and squander,
And x and y or zodiac
Excreting wizard mathematics
Like a slew of ebbtide worms
Won't solve it. The sand is miles and packt
And moonlights wash the gnawings of
A million years. The globe cants so,
It's miracle a man can walk it.
Listen to him: *I'll say my prayers*
And set mine eyes on kingdom come.
I'll jump the prickly hedge and scratch
Them in again. I'll. I'll.
Not Hesperides. I warrant,
No matter what you will. Try,
Scour this heaven-hung kettle of fish—
The sweep has greater satisfaction

Up a chimney cleaning soot
With good soap after. Oh, you'll hoist
And heft your stature by a hair,
No one but the Barber wiser.
   Hear how this ocean thurls and thunders!
   Crashing foams and ravels once
   Was muted marble Athens owned.

DOROTHY LIVESAY

b. 1909

206   *Fantasia*

FOR HELENA COLEMAN

And I have learned how diving's done
How breathing air, cool wafted trees
Clouds massed above the man-made tower
How these
Can live no more in eye and ear:
And mind be dumb
To all save Undine and her comb.

Imagination's underworld! where child goes down
Light as a feather. Water pressure
Hardly holds him, diving's easy
As the flight of bird in air
Or bomber drumming to his lair.

Child goes down, and laughingly
(He's not wanted yet, you see)
Catches fishes in his hand

Burrows toe in sifting sand
Seizes all the weeds about
To make a small sub-rosa boat

Then up he bobs, as easily
As any blown balloon
To greet the bosky, brooding sky
And hunger for the sun.

.   .   .

And child grown taller, clothed in man's
Long limbs, and shaggy hair, his chin outthrust
Searches for years the rounded world
Climbs to its peaks, falls to its valleys green
Striding the trim and trailing towns
Fingering the fond arteries
Possessing things, and casting them
Cloakwise to earth for sleeping time. . . .

Sometime the lust wanderer
Will sleep, will pause; will dream of plunging deep
Below it all, where he will need
No clock companion, thorn in flesh, no contact man
To urge him from the ground.
For flying's easy, if you do it diving
And diving is the self unmoored
Ranging and roving—man alone.

.   .   .

And I have learned how diving's done
Wherefore the many, many
Chose the watery stair
Down, down Virginia
With your fêted hair
Following after Shelley

Or wordcarvers I knew
(Bouchette; and Raymond, you)—
Here is the fascination
Of the salty stare:
And death is here.
Death courteous and calm, glass-smooth
His argument so suave, so water-worn
A weighted stone.
And death's deliberation, his
Most certain waiting-room
His patience with the patient, who will be
His for infinity. . . .

So no astounded peerers
On the surface craft
No dragging nets, no cranes
No gnarled and toughened rope
Not any prayer nor pulley man-devised
Will shake the undersea
Or be
More than a brief torpedo, children's arrow
More than a gaudy top outspun
Its schedule done. . . .

.   .   .

Wise to have learned: how diving's done
How breathing air, cool wafted trees
Clouds massed above the man-made tower
How these
Can live no more in eye and ear:
And mind be dumb
To all save Undine and her comb. . . .

DOROTHY LIVESAY

Signature

LIVESAY THE NAME GOD THEM GAVE
AND NOW LIVES AYE INDEED THEY HAVE.
> —*Lines on an English tombstone*

Born by a whim
This time
On a blowing plain
I am as wind
Playing high sky
With a name—
Winnipeg!

So prairie gave breath:
Child head, anemone
Raised from the winter grass
Pushing the mauve-veined cup
Upward to world all sky
Peopled with cloud.

Ages before
These violet veins
Fingered their mauve
Through England's green;
These crocus eyes
Glowed in stone
Or a poplar row
Sturdy with Normandy;
Or a sea-wall—
War's peep-hole.

DOROTHY LIVESAY

And longer than summers
Of conquering blood
Were my feet running
In a Roman wood
And my hair bound
In a vestal hood.

Stretched on the solitary sand
Of Egypt, I lay asunder:
Till the lover came,
The flowering night
Shaped me a name
And the earth shook under.

Now when I waken here,
Earthbound
Strapped to the sound
Of a Winnipeg wind;
I dream of the next step
On into time—
Casting off skin,
Bones, veins and eyes,
Flower without root,
Dancer without feet—
Gone in a cone of spiralled air,
And I only wind
Sucked to the sun's fire!

THE PRAIRIE GAVE BREATH; I GREW AND DIED:
ALIVE ON THIS AIR THESE LIVES ABIDE.

On Looking into Henry Moore

I

Sun, stun me, sustain me
Turn me to stone:
Stone, goad me and gall me
Urge me to run.

When I have found
Passivity in fire
And fire in stone
Female and male
I'll rise alone
Self-extending and self-known.

II

The message of the tree is this:
Aloneness is the only bliss

Self-adoration is not in it
(Narcissus tried, but could not win it)

Rather, to extend the root
Tombwards, be at home with death

But in the upper branches know
A green eternity of fire and snow.

III

The fire in the farthest hills
Is where I'd burn myself to bone:
Clad in the armour of the sun
I'd stand anew, alone.

DOROTHY LIVESAY

Take off this flesh, this hasty dress
Prepare my half-self for myself:
One unit, as a tree or stone
Woman in man, and man in womb.

ANNE WILKINSON

1910-1961

209   *Carol*

I was a lover of turkey and holly
But my true love was the Christmas tree
We hung our hearts from a green green bough
And merry swung the mistletoe

He decked the tree with a silver apple
And a golden pear,
A partridge and a cockle shell
And a fair maiden

No rose can tell the fumes of myrrh
That filled the forest of our day
Till fruit and shell and maid fell down
And the partridge flew away

Now I swing from a brittle twig
For the green bough of my true love hid
A laily worm. Around my neck
The hangman ties the holly.

Lens

I

The poet's daily chore
Is my long duty;
To keep and cherish my good lens
For love and war
And wasps about the lilies
And mutiny within.

My woman's eye is weak
And veiled with milk;
My working eye is muscled
With a curious tension,
Stretched and open
As the eyes of children;
Trusting in its vision
Even should it see
The holy holy spirit gambol
Counterheadwise,
Lithe and warm as any animal.

My woman's iris circles
A blind pupil;
The poet's eye is crystal,
Polished to accept the negative,
The contradictions in a proof
And the accidental
Candour of the shadows;
The shutter, oiled and smooth
Clicks on the grace of heroes
Or on some bestial act

When lit with radiance
The afterwords the actors speak
Give depths to violence,

Or if the bull is great
And the matador
And the sword
Itself the metaphor.

II

In my dark room the years
Lie in solution,
Develop film by film.
Slow at first and dim
Their shadows bite
On the fine white pulp of paper.

An early snap of fire
Licking the arms of air
I hold against the light, compare
The details with a prehistoric view
Of land and sea
And cradles of mud that rocked
The wet and sloth of infancy.

A stripe of tiger, curled
And sleeping on the ribs of reason
Prints as clear
As Eve and Adam, pearled
With sweat, staring at an apple core;
And death, in black and white
Or politic in green and Easter film,

Lands on steely points, a dancer
Disciplined to the foolscap stage,
The property of poets
Who command his robes, expose
His moving likeness on the page.

211   *A Cautionary Tale*

. . . we had sold our death . . . for the sum of £70 : 18 : 6d and lent our fear . . . on interest of £3 : 10 : 0d per month, so we did not care about death and we did not fear again.—FROM *The Palm Wine Drinkard* BY AMOS TUTUOLA

She met a lion face to face
As she went walking
Up to her hips in grass
On the wild savannah.
So close they stood they touched
If she put out her thumb
Or he his soft ferocious paw.
She bore no weight of fear,
For only yesterday
She'd leased it to a rich man, poor
In that commodity.
Without her terror she was free
From the alarming smell
That irritates a lion
And makes him lash his tail.
And so he yawned, and stretched
On the long stemmed grasses,
And in the pouring sun
She sat beside his royalty
And sang to him a tale of moon.

ANNE WILKINSON

Before he rose to go
He opened wide his jaw
And took between his teeth
Her wishing bone, as if to say,
I could, you know.
A rich man had her caution
So she laughed; cool,
In the lion's ear, her pretty breath.
What happened next happens
To every maiden fair
Who lends her fear
But forgets to sell her death:
The lion ate her up, and down
To the smallest crumb.
Lord have mercy upon
Her sweet white bones. Amen.

Nature Be Damned

I

Pray where would lamb and lion be
If they lay down in amity?
Could lamb then nibble living grass?
Lamb and lion both must starve;
For none may live if all do love.

II

I go a new dry way, permit no weather
Here, on undertaker's false green sod
Where I sit down beneath my false tin tree.
There's too much danger in a cloud,

In wood or field, or close to moving water.
With my black blood—who can tell?
The dart of one mosquito might be fatal;

Or in the flitting dusk a bat
Might carry away my destiny,
Hang it upside down from a rafter
In a barn unknown to me.

I hide my skin within the barren city
Where artificial moons pull no man's tide,
And so escape my green love till the day
Vine breaks through brick and strangles me.

III

I was witch and I could be
Bird or leaf
Or branch and bark of tree.

In rain and two by two my powers left me;
Instead of curling down as root and worm
My feet walked on the surface of the earth,
And I remember a day of evil sun
When forty green leaves withered on my arm.

And so I damn the font where I was blessed,
Am unbeliever; was deluded lover; never
Bird or leaf or branch and bark of tree.
Each, separate as curds from whey,
Has signature to prove identity.

And yet we're kin in appetite;
Tree, bird in the tree and I.

We feed on dung, a fly, a lamb
And burst with seed
Of tree, of bird, of man,
Till tree is bare
And bird and I are bone
And feaster is reborn
The feast, and feasted on.

IV

I took my watch beside the rose;
I saw the worm move in;
And by the tail I yanked him out
And stamped him dead, for who would choose
To leave alive a sin?

The pale rose died of grief. My heel
Had killed its darling foe,
Worm that cuddles in the heart
To ravish it. If worm not tell
How should rose its fairness know?

V

Once a year in the smoking bush
A little west of where I sit
I burn my winter caul to a green ash.
This is an annual festival,
Nothing to stun or startle;
A coming together—water and sun
In summer's first communion.

Today again I burned my winter caul
Though senses nodded, dulled by ritual.

One hundred singing orioles
And five old angels wakened me;
Morning sky rained butterflies
And simple fish, bass and perch,
Leapt from the lake in salutation.
St Francis, drunk among the daisies,
Opened his ecstatic eye.

Then roused from this reality I saw
Nothing, anywhere, but snow.

213   *Falconry*

'*The* Boke of St. Albans *had laid down precisely the classes of people
to whom any proper-minded member of the Falconidae might belong
. . . The list had defined itself meticulously downward to the kestrel,
and he, as a crowning insult, was allowed to belong to a mere knave—
because he was useless to be trained.*'—FROM T. H. WHITE's *The Goshawk.*

I

Eagle for an Emperor
Peregrine is due an earl
Goshawk is the right of yeoman
Kestrel for a knave or no-man.

God's left hand must bear them all:
Eagle of the emperor,
Peregrine that's due an earl,
Yeoman's goshawk, and the knave's
Bating kestrel, no-man's slave.

Rather bating kestrel, I,
Than mind the fist beneath the glove.
I, a kestrel, God, the Knave—

ANNE WILKINSON

And I will bate[1] until I die,
And bite the leather of my jesses,
And starve before I eat His messes.
Can I do more? Sweet Knave, I'll try.

Yet that fist and glove are home,
For, banished, what could I bate from?

II

As falcon on a falconer's wrist,
So should I, on God's big fist;
Yet will I not or preen or sit
Or take His lure, the rabbit skull,
And dip my hawking beak in hell.
Rather would I bate:
Head-down hang and scream and squawk
And churn the air and rough my feathers,
For though the leash that holds my jesses
Ties me to the precincts of His glove,
I will not love.

If tidbits do not tame His falcon
God remembers Babylon
And proper ways to tease and starve
The lust upon His leather glove.
Regard me now; I quiet sit,
Brooding on the skulls I'll split.
Or watch my flight; its easy pause,
Angle of incidence inclined
Against the bitter wind
Before I dive, God's mercy in my claws.

[1] To beat the wings impatiently and flutter away from the fist or perch.

b. 1911

214 *The Eye of Humility*

In the dream, in the charmed dream we are flying
not as a kite held at the other end by hand of flesh,
rich in the smell of grass and colts munching
in the sunned field and air smooth as milk,
but with the limbs and torso webbed with a metal boldness,
scorning the matters of earth, the mole, the blind mole's wis-
    dom,
bodies under the tree and a sweetness clouding the tongue.
In the dream, in the charmed dream, we alone have motion,
the world below a still life bathed in a green pre-thunder light,
hand on the wheel stuck like a fly in syrup,
the shovel raised never to fall, eyelid staid as a stone.

In the awakening, in the crash of awakening,
the heart is jolted into its eye,
the ancient oak in the dream an acorn
crowds into the eye,
the seed of Adam enters, Man of Sorrows,
with the eternal stars of wounds in His thigh;
in the dream, in the charmed dream we were flying
out of mind, who now are grounded with the slow root
in the invaded womb of time.

215 *When a Girl Looks Down*

When a girl looks down out of her cloud of hair
And gives her breast to the child she has borne,
All the suns and the stars that the heavens have worn
Since the first magical morning
Rain through her milk in each fibre and cell of her darling.

KAY SMITH

Hand baring the gift touches the hidden spring,
Source of all gifts, the womb of creation;
From the wide-open door streams the elation
Shaping all things, itself shapeless as air,

That models the nipple of girl, of bud, the angel
Forms unscrolling their voices over fields of winter,
That whittles the ray of a star to a heart's splinter
For one lost in his palace of breath on the frozen hill,
Flying the big-bellied moon for a sail,

And releases the flood of girl, of bud, of the horn
Whose music starts on a morning journey.
In mother, child and all, the One-in-the-many
Gathers me nearer to be born.

WILFRED WATSON

b. 1911

216   *The Windy Bishop*

There are seven hills
Stood like hunched
Cattle with their tails
Curled in, enduring
The pasture of days,
Stood in the morning
Light of my town
When the windy bishop preached me my dust

A sermon of snow
On a text of cold.

WILFRED WATSON

The sun was his
Wandering candle
Flame and the sky
His draughty cathedral
And even the busy worm
Was glum at my feet
When the windy bishop preached me my dust—

Me?—Me, I hurried my
Deaf heart home
And sure—I could
Have reached it safe
But stumbled, came
To my harm and there
Was no mercy in what
He was saying—none,
When the windy bishop preached me my dust

A sermon of snow.
His slippery phrase
Chattered in my teeth
Sank into my gums
Drew tears from my eyes
Sucked dry my marrow
Drilled my breastbone—
And the windy bishop preached at my heart

Through the hole
In my life. Flakes of cold
Curdled my blood
Into sleet, my limb
Stiffened, and I stood dumb
In the sick of fear.

Even the fox shuddered
In his pelt and the hills
Huddled like cattle
When the windy bishop lashed me with his word,
When the windy bishop preached my heart home.

O son of Mary, merciful
Father, and ghost all
Holy, save us from
The wrath of Calvin,
From the wrath of Rome;
Save us from good priests
And your many churches—
But above and beyond all
Save us from the terrible
Words and text
Of the windy bishop who'd preach our dust home.

217   *Emily Carr*

Like Jonah in the green belly of the whale
Overwhelmed by Leviathan's lights and liver
Imprisoned and appalled by the belly's wall
Yet inscribing and scoring the uprush
Sink vault and arch of that monstrous cathedral,
Its living bone and its green pulsing flesh—
Old woman, of your three days' anatomy
Leviathan sickened and spewed you forth
In a great vomit on coasts of eternity.
Then, as for John of Patmos, the river of life
Burned for you an emerald and jasper smoke

WILFRED WATSON

And down the valley you looked and saw
All wilderness become transparent vapour,
A ghostly underneath a fleshly stroke,
And every bush an apocalypse of leaf.

SAINT-DENYS-GARNEAU

1912–1943

218   *Le Jeu*

Ne me dérangez pas je suis profondément occupé

Un enfant est en train de bâtir un village
C'est une ville, un comté
Et qui sait
          Tantôt l'univers.

Il joue

Ces cubes de bois sont des maisons qu'il déplace
                              et des châteaux
Cette planche fait signe d'un toit qui penche
                         ça n'est pas mal à voir
Ce n'est pas peu de savoir où va tourner la route
                                   de cartes
Cela pourrait changer complètement
                              le cours de la rivière
A cause du pont qui fait un si beau mirage
                         dans l'eau du tapis
C'est facile d'avoir un grand arbre
Et de mettre au-dessous une montagne
                         pour qu'il soit en-haut.

SAINT-DENYS-GARNEAU

Joie de jouer ! paradis des libertés !
Et surtout n'allez pas mettre un pied dans la chambre
On ne sait jamais ce qui peut être dans ce coin
Et si vous n'allez pas écraser la plus chère
des fleurs invisibles

Voilà ma boîte à jouets
Pleine de mots pour faire de merveilleux enlacements
Les allier séparer marier,
Déroulements tantôt de danse
Et tout à l'heure le clair éclat du rire
Qu'on croyait perdu

Une tendre chiquenaude
Et l'étoile
Qui se balançait sans prendre garde
Au bout d'un fil trop ténu de lumière
Tombe dans l'eau et fait des ronds.

De l'amour de la tendresse qui donc oserait en douter
Mais pas deux sous de respect pour l'ordre établi
Et la politesse et cette chère discipline
Une légèreté et des manières à scandaliser les grandes
personnes

Il vous arrange les mots comme si c'étaient de
simples chansons
Et dans ses yeux on peut lire son espiègle plaisir
A voir que sous les mots il déplace toutes choses
Et qu'il en agit avec les montagnes
Comme s'il les possédait en propre.
Il met la chambre à l'envers et vraiment l'on ne s'y
reconnaît plus
Comme si c'était un plaisir de berner les gens.

Et pourtant dans son œil gauche quand le droit rit
Une gravité de l'autre monde s'attache à la feuille
d'un arbre
Comme si cela pouvait avoir une grande importance
Avait autant de poids dans sa balance
Que la guerre d'Éthiopie
Dans celle de l'Angleterre.

Nous ne sommes pas des comptables

Tout le monde peut voir une piastre de papier vert
Mais qui peut voir au travers
si ce n'est un enfant
Qui peut comme lui voir au travers en toute liberté
Sans que du tout la piastre l'empêche
ni ses limites
Ni sa valeur d'une seule piastre

Mais il voit par cette vitrine des milliers de jouets
merveilleux
Et n'a pas envie de choisir parmi ces trésors
Ni désir ni nécessité
Lui
Mais ses yeux sont grands pour tout prendre.

219   *Accompagnement*

Je marche à côté d'une joie
D'une joie qui n'est pas à moi
D'une joie à moi que je ne puis pas prendre

Je marche à côté de moi en joie
J'entends mon pas en joie qui marche à côté de moi
Mais je ne puis changer de place sur le trottoir
Je ne puis pas mettre mes pieds dans ces pas-là
           et dire voilà c'est moi

Je me contente pour le moment de cette compagnie
Mais je machine en secret des échanges
Par toutes sortes d'opérations, des alchimies,
Par des transfusions de sang
Des déménagements d'atomes
         par des jeux d'équilibre

Afin qu'un jour, transposé,
Je sois porté par la danse de ces pas de joie
Avec le bruit décroissant de mon pas à côté de moi
Avec la perte de mon pas perdu
         s'étiolant à ma gauche
Sous les pieds d'un étranger
        qui prend une rue transversale.

220   *Cage d'oiseau*

Je suis une cage d'oiseau
Une cage d'os
Avec un oiseau

L'oiseau dans sa cage d'os
C'est la mort qui fait son nid

Lorsque rien n'arrive
On entend froisser ses ailes

Et quand on a ri beaucoup
Si l'on cesse tout à coup
On l'entend qui roucoule
Au fond
Comme un grelot

C'est un oiseau tenu captif
La mort dans ma cage d'os

Voudrait-il pas s'envoler
Est-ce vous qui le retiendrez
Est-ce moi
Qu'est-ce que c'est

Il ne pourra s'en aller
Qu'après avoir tout mangé
Mon cœur
La source du sang
Avec la vie dedans

Il aura mon âme au bec.

221   *Petite fin du monde*

Oh ! Oh !
Les oiseaux
morts

Les oiseaux
les colombes
nos mains

296

SAINT-DENYS-GARNEAU

Qu'est-ce qu'elles ont eu
qu'elles ne se reconnaissent plus

On les a vues autrefois
Se rencontrer dans la pleine clarté
se balancer dans le ciel
se côtoyer avec tant de plaisir
                      et se connaître
dans une telle douceur

Qu'est-ce qu'elles ont maintenant
quatre mains sans plus un chant
que voici mortes
désertées

J'ai goûté à la fin du monde
et ton visage a paru périr
devant ce silence de quatre colombes
devant la mort de ces quatre mains
       Tombées
en rang côte à côte

Et l'on se demande
   A ce deuil
quelle mort secrète
quel travail secret de la mort
par quelle voie intime dans notre ombre
où nos regards n'ont pas voulu descendre
   La mort
a mangé la vie aux oiseaux
a chassé le chant et rompu le vol
à quatre colombes
alignées sous nos yeux

de sorte qu'elles sont maintenant
                              sans palpitation
et sans rayonnement de l'âme.

222   *Accueil*

Moi ce n'est que pour vous aimer
Pour vous voir
Et pour aimer vous voir

Moi ça n'est pas pour vous parler
Ça n'est pas pour des échanges
                              conversations
Ceci livré, cela retenu
Pour ces compromissions de nos dons

C'est pour savoir que vous êtes,
Pour aimer que vous soyez

Moi ce n'est que pour vous aimer
Que je vous accueille
Dans la vallée spacieuse de mon recueillement
Où vous marchez seule et sans moi
Libre complètement

Dieu sait que vous serez inattentive
Et de tous côtés au soleil
Et tout entière en votre fleur
Sans une hypocrisie
en votre jeu

Vous serez claire et seule
Comme une fleur sous le ciel
Sans un repli
Sans un recul de votre exquise pudeur

Moi je suis seul à mon tour
autour de la vallée
Je suis la colline attentive
Autour de la vallée
Où la gazelle de votre grâce évoluera
Dans la confiance et la clarté de l'air

Seul à mon tour j'aurai la joie
Devant moi
De vos gestes parfaits
Des attitudes parfaites
De votre solitude

Et Dieu sait que vous repartirez
Comme vous êtes venue
Et je ne vous reconnaîtrai plus

Je ne serai peut-être pas plus seul
Mais la vallée sera déserte
Et qui me parlera de vous?

223 *La Mort grandissante*

II

Nous avons attendu de la douleur
qu'elle modèle notre figure
     à la dureté magnifique de nos os
Au silence irréductible et certain de nos os

SAINT-DENYS-GARNEAU

Ce dernier retranchement inexpugnable de notre être
qu'elle tende à nos os clairement la peau de nos figures
La chair lâche et troublée de nos figures
qui crèvent à tout moment et se décomposent
Cette peau qui flotte au vent de notre figure
                                        triste oripeau.

Faible oripeau à tous les vents qui nous trahit
Qu'elle l'assujettisse décidément
                        à la forme certaine de nos os clairs.

Mais la douleur fut-elle devancée
Est-ce que la mort serait venue secrètement
                        faire son nid dans nos os mêmes
Aurait pénétré, corrompu nos os mêmes
Aurait élu domicile dans la substance même de nos os
Parmi nos os
De sorte qu'arrivée là après toute la chair traversée
Après toutes les épaisseurs traversées
                        qu'on lui avait jetées en pâture
Après toutes ces morsures dans notre chair molle
                                et comme engourdie
La douleur ne trouve pas non plus
                        de substance ferme à quoi s'attaquer
De substance ferme à quoi s'agripper
                                d'une poigne ferme
Densité à percer d'un solide aiguillon
Un silence solide à chauffer à blanc
Une sensibilité essentielle et silencieuse
                        à torturer sans la détruire

SAINT-DENYS-GARNEAU

Mais elle ne rejoint encore qu'une surface qui s'effrite
Un édifice poreux qui se dissout
Un fantôme qui s'écroule et ne laisse plus que poussière.

Nous des ombres de cadavres elles des réalités
                      de cadavres, des os de cadavres,
Et quelle pitié nous prend (et quelle admiration)
                      ombres consciences de cadavres
Et terreur fraternelle nous prend
Devant cette réponse faite
Cette image offerte
Os de cadavres.

Quand on est réduit à ses os
Assis sur ses os
couché en ses os
avec la nuit devant soi.

Nous allons détacher nos membres
            et les mettre en rang pour en faire un inventaire
Afin de voir ce qui manque
De trouver le joint qui ne va pas
Car il est impossible de recevoir assis tranquillement
            la mort grandissante.

Et cependant dressé en nous
Un homme qu'on ne peut pas abattre
Debout en nous et tournant le dos à la direction
                                 de nos regards
Debout en os et les yeux fixés sur le néant
Dans une effroyable confrontation obstinée et un défi.

Quitte le monticule impossible au milieu
Et le manteau gardant le silence des os
Et la grappe du cœur enfin désespéré
Où pourra maintenant s'incruster cette croix
A la place du glaive acide du dépit
A l'endroit pratiqué par le couteau fixé
Dont le manche remue un mal encore aigu
Chaque fois que ta main se retourne vers toi
Où s'incruste la croix avec ses bras de fer
Comme le fer qu'on cloue à l'écorce d'un arbre
Qui blesse la surface, mais la cicatrice
De l'écorce bientôt le submerge et le couvre
Et plus tard le fil dur qui blessait la surface
On le voit assuré au bon centre du tronc
C'est ainsi que la croix sera faite en ton cœur
Et la tête et les bras et les pieds qui dépassent
Avec le Christ dessus et nos minces douleurs.

Quitte le monticule impossible au milieu
Place-toi désormais aux limites du lieu
Avec tout le pays derrière tes épaules
Et plus rien devant toi que ce pas à parfaire
Le pôle repéré par l'espoir praticable
Et le cœur aimanté par le fer de la croix.

SAINT-DENYS-GARNEAU

Mon cœur cette pierre qui pèse en moi
Mon cœur pétrifié par ce stérile arrêt
Et regard retourné vers les feux de la ville
Et l'envie attardée aux cendres des regrets
Et les regrets perdus vers les pays possibles

Ramène ton manteau, pèlerin sans espoir
Ramène ton manteau contre tes os
Rabats tes bras épars de bonheurs désertés

Ramène le manteau de ta pauvreté contre tes os
Et la grappe séchée de ton cœur pour noyau
Laisse un autre à présent en attendrir la peau

Quitte le monticule impossible au milieu
D'un pays dérisoire et dont tu fis le lieu
De l'affût au secret à surprendre de nuit
Au secret d'un mirage où déserter l'ennui.

IRVING LAYTON

b. 1912

224   *The Birth of Tragedy*

And me happiest when I compose poems.
  Love, power, the huzza of battle
  are something, are much;
yet a poem includes them like a pool
  water and reflection.
In me, nature's divided things—
  tree, mould on tree—
  have their fruition;

I am their core. Let them swap,
bandy, like a flame swerve
I am their mouth; as a mouth I serve.

And I observe how the sensual moths
    big with odour and sunshine
    dart into the perilous shrubbery;
or drop their visiting shadows
    upon the garden I one year made
of flowering stone to be a footstool
    for the perfect gods
    who, friends to the ascending orders,
will sustain this passionate meditation
and call down pardons
for the insurgent blood.

A quiet madman, never far from tears,
    I lie like a slain thing
    under the green air the trees
inhabit, or rest upon a chair
    towards which the inflammable air
tumbles on many robins' wings;
    noting how seasonably
    leaf and blossom uncurl
and living things arrange their death,
while someone from afar off
blows birthday candles for the world

225 *The Cold Green Element*

At the end of the garden walk
the wind and its satellite wait for me;
their meaning I will not know
    until I go there,
but the black-hatted undertaker

who, passing, saw my heart beating in the grass,
is also going there. Hi, I tell him,
a great squall in the Pacific blew a dead poet
    out of the water,
who now hangs from the city's gates.

Crowds depart daily to see it, and return
with grimaces and incomprehension;
if its limbs twitched in the air
    they would sit at its feet
peeling their oranges.

And turning over I embrace like a lover
the trunk of a tree, one of those
for whom the lightning was too much
    and grew a brilliant
hunchback with a crown of leaves.

The ailments escaped from the labels
of medicine bottles are all fled to the wind;
I've seen myself lately in the eyes
    of old women,
spent streams mourning my manhood,

in whose old pupils the sun became
a bloodsmear on broad catalpa leaves
and hanging from ancient twigs,
   my murdered selves
sparked the air like the muted collisions

of fruit. A black dog howls down my blood,
a black dog with yellow eyes;
he too by someone's inadvertence
   saw the bloodsmear
on the broad catalpa leaves.

But the furies clear a path for me to the worm
who sang for an hour in the throat of a robin,
and misled by the cries of young boys
   I am again
a breathless swimmer in that cold green element.

226   *Bacchanal*

You there, and you, and you
Come, I want to embrace you
With beer on your breath and halitosis
Come with your Venus-rotted noses

Here is man's true temple, cool
Gloom, sincere worshippers—
Before them the tapers of beer
Like lights lit on many altars

Come, pleasure's my god and yours
Too, to go by your charming noises

Let's hiccup our happiness
And belch our ecstasies to Bacchus

He hears us and sends the room
Spinning. May his touch be always upon us.
May we, as he spins us in the cool gloom,
Be forever in his keeping.

227   *The Fertile Muck*

There are brightest apples on those trees
     but until I, fabulist, have spoken
they do not know their significance
or what other legends are hung like garlands
     on their black boughs twisting
like a rumour. The wind's noise is empty.

Nor are the winged insects better off
     though they wear my crafty eyes
wherever they alight. Stay here, my love;
you will see how delicately they deposit
     me on the leaves of elms
or fold me in the orient dust of summer.

And if in August joiners and bricklayers
     are thick as flies around us
building expensive bungalows for those
who do not need them, unless they release
     me roaring from their moth-proofed cupboards
their buyers will have no joy, no ease.

I could extend their rooms for them without cost
   and give them crazy sundials
to tell the time with, but I have noticed
how my irregular footprint horrifies them
   evenings and Sunday afternoons:
they spray for hours to erase its shadow.

How to dominate reality? Love is one way;
   imagination another. Sit here
beside me, sweet; take my hard hand in yours.
We'll mark the butterflies disappearing over the hedge
   with tiny wristwatches on their wings:
our fingers touching the earth, like two Buddhas.

228   *Boys in October*

Like Barbarossa's beard bright with oil
The maples glisten with the season's rain;
The day's porous, as October days are,
And objects have more space about them.

All field things seem weightless, abstract,
As if they'd taken one step back
To see themselves as they literally are
After the dementia of summer.

Now hale and sinewy my son, his friend
(The construction sand making a kind
Of festival under their feet while leaves
Fall and heave about them, drift and curl)

In their absorbed arm-on-shoulder stance
Look I think for all the world
Like some antique couple in a wood
Whom unexpected sibyls have made rich

— Something perhaps tricked out by Ovid!
On one condition, alas: they'll not use
The gold but hold it as a memorial
To Chance and their own abstinence.

229   *The Bull Calf*

The thing could barely stand. Yet taken
from his mother and the barn smells
he still impressed with his pride,
with the promise of sovereignty in the way
his head moved to take us in.
The fierce sunlight tugging the maize from the ground
licked at his shapely flanks.
He was too young for all that pride.
I thought of the deposed Richard II.

'No money in bull calves,' Freeman had said.
The visiting clergyman rubbed the nostrils
now snuffing pathetically at the windless day.
'A pity,' he sighed.
My gaze slipped off his hat toward the empty sky
that circled over the black knot of men,
over us and the calf waiting for the first blow.

IRVING LAYTON

Struck,
the bull calf drew in his thin forelegs
as if gathering strength for a mad rush . . .
tottered . . . raised his darkening eyes to us,
and I saw we were at the far end
of his frightened look, growing smaller and smaller
till we were only the ponderous mallet
that flicked his bleeding ear
and pushed him over on his side, stiffly,
like a block of wood.

Below the hill's crest
the river snuffled on the improvised beach.
We dug a deep pit and threw the dead calf into it.
It made a wet sound, a sepulchral gurgle,
as the warm sides bulged and flattened.
Settled, the bull calf lay as if asleep,
one foreleg over the other,
bereft of pride and so beautiful now,
without movement, perfectly still in the cool pit,
I turned away and wept.

ANNE MARRIOTT

b. 1913

230   *Prairie Graveyard*

Wind mutters thinly on the sagging wire
binding the graveyard from the gouged dirt road,
bends thick-bristled Russian thistle,
sifts listless dust
into cracks in hard grey ground.

ANNE MARRIOTT

Empty prairie slides away
on all sides, rushes toward a wide
expressionless horizon, joined
to a vast blank sky.

    Lots near the road are the most expensive
    where heavy tombstones lurch a fraction
    tipped by splitting soil.
    Farther, a row of aimless heaps
    names weather-worn from tumbled sticks
    remember now the six thin children
    of a thin, shiftless home.

Hawk, wind-scouring, cuts
a pointed shadow on the drab scant grass.

    Two graves apart by the far fence
    are suicides, one with a grand
    defiant tombstone, bruising at the heart
    'Death is swallowed up in victory.'
    (And may be, God's kindness being more large
    than man's, to this, who after seven years
    of drought, burned down his barn,
    himself hanged in it.)
    The second, nameless, set around
    with even care-sought stones
    (no stones on this section)
    topped with two plants, hard-dried,
    in rust-thick jam tins in the caked drab pile.

A gopher jumps from a round cave,
springs furtively, spurts under fence, is gone.

ANNE MARRIOTT

Wind raises dead curls of dust and whines
under its harsh breath on the limp dragged wires,
then leaves the graveyard stiff with silence, lone
in the centre of the huge lone land and sky.

DOUGLAS LE PAN

b. 1914

231   *Canoe-Trip*

What of this fabulous country
Now that we have it reduced to a few hot hours
And sun-burn on our backs?
On this south side the countless archipelagoes,
The slipway where titans sent splashing the last great glaciers;
And then up to the foot of the blue pole star
A wilderness,
The pinelands whose limits seem distant as Thule,
The millions of lakes once cached and forgotten,
The clearings enamelled with blueberries, rank silence about
    them;
And skies that roll all day with cloud-chimeras
To baffle the eye with portents and unwritten myths,
The flames of sunset, the lions of gold and gules.
Into this reservoir we dipped and pulled out lakes and rivers,
We strung them together and made our circuit.
Now what shall be our word as we return,
What word of this curious country?

It is good,
It is a good stock to own though it seldom pays dividends.
There are holes here and there for a gold-mine or a hydro-
    plant.

DOUGLAS LE PAN

But the tartan of river and rock spreads undisturbed,
The plaid of a land with little desire to buy or sell.
The dawning light skirls out its independence;
At noon the brazen trumpets slash the air;
Night falls, the gulls scream sharp defiance;
Let whoever comes to tame this land, beware!
Can you put a bit to the lunging wind?
Can you hold wild horses by the hair?
Then have no hope to harness the energy here,
It gallops along the wind away.
But here are crooked nerves made straight,
The fracture cured no doctor could correct.
The hand and mind, reknit, stand whole for work;
The fable proves no cul-de-sac.
Now from the maze we circle back;
The map suggested a wealth of cloudy escapes;
That was a dream, we have converted the dream to act.
And what we now expect is not simplicity,
No steady breeze, or any surprise,
Orchids along the portage, white water, crimson leaves.
Content, we face again the complex task.

And yet the marvels we have seen remain.
We think of the eagles, of the fawns at the river bend,
The storms, the sudden sun, the clouds sheered downwards.
O so to move! With such immaculate decision!
O proudly as waterfalls curling like cumulus!

Lion, Leopard, Lady

It was through a mucous membrane, a kind of mouth
Most tender to the touch, that dreamily
I swam into my own sick-room, south
Of this tropic, in a soft wind, a lymphatic sea.

Lying on the bed as though flayed
And stretched in an anatomical chart, muscles
Cross-hatched with nerves to the shamed air splayed
Rant as red as a cock's comb. Around me rustles

Translucent drapery disposed in a paper-thin
Illusion of late afternoon, a bland and blond
Stockade that stems the murk it dabbles in,
Though slimed like film where a serpent brood is spawned.

What was it made ensanguined fury cease?
By the bed two animals arrested stand,
A lion holding up a blood-stained fleece
And a leopard with an hour-glass in its hand.

Gold has been blown into the air. As the onset waned
Gold fleeced from the flesh and gold from the sliding hour
Have branched in the air and stiffened. Was it this restrained
The scathing lion and tranced the leopard's power?

But daylight darkens into deep gold, dark gold, black.
As the pale stockade is overwhelmed, I know
Red craving after one more night attack
Would be devoured—or left for flies to blow.

Then comes a lady in the failing light
With black lawn over sheerest, golden tissue,
Unknown where she comes from, daughter of night,
And like the beasts one of the shadows' issue.

Gliding from nowhere in the dying truce
Her gaze above the red flayed patient dwells,
A gaze of mildness, of the flower-de-luce,
That hovering, treats with savagery, compels,

To mildness lecherous tongues impatiently lolling.
She soothes the lion and the leopard calms.
Now both are feeding as the dew is falling,
Lapping contentment from her milk-white palms.

And ravening tongues now moonily caress
The form they butchered; now gentled, salve and save;
The stars their lost dominions repossess.
Again in fleecy skies the lilies wave.

233 *The New Vintage*

Wine of the new vintage they brought us
Bitter but the best they had
And by the wine or their kindness translated back to men,
Un-Circed, we sat at ease in a spell of daylight
That we knew could never last. Though it did.
Day after day through amber richness dawdling
We hardly noticed the thin trickle of acidity
As one sun-caverned green-glass flask succeeded another
And the battle moved further away. It was an autumn solstice
Where we lay forgotten to play with children

In a vine-blessed house, a beatitude of husbandry
Discussing with the farmer crops and legends;
And returning rarely to our own sour dispensation
When tending the vehicles that sulked under leafy nettings.

Sons we were
Re-entered into a patrimony from which
Many of our fathers, grandfathers even, had been dispossessed.
And we moved through the house discovering family heir-
    looms,
Shocks of Indian corn that blazed from the rafters
And above the stairway tomatoes skeined in ruby clusters;
Or gazed through windows at fields and furrows
Where a woman switched on two milk-white oxen
Through bare fruit-trees, blue with copper sulphate,
That offered to the bare, blue sky fruits of repentance.
These things like the word of life we handled then.

But there is not a happy ending.
(Nor in the parable is mention made
Of the morning when the prodigal, redeemed and feasted,
Was sought in vain, once more a prey to bestial craving;
When his father found only a robe and mocking ring.)
One morning a signal came and in half an hour
We had loaded the vehicles and tied on extra gear,
Enough to make us at home in the winds and smoke
Where we would be coiled like wraiths through a new
    campaign.
We took the farmer's address and promised to write
And as he poured out the final viaticum
The new wine in our lying throats stung sharp and bitter,
There was no ray left of its sun-burnt, august sweetness.

He watched us to the last from the middle of the road
Staring along that barren tunnel as though down a rifle-barrel
Where the rifling circled in a glassy, baffling pool
Too deep with future for his aching temples,
A leaden pool that sucked down to he knew not what,
And shimmered with unheard-of consummations sterile.

234   *Nimbus*

    To dive for the nimbus on the sea-floor
       Or seek it in the sun
    Calls for a plucky steeplejack
       Scaling sky's giddy ocean
    Or dolphin-hearted journeyman
    To swim from the foundered sunburst's roar
       With lost treasure on his back.

    Ocean that slovens and sidles in vast
       Indifference, hides
    In its sludge a wreath of drowning bells.
       Who in those tricky tides
    Or up the slippery daybreak's sides
    Can grapple the spices of morning fast
       That waste on the listless swells?

    Smothered beneath a lowering ceiling
       All cock-crow crispness dies.
    Bleary hordes are afraid to wake
       Into the mists that rise
    From a palsied swamp where a marsh-bird cries.
    Stranger, reconquer the source of feeling
       For an anxious people's sake.

Plunder the mind's aerial cages
   Or the heart's deep catacombs.
O daring's virtuoso, tossed
   Where the furious sunlight foams
Or through the instinct's twilit glooms,
Return with the sunburst's glistering pledges
   As a garland for the lost.

A bittern rustling in the reeds
   Is startled, and through the mist
Whirs screaming. Now, if now only, come
   With the nimbus in your fist.
Strike, strike the rust like a rhapsodist
And burnish gold each throat that pleads
   For dawn's encomium.

PATRICK ANDERSON

b. 1915

235   *Capital Square*

Danger is silent in the bloodless square:
the boxing brute of stone half hides his fist,
the moon in the haunt of weight is a heavy ghost
and the sun is a toastmaster,
the punishing façades disguise their skill
and fountains play before the parliament of standstill.

You may go freely through the paved immense
slowness, the architectural snow;
admire the statues stiffened in the silence

with No upon their lips and the heart at zero,
until having made some circles you understand
you are a pigmy held in a stone hand.

No warmth is here, only an abstract good;
your dead shall never bleed nor your love return;
children ask here no gifts nor the hungry food . . .
but now and then four walls of added men
swing into symmetry, with a stone noise
harden and echo at a statue's voice.

236   *Sleighride*

In front the horse's rump bright as a lantern
goes its gauche way—the runners squeak
on the cobbled ice. With hands plunged in the hair
of my muffled rug and a clown's red nose, I leave.

I kick my feet on the boards to keep them warm,
and pull my headband over the rims of my ears
while the driver trails his whip in the banks of snow
a-glow at the sides like waves of wonderful summers.

And my eyes cry, I smile an archaic smile
and my cheeks are rouged with aliveness and mad love
while around in a settled circle the dull hills
control the valley whose applegreen ice I leave.

Goodbye Goodbye I say and the sleigh keeps on
like shuttle in slot but crazily all the same,
working its roughhouse wood, retching its iron—
I am not anywhere now but an Adam in Time.

I wrinkle my face for the cold and cuff my flesh
and watch the fringe of the rug flap over the sides
and the shadow that slides on the drift, the quick compelled
shape of the two in blue with velvet heads.

Is anyone ever so new as upon a journey,
so full of physical news or so flashy with nerves
as one who is moved, and nakedly, freely
watches his body reel in the straight and the curves?

So I submit to this lane, to this alteration,
I cough with faith and my breath is a bulging prayer,
and I drowse in the pleasure as well as the terror of Time
with a hallelujah hello from a nest of fur.

237   *Camp*

It happened on a Sunday
in a country of the sun
that our journey sank below
the patterns made on maps:
wherever we were going
was suddenly the green
ferns by the river bank
where our car nosed in.

It was below all blowing
and great shows of the hills,
we happened there and were
in tunnels of the summer

PATRICK ANDERSON

where the flower fills
with honey and with wind
and insects open up
their warm enormous ground.

We were not high and clever
but low and to be glad
beside the water's race
and islands to explore
that grass outrustled place
and plan and map together
and flies designed the air
about the roaring flower.

And there were beds of stones
baked white by the brown water
and feathery islands where
the birds chilled with their beaks
the beaches of white stones
but when we waded there
one great bird in a fright
and turret of air
came angry over,
crier and diver.

So all a summer's day
of a Sunday drowned in green,
we flourished in that country
and no one ever came
but the sun with a hand of brass
stood in his height of sky
and poured the map like a cup
to run upon the place,
spilling it carelessly.

PATRICK ANDERSON

And no one ever came
where we were down so far
with our heads in our arms
sleeping on the grass
except some children who
ran naked through the blurred
noon to the blazing pool
and spoke into our dream
by being beautiful
and never spoke a word.

FREDERICK E. LAIGHT

b. 1915

238   *[Drought]*

I have seen tall chimneys without smoke,
   And I have seen blank windows without blinds,
   And great dead wheels, and motors without minds,
And vacant doorways grinning at the joke.

I have seen loaded wagons creak and sway
   Along the roads into the North and East,
   Each dragged by some great-eyed and starving beast
To God knows where, but just away—away.

And I have heard the wind awake at nights
   Like some poor mother left with empty hands,
   Go whimpering in the silent stubble lands
And creeping through bare houses without lights.

FREDERICK E. LAIGHT

These comforts only have I for my pain:
   The frantic laws of statesmen bowed with cares
   To feed me, and the slow, pathetic prayers
Of godly men that somehow it shall rain.

RINA LASNIER

239   *Escales*

I

Je n'ai pas survolé les escales d'amour
Plus basses et plus obscures au bout de la lumière
Que les eaux obstinément ternies des ornières.
Je n'ai pas dédaigné vos battures en fêtes
Que la marée submerge et noie amèrement;
J'ai quitté le risque farouche des tempêtes
Pour le faux arroi de vos émerveillements;
J'ai oublié la hauteur et ses gradins nus,
L'élargissement de ses voies sans affût
Pour éprouver le poids de vos amours brèves,
Comme une cime qui prend le joug de la neige.

Les paupières vidées des soleils abaissés
Par mes altitudes plus aiguës que la flèche.
J'ai touché la pierre où l'homme assis dessèche
Son ombre stagnante comme les nuits borées.

Le cœur angélisé par les aubes natales
Et les vents mêlés aux gémissements des dieux,
— Ô dieux! toutes vos solitudes musicales

RINA LASNIER

Soupirées au cœur de l'oiseau cimé de bleu ! —
J'ai cherché l'île polie du feu tropical
Et le murmure d'amour dont frémit la mer nuptiale
Autour de Vénus plus parfaite que le jour . . .

J'ai cherché le chanteur des îles; toi seul, Olen,
Dont la narine enflée d'aromes diffus
Leur imposait le divin contour du chant
Comme à mes désirs le cri d'amour absolu !

J'ai trouvé les îles et les siècles mystérieux
Des instants où le violier réduit son âme
En larmes plus transfigurantes que le feu,
Telle la noyalle au soleil oriflamme.
J'ai trouvé la corbeille de mes purs cheveux
Et le rosier de mes joues tout fleuri d'innocence,
Et les ormes obstinés dans la patience
A élever la terre jusqu'au bord des cieux.

.   .   .

Je sais l'écart de l'aile à l'aile fraternelle
Et la douleur de l'envergure, plus fidèle
À l'essor qu'à la lèvre le retour du baiser;
L'étouffement entre les roseaux entrecroisés
De l'oiseau qui de ses deux pattes palmées
Laisse une trace étoilée, par un peu d'eau sublimée.

Îles ! forfaitures des chemins intérieurs
De la mer, appeau et trémail de l'oiseleur,
Voici lié à la rancœur de mon sang
Le souffle dur des quatre bouches du vent.
Escales ! la Voix me ceint et me sépare,
Voici le dépeuplement de mon départ.

Olen, chanteur des îles et des battures fécondes,
J'ai entendu le cri de mon Goéland Noir,
C'est vers cette île à la dérive des mondes
Que j'élargirai mon âme jusqu'au soir !

II

Goéland ! Goéland ! toi qui ombrageais
Le zénith de la solitude où l'ange se dit,
Toi qui as détruit la proximité de la mort
Par ce très saint épaulement de ta jalousie,
Toi qui de ton essor édifiais le vertige
D'une tour où l'éblouissement est vision,
Toi qui avais tari dans ta chair d'ascension
L'amour pourpre et royal vestige,
Savais-tu donc le souffle trop léger d'Olen
Qui porte l'âme à un terme toujours absent ?

Goéland ! qu'as-tu vu de si beau dans ta pitié
Pour me contraindre et m'appeler à ce survol
Par lequel la terre à nouveau rassemblée
N'est plus qu'une liesse lointaine et sans parole ?
Quel vent, quelle main joueuse et puissante
A travers la savane de ta douceur
Fana cette sente sonore et montante
A mon chant sans trajet du cœur au cœur ?

Je m'étais couchée sous les océans du vent
Dans la toundra de mes affalements
Et j'avais ma bassesse pour cacher ma face,
La ténèbre des larmes pour abolir les espaces.
Pourquoi m'as-tu épousée en la navrance
De nos deux cris reconnus dans la souffrance ?

Pourquoi m'as-tu apprivoisée sous ta prunelle
Conjuguant en moi les angoisses antérieures
Et les effrois des nuits dissoutes sous mes ailes;
Pourquoi m'as-tu rendue vivante à mon cœur?

Je ne peux plus passer au centre de mon âme
Sans te susciter infiniment à l'orée
De mes désirs, comme le fruit courbe réclame
L'identique courbure du ciel sur lui seul appuyé.

Ô mon Goéland Noir, l'aube est déjà sur nous
Comme une palme de soie levant le jour;
Voici formé pour nous le long exil de l'amour,
La servile espérance retombe à nos genoux!

Reprenons le voyage icarien et radieux
Toujours puni de gloire et comblé de douleur,
Que notre aile brûlée de nouvelles profondeurs
Referme sur soi la blessure des dieux . . .

240 *Le Canard blanc*

Visa le noir, tua le blanc.

Si tu casses ses ailes sur ton étang sédentaire
Et fais ton déduit de lui jeter le pain d'hier,
Ou si tu le saignes au piège dans la faim de l'hiver,
L'ombre blanche du songe s'effacera de la neige.

Ô fils du roi, tu es méchant!
Par dessous l'aile il perd son sang.

En vain tu fonds la neige pour oublier ta proie.
— La neige épandue en espace pour laver ton regard —
En vain tu fracasses l'oiseau pour disperser sa blancheur,
En tumulte de chasse et de chiens roule ton cœur.

Ô fils du roi, tu es méchant!
Toutes ses plum' s'en vont au vent.

L'ombre et l'aile hâlaient le songe au dédale de l'air,
Mais l'aile retendait ton sillage dans la lumière,
— A chaque essor l'oiseau rédime le sang pour une brasée de
     vent —
Ramasse cet oiseau de plomb et pèse le poids de tes mains . . .

Ô fils du roi, tu es méchant!
Visa le noir, tua le blanc.

241   *Jungle de feuilles*

Absence de la forêt suffoquée de feuilles,
luxuriance à pourrir l'armature de l'arbre,
toison sans tête, sans ossature, monstre de pelage;
frondaisons sans sursis de ciel aux bras des branches.

Chaque feuille grasse collée à la graisse de la moiteur,
enchevêtrement poisseux de tous les rampements mous,
chair de chair sans retentissement de cris et de flèches;
marécage moisissant le socle de la cité.

Labyrinthe des léthargies sans fuite de rêve,
nuit verdâtre sans plumage d'étoiles, sans corne de lune
     brameuse.

RINA LASNIER

Ramas de feuilles refusant d'essuyer les pieds de la pluie,
chaque feuille refusant l'assaut de la pluie et du vent,
chaque feuille serait note de pluie, hymne de vent;
chaque arbre serait l'armature du feu futur.

Fermentation sans fruit entamé de faim fiévreuse,
stérile gravitation de l'identité sans issue de mort.

La forêt marcherait vers un seul apeurement d'eau,
la forêt s'évaserait pour une seule coulée d'oiseaux,
la forêt s'ordonnerait autour du péril de l'étincelle;
jungle tiède où manque la gloire amoureuse d'un corps
    incendié.

ANNE HÉBERT

b. 1916

242   *Les Deux Mains*

> Ces deux mains qu'on a,
> La droite fermée
> Ou ouverte;
>
> La gauche ouverte
> Ou fermée.
>
> Et les deux
> Ne s'attendant pas
> L'une l'autre.
>
> Ces deux mains immêlées,
> Ces deux mains immêlables.

Celle qu'on donne
Et celle qu'on garde;

Celle qu'on connaît
Et l'autre, l'inconnue.

Cette main d'enfant,
Cette main de femme.
Et parfois cette main travailleuse,
Simple comme une main d'homme.

Cela fait donc trois!
Et je découvre un nombre infini
En moi
De mains qui se tendent
Vers moi,
Comme des étrangères
Dont on a peur.

Ah! qui me rendra
Mes deux mains unies?
Et le rivage
Qu'on touche
Des deux mains,
Dans le même appareillage,
Ayant en cours de route
Éparpillé toutes ces mains inutiles . . .

243   *Ballade d'un enfant qui va mourir*

Je suis cet enfant qui joue du triangle;
Ah! que le son est aigu,
Ah! qu'il est d'argent.

ANNE HÉBERT

Ma voix vibre et tremble
Dans le monde vide.
Ah! que le monde est sourd,
Ah! que ma voix tremble.

Le son le plus haut,
Le plus clair
Qui déchire l'air
Comme des grelots de cristal,
Des larmes cristallisées
Qui s'entrechoquent dans leur transparence.

Je marche en chantant.
Ah! que l'écho est long
Derrière moi.

Les rues sont pavées de galets ronds,
Mes pieds tournent,
Les maisons sont mortes
Et tout le monde aussi;
Je n'entends plus leurs voix,
Leurs voix graves et fortes.

Il n'y a plus dans la ville
Que ma voix aiguë,
Que ma voix haute,
Que ma voix d'argent.

Déjà je sens l'odeur de la mer.
Ah! qu'elle est amère,
Et que je suis seul ici.

ANNE HÉBERT

Où est la Mort?
A-t-elle emporté tous les morts?
Pourquoi sont-ils silencieux
S'ils sont encore ici?

Voilà que j'ai traversé la ville
Où pas un mort ne m'a souri.
Où donc sont-ils?

Ma voix tremble
Et se perd
Dans la mer
Sonore de tous les vents intérieurs,
De toutes les immortelles tempêtes.
Ah! que son odeur est amère.

Ma voix est perdue;
Ah! que la voix de la mer
Est puissante.

Je ne me souviens plus
Ni de la voix des autres,
Ni de la mienne.

Je n'ai jamais vu la Mort.
Son visage est-il beau
Comme celui de ma mère?
Je ne sais pas,
Je ne sais pas.

Voilà que j'ai perdu
Le visage de ma mère;
Dans ma mémoire

ANNE HÉBERT

Je ne le retrouve plus.
Je ne sais plus,
Je ne sais plus.

Je n'ai jamais vu le visage de la Mort.
Ah ! que la mer est caressante ;
Elle baise mes pieds
En lames douces.

Elle monte vers moi
En me caressant.
J'ai pris sur moi son odeur amère.

Je suis en elle,
Mêlée à elle
Comme le sel.

Je marche au fond de la mer,
Je respire l'eau,
Calmement, comme de l'air.
Tout est vert et translucide ;
J'habite un palais vert.

J'ai tendu un hamac
Aux lâches mailles liquides,
Entre deux branches marines.
Je dors.

Demain j'explorerai l'immensité
Aux pentes douces,
J'irai à la recherche des morts,
J'enfoncerai dans le profond désert

Sans aventure de l'Éternité,
J'irai tout au long des jours confondus,
À la rencontre de ce visage inconnu
Dont je goûte déjà sur moi l'odeur amère.

244   *Vie de château*

C'est un château d'ancêtres
Sans table ni feu
Ni poussière ni tapis.

L'enchantement pervers de ces lieux
Est tout dans ses miroirs polis.

La seule occupation possible ici
Consiste à se mirer jour et nuit.

Jette ton image aux fontaines dures
Ta plus dure image sans ombre ni couleur.

Vois, ces glaces sont profondes
Comme des armoires.
Toujours quelque mort y habite sous le tain
Et couvre aussitôt ton reflet,
Se colle à toi comme une algue.

S'ajuste à toi, mince et nu,
Et simule l'amour en un lent frisson amer.

245 *La Chambre fermée*

Qui donc m'a conduite ici ?
Il y a certainement quelqu'un
Qui a soufflé sur mes pas.
Quand est-ce que cela s'est fait ?
Avec la complicité de quel ami tranquille ?
Le consentement profond de quelle nuit longue ?

Qui donc a dessiné la chambre ?
Dans quel instant calme
A-t-on imaginé le plafond bas
La petite table verte et le couteau minuscule
Le lit de bois noir
Et toute la rose du feu
En ses jupes pourpres gonflées
Autour de son cœur possédé et gardé
Sous les flammes oranges et bleues ?

Qui donc a pris la juste mesure
De la croix tremblante de mes bras étendus ?
Les quatre points cardinaux
Originent au bout de mes doigts
Pourvu que je tourne sur moi-même
Quatre fois
Tant que durera le souvenir
Du jour et de la nuit.

Mon cœur sur la table posé,
Qui donc a mis le couvert avec soin,
Affilé le petit couteau
Sans aucun tourment
Ni précipitation ?

Ma chair s'étonne et s'épuise
Sans cet hôte coutumier
Entre ses côtes déraciné.
La couleur claire du sang
Scelle la voûte creuse
Et mes mains croisées
Sur cet espace dévasté
Se glacent et s'enchantent de vide.

Ô doux corps qui dort
Le lit de bois noir te contient
Et t'enferme strictement pourvu que tu ne bouges.
Surtout n'ouvre pas les yeux!
Songe un peu
Si tu allais voir
La table servie et le couvert qui brille!

Laisse, laisse le feu teindre
La chambre de reflets
Et mûrir et ton cœur et ta chair;
Tristes époux tranchés et perdus.

246   *Le Tombeau des rois*

J'ai mon cœur au poing
Comme un faucon aveugle.

Le taciturne oiseau pris à mes doigts
Lampe gonflée de vin et de sang,
Je descends
Vers les tombeaux des rois
Étonnée
A peine née.

ANNE HÉBERT

Quel fil d'Ariane me mène
Au long des dédales sourds?
L'écho des pas s'y mange à mesure.

(En quel songe
Cette enfant fut-elle liée par la cheville
Pareille à une esclave fascinée?)

L'auteur du songe
Presse le fil,
Et viennent les pas nus
Un à un
Comme les premières gouttes de pluie
Au fond du puits.

Déjà l'odeur bouge en des orages gonflés
Suinte sous le pas des portes
Aux chambres secrètes et rondes,
Là où sont dressés les lits clos.

L'immobile désir des gisants me tire.
Je regarde avec étonnement
A même les noirs ossements
Luire les pierres bleues incrustées.

Quelques tragédies patiemment travaillées,
Sur la poitrine des rois, couchées,
En guise de bijoux
Me sont offertes
Sans larmes ni regrets.

Sur une seule ligne rangés:
La fumée d'encens, le gâteau de riz séché

ANNE HÉBERT

Et ma chair qui tremble:
Offrande rituelle et soumise.

Le masque d'or sur ma face absente
Des fleurs violettes en guise de prunelles,
L'ombre de l'amour me maquille à petits traits précis;
Et cet oiseau que j'ai respire
Et se plaint étrangement.

Un frisson long
Semblable au vent qui prend, d'arbre en arbre,
Agite sept grands pharaons d'ébène
En leurs étuis solennels et parés.

Ce n'est que la profondeur de la mort qui persiste,
Simulant le dernier tourment
Cherchant son apaisement
Et son éternité
En un cliquetis léger de bracelets
Cercles vains jeux d'ailleurs
Autour de la chair sacrifiée.

Avides de la source fraternelle du mal en moi
Ils me couchent et me boivent;
Sept fois, je connais l'étau des os
Et la main sèche qui cherche le cœur pour le rompre.

Livide et repue de songe horrible
Les membres dénoués
Et les morts hors de moi, assassinés,
Quel reflet d'aube s'égare ici?
D'où vient donc que cet oiseau frémit
Et tourne vers le matin
Ses prunelles crevées?

BERTRAM WARR

247 *Working Class*

We have heard no nightingales singing
in cool, dim lanes, where evening
comes like a procession through the aisles at passion-tide,
filling the church with quiet prayer dressed in white.
We have known no hills where sea-winds sweep up thyme
    perfume,
and crush it against our nostrils, as we stand by hump-backed
    trees.

We have felt no willow leaves pluck us timidly
as we pass on slack rivers;
a kiss, and a stealing away, like a lover who dares no more.
For we are the walkers on pavement,
who go grey-faced and given-up through the rain;
with our twice turned collars crinkled,
and the patches bunched coarsely in our crotches.
They have gashed the lands with cities,
and gone away afraid when the wounds turned blue.
Beauty has crept into the shelves of squat buildings,
to stare out strangely at us from the pages of Keats,
and the wan and wishful Georgian leaves.
These are our birthright, smoke and angry steel,
and long stern rows of stone, and wheels.
We are left with the churches, the red-necked men who eat
    oysters,
and stand up to talk at us in the approved manner.
We are left with the politicians who think poorly of us,
and who stand back with chaos in their pale old eyes
whimpering, 'That is not what we wanted. No,
it was not to have gone that way.'

They are very old, but we have been very ill,
and cannot yet send them away.

But there are things that still matter, something yet within us;
nights of love, bread and the kids,
and the cheek of the woman next door,
thoughts that glitter sometimes like a ruby on a mud-flat,
dreams that stir, and remind us of our blood.

Though the cities straddle the land like giants, holding us
        away.
we know they will topple some day,
and will lie over the land, dissolving and giving off gases.
But a wind will spring up to carry the smells away
and the earth will suck off the liquids and the crumbling flesh,
and on the bleached bones, when the sun shines, we shall
        begin to build.

248   *The Deviator*

I sat here this morning, detached, summoning up, I think
Something metaphysical;
And wishing peevishly for a thick fur to parcel up the many
        distractions:
All that I felt, which was not to be released;
All that I saw, blue-blotched wallpaper, the wooden bear,
And the mirror, mirror on the wall;
All that I heard—all that I hear now, for today I hear sounds:
The hungry, unhopeful wail of a rag-and-bone man in the
        street;
His cart will be filled before nightfall, if God will.

The hover and drift of a voice through a sluggish gypsy
    lament;
She is from home, and the distance beats like a piston against
    her.
Plate and knife discord, fulfilling, and water rushing down-
    ward through pipes.
The satisfied slam of a door returning, adjusted again.
And the words of the woman across the court,
Muted through the vibrating films of phlegm in her throat.
In resignation, for the phlegm has long been with her,
Belonging, not to be cleared, and only strangers mind.
And as I sat here this morning, thinking my thoughts amid the
    sounds,
Suddenly, all these, the definables, began telling their mean-
    ings to me,
Saying there is no aloneness, there can be no dark cocoon,
With room for one, and an empty place, if love should come.

249   *On a Child with a Wooden Leg*

See, in the garden there, it hops and lurches about;
Different in species almost, from its associates;
Sourness in the symphony, a toad floundering among ferns,
Dead Wood.

In the evening after prayers,
Probably the parent observes
How incongruous, on the chair,
Is the single, folded sock;
And on the floor
The one shoe,
Dissatisfied, perhaps, in the incomplete life.

RONALD HAMBLETON

b. 1917

Sockeye Salmon

Caught in the glib catcher's net
With the fly that wanders, is the wonder fish;
Threshes a moment in the windowed lace
Till the eye is opaque and supremely glazed.
Not projects outward no tangent beam,
Not gets the increase of scenery
Passing to afflict the retina.
Being unfit to negotiate
The invisible livelihood of lungs,
It flails in a harder-to-swim-in sea.
Outward in material lies its wherewithal,
And the gills adjust, discriminate,
But is caught by the introspective air
That moves captor's brain and viscera.

Hung like a murderer with stretched-out neck,
Prepared for dissection, absorption, use,
Subject to putrefactive air,
In gaunt symmetry lies the wonder fish;
The trip from the egg to the waterfall,
Leaping lively or lying sunned,
The spawning, the schooling, the quick increase
Are value and profit and capital.
No natural course is dissatisfied,
No function corrupted, there is no waste.
Use has been served up with vinegar,
The matter discussed with great dispatch.

In the ribbed lucent shallows is the window clear;
And the eyes' connection established there

RONALD HAMBLETON

All harmony, because all enmity
Has logically come to stay;
Cements by its close attractive gaze;
For man and fish find purest pleasure
In their prostituting mutual sight.

MIRIAM WADDINGTON

b. 1917

Thou Didst Say Me

Late as last summer
thou didst say me, love
I choose you, you, only you.
oh the delicate del-
icate serpent of your lips
the golden lie bedazzled
me with wish and flash
of joy and I was fool.

I was fool, bemused
bedazed by summer, still
bewitched and wandering
in murmur hush in green-
ly sketched-in fields
I was, I was, so sweet
I was, so honied with
your gold of love and love
and still again more love.

late as last autumn
thou didst say me, dear

my doxy, I choose you and
always you, thou didst pledge
me love and through the red-
plumed weeks and soberly
I danced upon your words
and garlanded these
tender dangers.

year curves to ending now
and thou dost say me, wife
I choose another love, and oh
the delicate del-
icate serpent of your mouth
stings deep, and bitter
iron cuts and shapes
my death, I was so fool.

252 *Catalpa Tree*

Catalpa, in you a song, a cache
A secret story hidden,
A cat, an alp to climb, an ahhh—
Winedrinker's joy and almost the apache
Of violent lunges, whisperings backstage.
And still the greenery, the lacings of the leaves
With quiet, wind outside
And inside cool, cool as caves
Or water, cool as waves
And welcome as water is
On salted skin and ankle.

343

Here is everness,
And gliding of the light
Into some brilliant world where it enjoys
Its own infinity, here I taste the grass
And touch the springy blossoms dry as silk,
Think such was I and such my child may be
If grace grows leaves and listening multiplies
And trees yield up their wordless therapy.

253 *The Season's Lovers*

In the daisied lap of summer
The lovers lay, they dozed
And lay in sun unending,
They lay in light, they slept
And only stirred
Each one to find the other's lips.
At times they sighed
Or spoke a word
That wavered on uneven breath,
He had no name and she forgot
The ransomed kingdom of her death.

When at last the sun went down
And chilly evening stained the fields,
The lovers rose and rubbed their eyes:
They saw the pale wash of grass
Heighten to metallic green
And spindly tongues of granite mauve
Lick up the milk of afternoon,
They gathered all the scattered light
Of daisies to one place of white,

MIRIAM WADDINGTON

And ghostly poets lent their speech
To the stillness of the air,
The lovers listened, each to each.

Into the solid wall of night
The lovers looked, their clearer sight
Went through that dark intensity
To the other side of light.
The lovers stood, it seemed to them
They hung upon the world's rim—
He clung to self, and she to him;
He rocked her with his body's hymn
And murmured to her shuddering cry,
You are all states, all princes I,
And sang against her trembling limbs,
Nothing else is, he sang, *but I.*

They lifted the transparent lid
From world false and world true
And in the space of both they flew.
He found a name, she lost her death,
And summer lulled them in its lap
With a leafy lullaby.
There they sleep unending sleep,
The lovers lie
He with a name, she free of death,
In a country hard to find
Unless you read love's double mind
Or invent its polar map.

b. 1917

254   *The Stenographers*

After the brief bivouac of Sunday,
their eyes, in the forced march of Monday to Saturday,
hoist the white flag, flutter in the snow storm of paper,
haul it down and crack in the midsun of temper.

In the pause between the first draft and the carbon
they glimpse the smooth hours when they were children—
the ride in the ice-cart, the ice-man's name,
the end of the route and the long walk home;

remember the sea where floats at high tide
were sea marrows growing on the scatter-green vine
or spools of grey toffee, or wasps' nests on water;
remember the sand and the leaves of the country.

Bell rings and they go and the voice draws their pencil
like a sled across snow; when its runners are frozen
rope snaps and the voice then is pulling no burden
but runs like a dog on the winter of paper.

Their climates are winter and summer—no wind
for the kites of their hearts—no wind for a flight;
a breeze at the most, to tumble them over
and leave them like rubbish—the boy-friends of blood.

In the inch of the noon as they move they are stagnant.
The terrible calm of the noon is their anguish;
the lip of the counter, the shapes of the straws
like icicles breaking their tongues are invaders.

Their beds are their oceans—salt water of weeping
the waves that they know—the tide before sleep;
and fighting to drown they assemble their sheep
in columns and watch them leap desks for their fences
and stare at them with their own mirror-worn faces.

In the felt of the morning the calico minded,
sufficiently starched, insert papers, hit keys,
efficient and sure as their adding machines;
yet they weep in the vault, they are taut as net curtains
stretched upon frames. In their eyes I have seen
the pin men of madness in marathon trim
race round the track of the stadium pupil.

255   *Adolescence*

In love they wore themselves in a green embrace.
A silken rain fell through the spring upon them.
In the park she fed the swans and he
whittled nervously with his strange hands.
And white was mixed with all their colours
as if they drew it from the flowering trees.

At night his two-finger whistle brought her down
the waterfall stairs to his shy smile
which, like an eddy, turned her round and round
lazily and slowly so her will
was nowhere—as in dreams things are and aren't.

Walking along the avenues in the dark
street lamps sang like sopranos in their heads

with a violence they never understood
and all their movements when they were together
had no conclusion.

Only leaning into the question had they motion:
after they parted were savage and swift as gulls.
Asking and asking the hostile emptiness
they were as sharp as partly sculptured stone
and all who watched, forgetting, were amazed
to see them form and fade before their eyes.

256   *Stories of Snow*

Those in the vegetable rain retain
an area behind their sprouting eyes
held soft and rounded with the dream of snow
precious and reminiscent as those globes—
souvenir of some never nether land—
which hold their snow storms circular, complete,
high in a tall and teakwood cabinet.

In countries where the leaves are large as hands
where flowers protrude their fleshy chins
and call their colours
an imaginary snow storm sometimes falls
among the lilies.
And in the early morning one will waken
to think the glowing linen of his pillow
a northern drift, will find himself mistaken
and lie back weeping.

P. K. PAGE

And there the story shifts from head to head,
of how, in Holland, from their feather beds
hunters arise and part the flakes and go
forth to the frozen lakes in search of swans—
the snow light falling white along their guns,
their breath in plumes.
While tethered in the wind like sleeping gulls
ice boats wait the raising of their wings
to skim the electric ice at such a speed
they leap the jet strips of the naked water,
and how these flying, sailing hunters feel
air in their mouths as terrible as ether.
And on the story runs that even drinks
in that white landscape dare to be no colour;
how, flasked and water clear, the liquor slips
silver against the hunters' moving hips.

And of the swan in death these dreamers tell
of its last flight and how it falls, a plummet,
pierced by the freezing bullet
and how three feathers, loosened by the shot,
descend like snow upon it.
While hunters plunge their fingers in its down
deep as a drift, and dive their hands
up to the neck of the wrist
in that warm metamorphosis of snow
as gentle as the sort that woodsmen know
who, lost in the white circle, fall at last
and dream their way to death.

And stories of this kind are often told
in countries where great flowers bar the roads
with reds and blues which seal the route to snow—

as if, in telling, raconteurs unlock
the colour with its complement and go
through to the area behind the eyes
where silent, unrefractive whiteness lies.

257 *Man with One Small Hand*

One hand is smaller than the other. It
must always be loved a little like a child;
requires attention constantly, implies
it needs his frequent glance to nurture it.

He holds it sometimes with the larger one
as adults lead a child across a street.
Finding it his and suddenly alien
rallies his interest and his sympathy.

Sometimes you come upon him unawares
just quietly staring at it where it lies
as mute and somehow perfect as a flower.

But no. It is not perfect. He admits
it has its faults: it is not strong or quick.
At night it vanishes to reappear
in dreams full-size, lost or surrealist.

Yet has its place like memory or a dog—
is never completely out of mind—a rod
to measure all uncertainties against.

Perhaps he loves it too much, sets too much stock
simply in its existence. Ah, but look!
It has its magic. See how it will fit
so sweetly, sweetly in the infant's glove.

T–Bar

Relentless, black on white, the cable runs
through metal arches up the mountainside.
At intervals giant pickaxes are hung
on long hydraulic springs. The skiers ride
propped by the axehead, twin automatons
supported by its handle, one each side.

In twos they move slow motion up the steep
incision in the mountain. Climb. Climb.
Somnambulists, bolt upright in their sleep
their phantom poles swing lazily behind,
while to the right, the empty T-bars keep
in mute descent, slow monstrous jigging time.

Captive the skiers now and innocent,
wards of eternity, each pair alone.
They mount the easy vertical ascent,
pass through successive arches, bride and groom,
as through successive naves, are newly wed
participants in some recurring dream.

So do they move forever. Clocks are broken.
In zones of silence they grow tall and slow,
inanimate dreamers, mild and gentle-spoken,
blood brothers of the haemophilic snow
until the summit breaks and they awaken
imagos from the stricture of the tow.

Jerked from her chrysalis the sleeping bride
suffers too sudden freedom like a pain.
The dreaming bridegroom severed from her side
singles her out, the old wound aches again.
Uncertain, lost, upon a wintry height
these two not separate yet no longer one.

But clocks begin to peck and sing. The slow
extended minute like a rubber band
snaps back to nothing and the skiers go
quickly articulate, while far behind
etching the sky-line, obdurate and slow
the spastic T-bars pivot and descend.

259 *Arras*

Consider a new habit—classical,
and trees espaliered on the wall like candelabra.
How still upon that lawn our sandalled feet.

But a peacock rattling its rattan tail and screaming
has found a point of entry. Through whose eye
did it insinuate in furled disguise
to shake its jewels and silk upon that grass?

The peaches hang like lanterns. No one joins
those figures on the arras.

352

P. K. PAGE

                    Who am I
or who am I become that walking here
I am observer, other, Gemini,
starred for a green garden of cinema?

I ask, what did they deal me in this pack?
The cards, all suits, are royal when I look.
My fingers slipping on a monarch's face
twitch and go slack.
I want a hand to clutch, a heart to crack.

No one is moving now, the stillness is
infinite. If I should make a break. . . .
take to my springy heels . . .? But nothing moves.
The spinning world is stuck upon its poles,
the stillness points a bone at me. I fear
the future on this arras.
                    I confess:
It was my eye.
Voluptuous it came.
Its head the ferrule and its lovely tail
folded so sweetly; it was strangely slim
to fit the retina. And then it shook
and was a peacock—living patina,
eye-bright—maculate!
Does no one care?

I thought their hands might hold me if I spoke.
I dreamed the bite of fingers in my flesh,
their poke smashed by an image, but they stand
as if within a treacle, motionless,
folding slow eyes on nothing. While they stare
another line has trolled the encircling air,
another bird assumes its furled disguise.

b. 1918

260 *The Butterfly*

An uproar,
a spruce-green sky, bound in iron,
the murky sea running a sulphur scum,
I saw a butterfly, suddenly.
It clung between the ribs of the storm, wavering,
and flung against the battering bone-wind.
I remember it, glued to the grit of that rain-strewn beach
that glowered around it, swallowed its startled design
in the larger iridescence of unstrung dark.

That wild, sour air, those miles of crouching forest, that moth
when all enveloping space
is a thin glass globe, swirling with storm
tempt us to stare, and seize analogies.
The Voice that stilled the sea of Galilee
overtoned by the new peace, the fierce subhuman peace
of such an east sky, blanched like Eternity.

The meaning of the moth, even the smashed moth, the
meaning of the moth—
can't we stab that one angle into the curve of space
that sweeps so unrelenting, far above,
towards the subhuman swamp of under-dark?

261 *Watershed*

The world doesn't crumble apart.
The general, and rewarding, illusion
Prevents it. You know what you know in your heart
But there is no traffic in that direction,

354

Only acres of stained quicksand,
         Stained by the sun
That lingers still at a Muscovite level, ignoring
The clocks in the wrists and the temples, and up in the towers
That you see as you walk, assuming the earth your floor
Though you know in your heart that the foothold really is
         gone.

(I saw you come out of the painted grove, my buck,
With the bruise of leaf-wet under your eyes,
         In a shy terrible blaze.
   The painted grove, hung stiffly with cold wax
   And fading pigments, issued you complete
And tissued them in myriad light-spots, swivelling
Into sheerest space. It was bright and spacious and neat
With everything moving, pricking from points of clear
         Day-bourne.)

There is a change in the air:
The rain and the dark and the bare
Bunched trees, in pewter fresco, square
From the window. Yes, and you know
In your heart what chill winds blow.
And the clocks in the temples, in all the towers, sound on
(Quarter, and half), and the gutters flow, and the sour
Rain pastes the leather-black streets with large pale leaves.

262 *Stray Dog, near Écully,*
Valley of the Rhône

The dog called Sesamë slewed out
   Under the Norman arch, open
For the gardener's walked bicycle. No doubt
   On some wild leash still, in three-legged loping

He circles the grey stone and barley fringe
   Of the Roman amphitheatre, canting
To miss the guide, the stopped sun, the mélange
   Of Rome's new coin-conducted legion. Panting

He sloughs all touring finally in the shade
   Of a wild apricot-tree, not glancing up.
Fire-points in his sad eyes fix on the fading
   Campagna ghost. A Rouault hoop,

The limited landscape wobbles down
   Its sandy track of planetary time.
Back in the courtyard, through the hills around
   Deployed, they search, shouting 'Sey-sahm, Sey-sahm'.

263 *Perspective*

   A sport, an adventitious sprout
   These eyeballs, that have somehow slipped
   The mesh of generations since Mantegna?

   Yet I declare, your seeing is diseased
   That cripples space. The fear has eaten back
   Through sockets to the caverns of the brain
      And made of it a sifty habitation.

356

We stand beholding the one plain
And in your face I see the chastening
Of its small tapering design
That brings up *punkt*.
    (The Infinite, you say,
      Is an unthinkable—and pointless too—
        Extension of that *punkt*.)

But do you miss the impact of that fierce
Raw boulder five miles off? You are not pierced
By that great spear of grass on the horizon?
    You are not smitten with the shock
      Of that great thundering sky?

Your law of optics is a quarrel
Of chickenfeet on paper. Does a train
Run pigeon-toed?

I took a train from here to Ottawa
On tracks that did not meet. We swelled and roared
Mile upon mightier mile, and when we clanged
Into the vasty station we were indeed
Brave company for giants.

    Keep your eyes though,
You, and not I, will travel safer back
               To Union station.
Your fear has me infected, and my eyes
That were my sport so long, will soon be apt
Like yours to press out dwindling vistas from
The massive flux massive Mantegna knew
And all its sturdy everlasting foregrounds.

357

New Year's Poem

The Christmas twigs crispen and needles rattle
Along the windowledge.
               A solitary pearl
Shed from the necklace spilled at last week's party
Lies in the suety, snow-luminous plainness
Of morning, on the windowledge beside them.
And all the furniture that circled stately
And hospitable when these rooms were brimmed
With perfumes, furs, and black-and-silver
Crisscross of seasonal conversation, lapses
Into its previous largeness.
                  I remember
Anne's rose-sweet gravity, and the stiff grave
Where cold so little can contain;
I mark the queer delightful skull and crossbones
Starlings and sparrows left, taking the crust,
And the long loop of winter wind
Smoothing its arc from dark Arcturus
To the bricked corner of the drifted courtyard,
And the still windowledge.
              Gentle and just pleasure
It is, being human, to have won from space
This unchill, habitable interior
Which mirrors quietly the light
Of the snow, and the new year.

265   *Meeting Together of Poles &*
            Latitudes: in Prospect

Those who fling off, toss head,
   Taste the bitter morning, and have at it—
   Thresh, knead, dam, weld,
   Wave baton, force
   Marches through squirming bogs,
   Not from contempt, but
   From thrust, unslakeably thirsty,
   Amorous of every tower and twig, and
   Yet like railroad engines with
   Longings for their landscapes (pistons pounding)
   Rock fulminating through
   Wrecked love, unslakeably loving—
   Seldom encounter at the Judgement Seat
Those who are flung off, sit
   Dazed awhile, gather concentration,
   Follow vapour-trails with shrivelling wonder,
   Pilfer, mow, play jongleur
   With mathematic signs, or
   Tracing the forced marches make
   Peculiar cats-cradles of telephone wire,
   Lap absently at sundown, love
   As the stray dog on foreign hills
   A bone-myth, atavistically,
   Needing more faith, and fewer miles, but
   Slumber-troubled by it,
   Wanting for death that
   Myth-clay, though
   Scratch-happy in these (foreign) brambly wilds;
But when they approach each other
   The place is an astonishment:

MARGARET AVISON

Runways shudder with little planes
Practising folk-dance steps or
Playing hornet,
Sky makes its ample ruling
Clear as a primary child's exercise-book
In somebody else's language,
And the rivers under the earth
Foam without whiteness, domed down,
As they foam indifferently every
Day and night (if you'd call that day and night)
Not knowing how they wait, at the node, the
Curious encounter.

LOUIS DUDEK

b. 1918

266   *A Street in April*

Look now, at this February street in April
where not a flower blossoms, or if one broke
would be like water from a blister, a yellow poke,
new bird lime on a rail, or jet from a yolk.

Neither the fire-escapes making musical patterns
nor the filigree of stone flowery and decorating
can now accompany young April; the iron grating
jars, someone dropped a kettle in the orchestrating.

There a pale head rising from an eyeless cavern
swivels twice above the street, and swiftly dips
back into the gloom of the skull, whose only lips
are the swinging tin plate and the canvas strips.

And here are infants too, in cribs, with wondrous eyes
at windows, the curtains raised upon a gasping room,
angelic in white diapers and bibs, to whom
the possibilities in wheels and weather—bloom.

But I have seen a dove gleaming and vocal with peace
fly over them, when his sudden wings stirred
and cast the trembling shadow of a metal bird;
so April's without flower, and no song heard.

267   *An Air by Sammartini*

It was something you did not know
            had existed—by a dead Italian.
Neither words nor a shape of flesh
            but of air;
                whose love it celebrated
                and 'cold passion'
Amoroso Canto, a crystal
            that fell from musical fingers—
As a cloud comes into the eye's arena,
            a certain new tree
                where the road turns,
            or love, or a child, is born,
                or death comes:
Whatever is found or is done
            that cannot be lost or changed.

LOUIS DUDEK

The Pomegranate

The jewelled mine of the pomegranate, whose hexagons of
    honey
The mouth would soon devour but the eyes eat like a poem,
Lay hidden long in its hide, a diamond of dark cells
Nourished by tiny streams which crystallized into gems.

The seeds, nescient of the world outside, or of passionate
    teeth,
Prepared their passage into light and air, while tender roots
And branches dreaming in the cell-walled hearts of plants
Made silent motions such as recreate both men and fruits.

There, in a place of no light, shone that reddest blood,
And without a word of order, marshalled those grenadiers:
Gleaming without a sun—what art where no eyes were!—
Till, broken by my hand, this palace of unbroken tears.

To wedding bells and horns howling down an alley,
Muffled, the married pair in closed caravan ride;
And then, the woman grown in secret, shining white,
Unclothed, mouth to mouth he holds his naked bride.

And there are days, golden days, when the world starts
    to life,
When streets in the sun, boys, and battlefields of cars,
The colours on a bannister, the vendors' slanting stands
Send the pulse pounding on like the bursting of meteors—

As now, the fruit glistens with a mighty grin,
Conquers the room; and, though in ruin, to its death
Laughs at the light that wounds it, wonderfully red,
So that its awful beauty stops the greedy breath.

And can this fact be made, so big, of the body, then?
And is beauty bounded all in its impatient mesh?
The movement of the stars is that, and all their light
Secretly bathed the world, that now flows out of flesh.

From *Europe*

269   *19*

The commotion of these waves, however strong, cannot
    disturb
    the compass-line of the horizon
nor the plumb-line of gravity, because this cross co-ordinates
    the tragic pulls of necessity
that chart the ideal endings, for waves, and storms
    and sunset winds:
the dead scattered on the stage in the fifth act—
Cordelia in Lear's arms, Ophelia, Juliet, all silent—
show nature restored to order and just measure.
    The horizon is perfect,
and nothing can be stricter
than gravity; in relation to these
    the stage is rocked and tossed,
kings fall with their crowns, poets sink with their laurels.

270   *95*

        The sea retains such images
            in her ever-unchanging waves;
        for all her infinite variety, and the forms,
        inexhaustible, of her loves,

LOUIS DUDEK

she is constant always in beauty,
    which to us need be nothing more
      than a harmony with the wave on which we move.
All ugliness is a distortion
of the lovely lines and curves
    which sincerity makes out of hands
      and bodies moving in air.
Beauty is ordered in nature
    as the wind and sea
  shape each other for pleasure; as the just
  know, who learn of happiness
    from the report of their own actions.

GILLES HÉNAULT

b. 1920

271   From *L'Invention de la roue*

Que j'entonne à ta gloire, ô cercle, forme pure,
Un chant qui soit l'écho du chant de la Nature!
Ta force virtuelle enfantera des lois,
Inondera la terre et mon être et ma voix
Ne seront que délire au seuil embryonnaire
D'un mirage devant mon œil visionnaire!
Pareils aux vents de mer pleins d'éclairs et de sel
Me poussent mes espoirs vers l'astre universel.
J'écoute en moi chanter le tourbillon des sphères!
Pensée! astre nouvel et qui me régénère
Voici que, dédaignant ma vie, enfin, je tends
Au delà de mon être entier vers toi! j'entends
Ton prophétique chant: ô puissance, puissance!
Envahir ma cervelle et combler le silence!

364

GILLES HÉNAULT

Nulle étoile du Nord au monde sidéral
Ne remarquera ma route, ô penser idéal,
Que toi! je vais créer l'avenir chimérique
A l'image de mon désir géométrique.
Verse-moi la science, ô rayon, comme une eau
Qui ravivant mon front, me tire du tombeau;
Que je me lève enfin pour dompter la nature
Et bâtir de mes mains cette Cité future
Où, courbe, s'inscrirait la marque du compas.
Qui parle d'ignorance et parle de trépas?
Mon cerveau traversé de clartés irréelles
Croit au pouvoir sans fin des pensées immortelles
Et, posant des leviers sur ces points d'appui sûrs,
Je ferai chavirer l'Univers dans l'azur!
Au creux de cet espoir mon œil jette la sonde
Pour mesurer en moi le devenir du monde.
Dès sa source, le fleuve anticipe la mer,
Et la fleur sait le fruit, savoureux ou amer,
Qui la prolongera dans le temps et l'espace.

.   .   .

Rien n'est plus que toi seul, astre de plénitude!
Rien n'est plus que toi seul, astre de certitude!
S'il nous faut dériver pour combler notre sort,
S'il nous faut louvoyer pour atteindre le port,
Nous roulerons quand même aux confins du mystère,
Nous voguerons quand même et crierons: terre! terre!
En voyant reparaître en notre humanité
Le paradis perdu de notre liberté.
Désancrons, pour courir les hautes aventures
Sur des mers reflétant de nouvelles natures;
Entends, ô mon ami, l'appel lointain des flots
Répondant à l'appel plus lointain des sanglots
Qui scandent dans ton cœur, jeune et déjà trop sage,

Le désir infini d'un infini voyage.
Contemple encor la mer en sa mobilité,
Et voit comme persiste et meurt sa volonté
Dans le strict retour de sa vague marine.
Ose à présent douter de ta force divine.
Liant et déliant son élan vers l'azur,
La mer, comme l'esprit, se ruant au futur,
Par les temps de marée et par les soirs d'orage
Veut abolir du ciel l'indestructible image.
Elle clame à la lune un secret souverain.
La lune ! nous l'aurons à nous, pauvres marins,
Nous l'aurons dans nos cœurs, dans nos bras, dans nos âmes
Et nous la bercerons à la plainte des lames.
Qui ne veut pas la lune est-il mort ou vivant ? . . .

272 *Je te salue*

I

Peaux-Rouges
Peuplades disparues
dans la conflagration de l'eau-de-feu et des tuberculoses
Traquées par la pâleur de la mort et des Visages-Pâles
Emportant vos rêves de mânes et de manitou
Vos rêves éclatés au feu des arquebuses
Vous nous avez légué vos espoirs totémiques
Et notre ciel a maintenant la couleur
des fumées de vos calumets de paix.

II

Nous sommes sans limites
Et l'abondance est notre mère.
Pays ceinturé d'acier

366

GILLES HÉNAULT

Aux grands yeux de lacs
A la bruissante barbe résineuse
Je te salue et je salue ton rire de chutes.
Pays casqué de glaces polaires
Auréolé d'aurores boréales
Et tendant aux générations futures
L'étincelante gerbe de tes feux d'uranium.
Nous lançons contre ceux qui te pillent et t'épuisent
Contre ceux que parasitent sur ton grand corps d'humus et
     de neige
Les imprécations foudroyantes
Qui naissent aux gorges des orages.

III

J'entends déjà le chant de ceux qui chantent:

Je te salue la vie pleine de grâces
le semeur est avec toi
tu es bénie par toutes les femmes
et l'enfant fou de sa trouvaille
te tient dans sa main
comme le caillou multicolore de la réalité.

Belle vie, mère de nos yeux
vêtue de pluie et de beau temps
que ton règne arrive
sur les routes et sur les champs
Belle vie
Vivent l'amour et le printemps.

Petite Genèse apocryphe

À ROLAND GIGUÈRE

I

Adam et Ève
ne sont que mirages
aux sources du temps.

II

Ève à dents
virginales
Ève et Adam
découvrent le pollen.
Adam et Ève à lèvres virginales
plantent l'arbre de la race humaine.

III

Femme acéphale
Fertile Vénus
Où l'homme prend racine
Seins, ventre, vagin
Cycle d'amour et d'argile
Femme, moitié d'ombre
Les deux pieds dans la terre
Et les bras au ciel
Tu es l'horizon de notre enfance
Et tu flambes au soleil
De notre amour charnel.

IV

Une vie sacrifiée
au plus haut de sa tige

GILLES HÉNAULT

Un bel arbre de vie émondé
Penche les fruits de ses mamelles
Vers les toujours croissantes générations
Pour que son esclavage
Fasse aux survivants
Une belle ombre calme.

v

Un Éden d'arbres à pain et de temps perdu
Se mêlait au sable
Les étoiles prises au filet
Jouaient aux feux-follets
C'était au temps de l'amour sans épines
De la jeunesse en fleurs
De la femme sans fard
Et de l'homme sans mémoire.

vi

Ce jour-là
Dieu se montra dans toute sa splendeur:
En robe violette
avec des boutons blancs
la barbe passée au bleu
et les cheveux ondulés en éclairs
Il alluma un chandelier à sept branches
et la lumière fut!
Adam à cheval sur l'horizon
Entre les océans du Bien et du Mal
Attendait le signal de plonger.
Satan faisait la sieste
Sur la plage du temps.

VII

Le cheval inventait sa race
de crinières et de galops
Il inventait le rythme et le saut
Mais déjà il rêvait de racines étrangères
De fouets, de labours et de guerre
Car l'homme . . .
Avait mangé la pomme.

VIII

Dieu mit son habit de gendarme
Son képi à trois galons
Au fourreau mit sa rapière
Sous sa tunique son cœur de pierre
Et s'achemina vers la terre
Suivi de l'archange, son adjudant
Le père allait châtier ses enfants
A cause d'une pomme sure
Qu'Adam avait mangée
Dieu protégeait son verger
Car s'il a de l'amour
pour ses enfants, les hommes
Il aime encore bien mieux
La confiture aux pommes.

IX

Puis nous avons connu
Des jours de bêtes féroces
Nous avons combattu
Des monstres presque humains
Nous avons inventé
L'éclatante raison

GILLES HÉNAULT

Nous avons découvert
Le coq et sa chanson
Nous avons chevauché
L'auroch et le bison
Nous avons allumé
le feu de l'espérance
au plus profond de nos cœurs.
Et un beau matin, le soleil s'est levé
au chant du coq !

X

L'homme a quitté la nuit de la préhistoire
L'âge de pierre et de cloportes
A l'entrée de la caverne
Il a planté le totem de son destin
Les chameaux ont inventé la caravane
Et l'homme a connu les mirages
d'âge en âge
Dans un désert de soif et de sable
et de désirs insatiables.

XI

Pourtant les oasis
mirent un avenir de palmes
dans le ciel intérieur de chaque homme
qui voit dans les hommes des frères
et dans la paix, l'eau qui désaltère.

XII

Totem ton ombre
décline à midi
La terre balance

ses flancs d'abondance
Les fleuves se bercent
au creux de leur lit
Les moissons se pâment
quand le vent les peigne
L'enfant ouvre des yeux
grands comme des mains
Il commence le jeu
d'aimer l'amour, la vie, le pain
Et la rose des vents
annonce du beau temps.

RAYMOND SOUSTER

b. 1921

274   *Search*

Not another bite, not another cigarette,
Nor a final coffee from the shining coffee-urn before you
    leave
The warmth steaming at the windows of the hamburger-joint
    where the Wurlitzer
Booms all night without a stop, where the onions are thick
    between the buns.
Wrap yourself well in that cheap coat that holds back the
    wind like a sieve,
You have a long way to go, and the streets are dark, you may
    have to walk all night before you find
Another heart as lonely, so nearly mad with boredom, so
    filled with such strength, such tenderness of love.

275   *The Man who Finds that his Son*
has Become a Thief

Coming into the store at first angry
At the accusation, believing in
The word of his boy who has told him:
I didn't steal anything, honest.

Then becoming calmer, seeing that anger
Will not help in the business, listening painfully
As the other's evidence unfolds, so painfully slow.

Then seeing gradually that evidence
Almost as if tighten slowly around the neck
Of his son, at first vaguely circumstantial, then gathering
    damage,
Until there is present the unmistakable odour of guilt
Which seeps now into the mind and lays its poison.

Suddenly feeling sick and alone and afraid,
As if an unseen hand had slapped him in the face
For no reason whatsoever: wanting to get out
Into the street, the night, the darkness, anywhere to hide
The pain that must show in the face to these strangers, the
    fear.

It must be like this.
It could hardly be otherwise.

276 *Not Wholly Lost*

John warns me of nostalgia
And I suppose he's right—but what the hell—
What are poems for but for celebration
Of our time on the earth the years behind us
And ahead? And I for one will leave
The future to others and plunge back gladly
Into the mist of old ghosts and places
Where these appear—

                              scarlet flame of Dosco's
Open hearth behind the jail, stench of the coke-ovens,
Poverty naked as the Newfie girl under the cheap dress
That November. Smell of fish and ocean
At the North Sydney piers. Lobsters on the half-shell
In Cormier's, the movie where a hundred was a crowd. And
    on from Shediac
The warm sands, blue waters of the Point; summer that
    seemed over
Before it had begun, and our youth with it, for that year
    anyway: but there was another year
And another summer (thank God there was always another).
    Remember, we never found any clams
But drank that bottle of rum sitting on the shell-heavy sand
    of Batouche
And came back hungry to camp

                              O what better days were
        there
Than mornings on the Bournemouth cliffs, blue above and
    blue below, each outshining
The other. Or nights walking Yorkshire roads, great trees on
    either side, good smell
Of hay in the fields.

    374

We would never do the things now
We did then, we've grown older, too serious; and what we
    did
For the plain simple hell of it we will not do now or in any
    other year. But we did them once,
Those things are not wholly lost; they linger in the heart, in
    the mind,
And nothing can take them from us or change them
Unless it is death.

277   *The Collector*

What she collects is men
As a bee honey, leaving out
The subtlety of that swift winger. There's little
In the way her eyes look into theirs (O take me)
Her body arches forward (possess me *now*).

At her age (other women say)
It's ridiculous: but how much envy
Mixes with fact? They will say: none,
But we know better, watching their faces. Still, admit
What she collects, finally, is pain.

278   *Ties*

New ties, fifteen each, ten
For a dollar (he said),
Holding them up in bunches of I suppose
Five each for us to see: and they did look new,
Like good ties, cheap at double the price.

375

But we didn't buy any; I because I had only
A dime left for a beer, the others—well,
They'd been stung too many times before, bargains
Not bargains, something like that. It's the same
As marriage or joining the army
They might have said, joking, but not really joking
As much as telling a fact, the essential fact
Of their lives: nothing wonderful, nothing in their favour
Liable ever to happen; life like these ties
Passed round in front of us, difficult to judge, uncertain, open
To the greatest suspicion, a jungle of dark-twisting lies.

E. W. MANDEL

b. 1922

Minotaur Poems

279   I

It has been hours in these rooms,
the opening to which, door or sash,
I have lost. I have gone from room to room
asking the janitors who were sweeping up
the brains that lay on the floors,
the bones shining in the wastebaskets,
and once I asked a suit of clothes
that collapsed at my breath and bundled
and crawled on the floor like a coward.
Finally, after several stories,
in the staired and eyed hall,
I came upon a man with the face of a bull.

II

My father was always out in the garage
building a shining wing, a wing
that curved and flew along the edge of blue air
in that streamed and sunlit room
that smelled of oil and engines
and crankcase grease, and especially
the lemon smell of polish and cedar.
Outside there were sharp rocks, and trees,
cold air where birds fell like rocks
and screams, hawks, kites, and cranes.
The air was filled with a buzzing and flying
and the invisible hum of a bee's wings was honey
in my father's framed and engined mind.
Last Saturday we saw him at the horizon
screaming like a hawk as he fell into the sun.

VI

Orpheus

The Welshman by the pit whose Sabbath voice
Would set the week to peace, or end a day,
Picked over coal and said he knew within
The inside of our god, his transformation
Out of tree, the face in black, faced out of coal,
Stamped on the walls he picked. His useful metaphor,
He said, the pit shaped underneath him into black
And pitied words that moved the leaves or sang
Together flocks, or shook the dull and herded animals.
His pity also took between the rocks
Some still alive who saw the black and second

Hand that clawed them, and he mocked in Welsh
Whatever shades fell back, and cursed and sang
Back to their second death those grave ghosts.

Who found his body and who found his head
And who wiped god from off his eyes and face?

282   *The Fire Place*

A furnace is of stone and clay,
A fire burns inside the stone,
Beside the flame Fuseli lay,
The heart within it was his own.

Fuseli, when the witch came in,
Raised the roof above his stone,
On her thighs he painted sin,
On her head a horse's mane.

From her lips a vocal moth
Issued screaming to the smoke,
Augustan ladies in their mirth
Gathered folds about her smock.

In the smoking cup a sea,
By the bed a painted ship,
In the door a massive key,
On the floor an open trap.

Coupled with a horse a man
Leans upon her breast and sighs,
Flaming curtains issue then,
Thus between the witch's thighs.

E. W. MANDEL

Song

When the echo of the last footstep dies
and on the empty street you turn empty eyes
   what do you think that you will see?
    A hangman and a hanging tree.

   When there are no more voices
   and yet you hear voices singing
    in the hot street,
what do you think will be their song?
Glory to the hangman who is never wrong.

When on the hot sands of your burning mind
   the iron footsteps clang no more
   and blind eyes no longer see
    and hot voices end,
what do you think will be your plea?
   Hanging isn't good enough for me.

ELIZABETH BREWSTER

b. 1922

In the Library

I

Believe me, I say to the gentleman with the pince-nez,
Framed forever with one hand in his pocket,
With passion, with intensity I say it—
Believe me, oh believe me, you are not I.
Making my chair squeak on the chilly floor,
Catching up my pencil, I say—

But of course I am myself
And all the while time flows, time flows, time flows;
The minutes ripple over the varnished tables.
This is June, I say, not yesterday or tomorrow.
This is I, not Byron or Vanessa. I am not in the moon.
I must differentiate my body from all other bodies,
Realizing the mole on my neck, the scar on my hand.
I must wind my watch, say it is ten o'clock.
But I know I am not convinced, feel uneasily the lie.
Because actually I am Byron, I am Vanessa,
I am the pictured man with the frigid smile,
I am the girl at the next table, raising vague eyes,
Flicking the ash from her cigarette, the thoughts from her
    mind.
The elastic moment stretches to infinity,
The elastic moment, the elastic point of space.
The blessed sun becomes the blessed moon.

II

Alone in the public room, listening to retreating footsteps,
Listening to a whistle and a scrap of song,
I who must always tiptoe over floors,
Stand with raised hand and thudding heart outside doorways,
Linger embarrassed in the corridors of life,
Apologizing, back out of rooms like an intruder—
I, who listen too nervously to the epoch-shattering stroke of
    the clock—
I would imitate if I could the staccato, assured footsteps,
The whistle unconscious of fear, scornful of time.
But is it worth it? I ask, is it worth it?
And think more respectfully of the fox's sincerity.

b. 1923

285   *Exequy*

TO PETER ALLT

non ci,
non là.

Departed friend, I do not come
With requiem or any glum
Taxidermy of public tears
Wherein the quick grace disappears
Of delicate cell, precarious blood,
That, fearsome now, become the food
Of creatures lower yet than I,
They only thrive when friends must die;
Strange sacrament! beneath the ground
Enacted, out of sight and sound
Of the first rites of priest and choir,
Of minute bell and candle fire.
Still less, my friend, do I upbraid
Our deadly case; when all is said
How could one love what cannot die?
And God (we read) this pain did try
Who, since beloved as man, before
Was feared in whirlwinds and the roar
Of seas on Asia Minor's shore.
I come, not with an impudent claim
To snatch from time a mortal name
Or grave it in a lasting brass
Of verse to outlive men—alas,
Poems are less immortal than
The slender spirit of a man—

But to pronounce my last goodbye.
The birde has flowne. And so you fly
Into the wind of death, and there
We'll follow in our own good year.

NORMAN LEVINE

b. 1924

286   *Crabbing*

TO W. S. GRAHAM

Timbers heaving to heaven we sailed at seven
With bait aboard wet so sliced for smell.
Gurnards stinking guts cut and skewered.
And our faces still fresh from the bundled bed.
We sailed alone and silent in the light of morning
From harbour shelter and a three sided bell.
Saw the wind yawn to stretch skin over water
Cough the white gossip, clot, into silence.
Sun over water. Sea sick with colour.

And hungry the gull with her turrow, turrow,
Gathered an escort of gliding white hulls.
Cherry splashed beaks plunged heads into water
Slitbeak smiles spread morning's laughter
They and the rudder looked for our marker
And by all the braille signs we found the stall.
There we circled, staring at landscape, waiting
For the tide to be well and truly in. Now sea, domestic
Broke skin for marker, and there, the flagstick, rose.

NORMAN LEVINE

We stood by the wheelhouse where spray was spitting
And lifted the black sheath on to the mizzen
Cupped up to heaven, steady for direction,
We cut the engine and steered with sail.
Soon the blue fullness laid out its carpet
In continual cadence of floor, wall, floor.
Silently we came forward, now weaving, now sliding
Slow as a boxer with hands cautious in rhythm
Pulling a rope's strength and wetness aboard.

And while we were heaving, now to horizon,
The winch kept turning as a potter's wheel:
Rope swung dripping, ourselves waiting. What lodger
Within prison wire turned chimney inside?
The first cage broke angry out of its grievance.
Craw, Craw, was shouted in simple alphabet.
(A Craw for a Crayfish, a Blue for a Lobster.)
Words of children, all sound and colour
Formed a sweated sentence with a hardworked verb.

After the first the others filled spaces:
Of Craw empty, Blue empty, and sometimes Crab.
Nervous jewels of colour, now covered, now hidden
As cage changed to parlour and prepared to receive
The new bait, now hanging, so silent by chimney.
And still in that rhythm the pots went over
Side to foam pulling, depth, under bubbles
Stretching ropes, straightened, behind us, dove.
And there we left them for tomorrow's tide.

Returning we let rudder find fast its direction
And running as a hurdler we rose, up, and over
Oak ribs to water keeled back those tons.
Shuddering we shot on, sometimes to heaven.

And land goes with us walking
In shapes the shadows formed. Where stone pierced bone
The earth made windows. Who watched our homecoming.

PIERRE TROTTIER

b. 1925

287   *Femme aux couleurs de mon pays*

Femme aux couleurs de mon pays
Voici qu'un peuple entier me porte
Sur les épaules de ses vagues
Et me remplit le cœur à déferler
D'amour d'un océan à l'autre

Ne vas pas replier sur toi-même les ailes
De ce château que tu habites que tu laisses
Envahir par la brousse et les ronces rebelles
Rebelles trop à mes caresses jardinières

Ne me refuse pas d'entendre ce poème
Que fait le vent d'automne aux flancs de tes montagnes
En vers émerveillants de couleurs et de chutes
De feuilles que j'emprunte aux vignes de tes murs
De feuilles dont tes pas redoutent la douceur

Reconnais-les de ton château de mon pays
Et ne crains point d'y perdre tes propres couleurs
N'impose plus à mes forêts
La pénible morsure d'une patience
Aux dents de jour aux dents de nuit qui rongent
Les arbrisseaux des heures virginales
Pour les abattre une à une aux rives du temps

PIERRE TROTTIER

Femme aux couleurs de mon pays
Ne vois-tu pas mes castors qui s'acharnent
A défaire les mailles des saisons
En opposant des digues à l'hiver
Pour retenir les larmes de ces lacs si beaux
Que pleure mon amour sur toi sur mon pays

Ne sens-tu pas des Laurentides aux Rocheuses
Les doigts du vent viril avides de peigner
Tes longs cheveux de blé au front de tes prairies

N'entends-tu pas venir la vaste chevauchée
Des nuages bruyants que l'amour éperonne
Avant d'éclabousser les chairs les plus fertiles
En piétinant ton ciel de sabots de tonnerre

Ne sens-tu pas aux bords du Saint-Laurent
Les amères marées d'un grand fleuve amoureux
Et qui pourtant coule d'une eau si douce
Au cœur des villes intérieures

Pourquoi donc demander aux pêcheurs de la côte
D'étendre sur tes villes leurs filets de brumes
Où ne se prennent que les poissons de ta crainte
Ta crainte qui vacille à tous les réverbères

Femme aux couleurs de mon pays
Ta chevelure écume sur des vagues
De religions de langues différentes
Ta chevelure écume en boucles
Où se trouve captive
L'étoile de mer de ma main
Qui ne parvient pas à les démêler

Dans tous ces vents contradictoires
Qui te font peur d'être une dans l'amour

Et je me perds en vous femme patrie
Tant que je ne distingue plus
Dans les brumes de vos parfums
Laquelle j'aime le plus en l'autre

Ah dites-moi répondez-moi
                                    De quel poème
Obtiendrai-je le Sésame-ouvrez-vous des brumes
De quel poème à fleur de chair à fleur de champs
Ferai-je éclater les épis de vos cœurs
Aux moissons de l'amour aux moissons de la terre

288   *Adam*

I

Jeunesse réjouie au temps d'avant le sexe
Jeunesse au corps de femme détaché de moi
A quel autel de Dieu monterai-je vers toi

Je gravis seul les marches des corps innombrables
Que fauche la mitraille impitoyable du péché
Ou qui se noient dans l'immense flaque du vice

Je gravis triste et seul cet escalier de chair
Et seul debout j'indique par mon ombre l'heure
Au soleil aujourd'hui que je n'ai plus en moi
Car mon cœur ne bat plus que dans le beffroi vide
D'une église interdite aux cloches envolées

Perdu dans les égouts d'un temps trop mécanique
J'ai nostalgie de toi originelle terre
Et du souffle premier qui gonfla tes poumons
J'ai nostalgie du sang d'une mère sans âge
Dont je voudrais que les veines me guident
A l'ombilic étincelant du premier jour

Plonge scaphandrier aux profondeurs du temps
Archéologue fouille aux ruines de l'Éden
Et toi mémoire cours en estafette
Jusqu'au songe parfait où je rendors en moi
La femme et le miroir qui refléta ma faute

II

Ô songe
En toi mon âme et mon regard intemporels
Embrassent plus que les rives du Styx
Ô songe
En toi commence la forêt où seul
A pas feutrés j'avance à la file indienne
Qui me répète à l'infini dans l'innocence

Je me repose en la Pensée complète

J'ouvre la Terre comme un dictionnaire
Où chaque fleur dans son parfum porte son nom
Où chaque fruit dans sa saveur porte le sien
Si bien inscrits qu'en un seul souffle tout est dit

Il règne une parole inutile à transcrire
L'âme pour converser prend la couleur du temps
Et le sexe s'ignore dans son monologue

PIERRE TROTTIER

Qui donc ici voudrait penser quand tout se pense
Sur la terre le ciel promène un doigt de lune
Que l'homme enfant susurre entre ses dents d'étoiles
Un doigt de lune au fond du verre de la nuit
Que je renverse et vide au fond de mon cœur d'aube

Dans le matin une femme se lève
Et trouble de son ombre mon réveil

Est-elle femme ou nuit cette ombre que je bois
A la cuiller du jour qui m'assoiffe de l'autre
En creusant à mon flanc le grand remous du sexe
Où se brouille en moi-même l'image de Dieu

Ô chair unique en toi je souffre division
Au delta de l'histoire qui par moi commence

III

N'entends-tu pas penser tout haut la lune chauve
A mon soleil qui prie agenouillé tout bas
Dans l'aube ou dans le crépuscule

Est-ce une vaine joie qu'il a brûlée
A l'heure adulte de midi
Ou n'est-il à genoux que pour subir
Dans la forêt l'épreuve des sentiers étroits
Où bifurque le sexe
                                à jamais
                                        divisé

A quel autel de Dieu monterai-je vers toi
Jeunesse réjouie au temps d'avant le sexe
Jeunesse au corps de femme détaché de moi

289 *A la claire fontaine*

Laisse-moi t'emmener à la claire fontaine
Laisse-moi te chanter des chansons anciennes

Il y a longtemps que je t'aime
Et jamais je ne t'oublierai

Laisse-moi consoler ton peuple-cendrillon
Puisqu'il ne peut pas oublier son prince
Et que ses souvenirs sont les mauvais brouillons
D'un rêve qui s'égare et d'un espoir trop mince

Il y a longtemps que je t'aime
Et jamais je ne t'oublierai

Laisse-moi consoler tes pauvres écoliers
Qui n'ont jamais gagné que des prix de mémoire
Et qui du temps se sentent prisonniers
Quand il faut prendre place dans l'histoire

Il y a longtemps que je t'aime
Et jamais je ne t'oublierai

Laisse-moi te chanter des chansons anciennes
Laisse-moi t'emmener à la claire fontaine

The Katzenjammer Kids

With porcupine locks
And faces which, when
More closely examined,
Are composed of measle-pink specks,
These two dwarf imps,
The Katzenjammer Kids,
Flitter through their Desert Island world.
Sometimes they get so out of hand
That a blue Captain
With stiff whiskers of black wicker
And an orange Inspector
With a black telescope
Pursue them to spank them
All through that land
Where cannibals cut out of brown paper
In cardboard jungles feast and caper,
Where the sea's sharp waves continually
Waver against the shore faithfully
And the yellow sun above is thin and flat
With a collar of black spikes and spines
To tell the innocent childish heart that
It shines
And warms (see where she stands and stammers)
The dear fat mother of the Katzenjammers.
Oh, for years and years she has stood
At the window and kept fairly good
Guard over the fat pies that she bakes
For her two children, those dancing heartaches.
Oh, the blue skies of that funny-paper weather!
The distant birds like two eyebrows close together!

And the rustling paper roar
Of the waves
Against the paper sands of the paper shore!

The Chough

291

The chough, said a dictionary,
Is a relation of the raven
And a relative of the crow.
It's nearly extinct,
But lingers yet
In the forests about Oporto.
So read I as a little child
And saw a young Chough in its nest,
Its very yellow beak already tasting
The delicious eyes
Of missionaries and dead soldiers;
Its wicked mind already thinking
Of how it would line its frowsy nest
With the gold fillings of dead men's teeth.
When I grew older I learned
That the chough, the raven and the crow
That rise like a key signature of black sharps
In the staves and music of a scarlet sunset
Are not to be feared so much
As that carrion bird, within the brain,
Whose name is Devouring Years,
Who gobbles up and rends
All odds and ends
Of memory, good thoughts and recollections
That one has stored up between one's ears
And whose feet come out round either eye.

The Horn

What is the horn that the dawn holds,
A soft shrill horn of feathers,
Cold as the dew on the grass by the paths,
Warm as the fire in the match in the box.
When this horn blows, in a sky of the sun
There rises our green star of earth
And the four evangelists who've borne
Thy bed down through the night
Now leave thee still thine eyes to see
The sun's separation of shadows.

Neither capons nor pullets nor hens
Can wake the sun and the world;
Only the prophets of the Old Testament
Huge old cocks, all speckled and barred,
Their wings like ragged pages of sermons,
Only they from their roosts in the henhouse
Can rouse the bread from its oven-sleep,
Raise the smoke from the haunted chimney.

Fierce old cock whose eyes look blind
So glaring and inspired are they,
Who live in this dungeon of cramp and dirt;
Fierce old fowl with shaking red wattles
Surrounding a beak like a kernel of wheat,
A yellow beak, plump, twisted and sharp
Which opens, hinged and prizing cry,
To show the sun's fistful of golden darts.

From *A Suit of Nettles*

January

ARGUMENT

In this first eclogue two geese, Branwell & Mopsus, discuss the different kinds of love. Branwell is wearing a suit made out of nettles.

With the other geese within the goosehouse
There lived, I know not how, various kinds
Of geese: some like a cat, some like a mouse,
Some like a groundhog and some like lions,
Some like two straight parallel lines,
Others more circular in character,
Some shallow and some deep as mines,
Others than chaos far more muddier,
And whether you should parcel fast or loose
Some could not be but simply described 'Goose'.

BRANWELL MOPSUS

You there, old Mopsus, you're no bird.
I see distinctly limbs beneath the feathers;
You've got a voice too that was never heard
Just in springtime, but in all the weathers.
Do not stand agog at these green tatters;
Crossed in love I'll wear them till my death.
Mopsus, is there purpose in the pulse one gathers
Wristful by wristful? Mopsus, spend thy breath
In talking as I hear you can of geese
And life and whether they and all and life should cease.

JAMES REANEY

It might! And no time's better than this month,
The two-faced time whose sun no more goes south,
And in its cold there comes a milk white moth
Of frozen breath from horse and warm cow mouth
As they run down to pond to cure their drouth;
Old Brown's crowbar breaks the ice beforehand
To give new life to their lives so uncouth,
But need not do so if you understand:
By next September we could stop all life—
Let no one break the ice, let no man take a wife.

BRANWELL

But should we smother all creation outright?

MOPSUS

Here stands a woman with attractive dugs
And here a dugless wise old anchorite;
She leads a life of grotesque scarecrow hugs,
His eyes slide over Bibles slow as slugs;
She tempts you down a well of luscious shame
That into world another funeral lugs,
Another longing for the whence it came,
More jumping in and out of needles' eyes,
More love poems, paradoxes, happy unions, lies.

From some old grim geneva-gowned bore
Proto-orthodox, the hermit lifts his eyes
And gelds you from the world with sermons frore
About the cleansing of the foul heart's sties
With fasts, with baking private humble pies,
Feeling fear, dread, repentance, god-desire,

394

God-terror, god-damnation till you rise
Downwards from your knees to worlds of dire
Pathless woods of rungless Jacob's ladders
Set in hollows filled with aspen-voiced adders.

But do not follow either of these devils,
Reject Elijah—swear off Jezebel,
Come to my ferny groves by calm canals
Where all is bland correct and rational;
Our friendship we'll develop cell by cell,
Investigating what one can't believe;
Attached to all that is unphysical
We'll talk and muse until we must take leave.
Some call that death, but our minds meshed together
Will note the new unbodied time as but a change in weather.

Here look at man. I'll draw him in this dung.
Here the arms like shrivelled legs that uphoist
Spoons of outside world for wet mouth-tongue.
Beneath here hear his bellows groan and hiss:
Dreary East Wind sucked in bladder moist,
Expelled in warm coughs, shrieks, words, cries, alarums:
This knot hides stomach's greedy frog-jump cess,
These legs look like great dropsy ogre arms,
Here Love has chosen Sewer for his mate,
You'd marry this, you'd copy this, you'd propagate!

Climb up with me into this peastraw loft
Where rustlings strange this afternoon have come.
Above the geese Ann and the hired boy coughed,
Their bodies adding up the lovers' sum.
What oneness is there now to this relation?
Their joined mouths comprise a sort of union,

His teeth against her teeth with skull tension.
So with a short leap now his passions come.
Look how she breathes him in and out thro' snout
Of Hell, and so were we from Heaven tumbled out!

I do not think he loves her nor she him;
They love the deed, but not I think each other.
You say you love through girl her elohim,
You love her soul and not your selfish pleasure,
But how be sure? With me your steadfast brother
Be certain of the soul's affection; never
Could we stoop to this foul mad disorder.
Come Light, Fire and Sun from planets sever,
Possess the Love and Light that does not use
This stake and heart-of-vampire sexual eye of ooze.

BRANWELL

But is this light, my dear friend Mopso,
That never falls on darkness but between
The nine sick planets would to nothing go?
Can I desire one whit of world I've seen
Displayed in your cartography of spleen?
I shiver at its top, that round cold sea.
Without some isle a sea's a dismal scene.
The world's hot middle where it's he and she
Has grown for me feverish stinging clothes.
Your favourite land is better I agree—
What a round concrete continent of snows!
But too round and too continent for me
For I want offspring summerson autumnman wintersage
And tricklerrain thawwind panetap upleaf windrage
Plow and seed and hoe, green, sucklepig, yellowripe,
    sicklestraw and all such glamourie.

396

294 *November*

ARGUMENT

Four birds discuss the calendar. Mopsus has certainly come a long way from the detachment & 'calm canals' he mentioned at first.

OOKPIK STARLING WILDGOOSE MOPSUS

Birdies, can there be any doubt
My master, Winter, turns the wheel,
  The Miller whom none love.
I at the spindle pole have been
And through the swarming shuddering snow
  Seen at work the God of Death;
Winter and Death turn all the world,
Man and continents come apart
  Like skin from flesh from bone.
The world was planned in cold arithmetic,
Numbers flapping like vultures fast & thick
Down and around my merry Master Zero
Like birds of prey about a stone dead hero.

STARLING

The year begins when it grows warm;
Then I once more do mate and chirp
  And fly out from the town.
It is not year or time at all
When all there's eatable is dung
  And all is frozen round.
Give me the eaves of a steam laundry
Where I dream of upperworld spring
  Above this grave of cold.

397

JAMES REANEY

Once I lived in a place of sun,
I wish I knew how there to run,
Migrationless I debris am
Yet know the world begins with warm.

WILDGOOSE

My wings tell me that September
Shall the year's beginning be;
   Up those wide rungs I climb
And fly a vigorous sabbath south
And find no winter in my year
   But live a summer seesaw;
Two summers like a figure eight
Two wings like tables of the law
   Are my four seasons.
The wobbling earth with its Goliath snows
I steady and defeat with feathered blows.
The year begins when death and chaos sprout
And I must with a new world beat them out.

MOPSUS

A sun, a moon, a crowd of stars,
A calendar nor clock is he
   By whom I start my year.
He is most like a sun for he
Makes his beholders into suns,
   Shadowless and timeless.
At the winter sunstill some say
He dared be born; on darkest day
   A babe of seven hours
He crushed the four proud and great directions
Into the four corners of his small cradle.
He made it what time of year he pleased, changed
Snow into grass and gave to all such powers.

b. 1927

Marvell's Garden

Marvell's garden, that place of solitude,
is not where I'd choose to live
yet is the fixed sundial
that turns me round
unwillingly,
in a hot glade
as closer, closer I come to contradiction,
to the shade green within the green shade.

The garden where Marvell scorned love's solicitude—
that dream—and played instead an arcane solitaire,
shuffling his thoughts like shadowy chance
across the shrubs of ecstasy,
and cast the myths away to flowering hours
as, yes, his mind, that sea, caught at green
thoughts shadowing a green infinity.

And yet Marvell's garden was not Plato's
garden—and yet—he did care more for the form
of things than for the thing itself—
ideas and visions,
resemblances and echoes,
things seeming and being
not quite what they were.

That was his garden, a kind of attitude
struck out of an earth too carefully attended,
wanting to be left alone.
And I don't blame him for that.
God knows, too many fences fence us out
and his garden closed in on Paradise.

On Paradise! When I think of his hymning
Puritans in the Bermudas, the bright oranges
lighting up that night! When I recall
his rustling tinsel hopes
beneath the cold decree of steel,
Oh, I have wept for some new convulsion
to tear together this world and his.

But then I saw his luminous plumèd wings
prepared for flight,
and then I heard him singing glory
in a green tree,
and then I caught the vest he'd laid aside
all blest with fire.

And I have gone walking slowly in
his garden of necessity
leaving brothers, lovers, Christ
outside my walls
where they have wept without
and I within.

296   *A Tall Tale*

              or, A Moral Song

The whale, improbable as lust,
carved out a cave
for the seagirl's rest;
with rest the seagirl, sweet as dust, devised
a manner for the whale
to lie between her thighs.

Like this they lay
within the shadowed cave
under the waters, under the waters wise,
and nested there, and nested there and stayed,
this coldest whale aslant this seagirl's thighs.

Two hundred years, perhaps, swam by them there
before the cunning waters so distilled the pair
they turned to brutal artifacts of stone
polished, O petrified prisoners of their lair.
And thus, with quiet, submerged in deathly calm,
the two disclosed a future geologic long,
lying cold, whale to thigh revealed
the secret of their comfort
to the marine weeds,
to fish, to shell, sand, sediment and wave,
to the broken, dying sun
which probed their ocean grave.
These, whale and seagirl, stone gods,
stone lust, stone grief,
interred on the sedimented sand
amongst the orange starfish,
these cold and stony mariners
invoked the moral snail
and in sepulchral voice intoned a moral tale:
'Under the waters, under the waters wise,
all loving flesh will quickly meet demise,
the cave, the shadow cave is nowhere wholly safe
and even the oddest couple can scarcely find relief:
appear then to submit to this tide and timing sea
but secrete a skilful shell and stone and perfect be.'

ROLAND GIGUÈRE

b. 1929

297   *Continuer à vivre*

S'avançaient sur la nappe mince du présent
un millier d'images déjà répudiées
et continuaient de nous solliciter ces mirages
d'un monde que nous savions ruiné

et le cancer fleurissait invulnérable

ce n'était pas la peur mais le dégoût
qui nous serrait la gorge

nous nous sentions virus
plaies béantes
pus poison plaies
mauvais sang et plaies
nous nous sentions plaies mal fermées
quand certaines paroles venaient pourrir
sur nos lèvres rouges et gercées

nous nous sentions coupables
coupables et lourds
de tout le sang versé qui avait fait croûte
des animaux dénaturés de la nature inanimée
des jours sans pain des années noires
de la vie dévisagée enfin
nous nous sentions coupables
corps et biens dans le désastre

et pour continuer à vivre
dans nos solitaires et silencieuses cellules
nous commencions d'inventer un monde
avec les formes et les couleurs
que nous lui avions rêvées.

Les Mots-flots

Les mots-flots viennent battre la plage blanche
où j'écris que l'eau n'est plus l'eau
sans ses lèvres qui la boivent

les mot-flots couronnant le plus désertique îlot
le lit où je te vois nager la nuit
et la paupière te couvre comme un drap
au versant abrupt du matin
quand tout vient se fracasser sur la vitre

les mots-flots qui donnent aux ruisseaux
cette voix mi-ouatée qu'on leur connaît
voix miroitée
vois comme je te vois moi qui pourtant ferme les yeux
sur le plus fragile de tes cheveux
moi qui ferme les yeux sur tout
pour voir tout en équilibre
sur la pointe microscopique du cœur
pointe diamantée des dimanches hantés
dis à m'enchanter et jusqu'à m'en noyer
de ces longs rubans de mots-flots
que tu déroules le soir entre tes seins
comme si tout un fleuve rampait à tes pieds
comme si les feuilles n'avaient pour les bercer
d'autre vent que celui de tes cils de soie lactée

les mots-flots toujours les mots-flots
sur le sable la mariée toute nue
attend la grande main salée de la marée
et un seul grain de sable déplacé démasque soudain
la montagne de la vie

403

avec ses pics neigeux ses arêtes lancinantes
ses monts inconquis ses cimes décimées
un seul grain de sable et ce sont aussitôt
des milliers de dunes qui apparaissent
puis des déserts sans mirages
un sphinx d'ébène
et trois cents pyramides humaines mortes de soif

un seul grain de sable et la mariée n'est plus à elle
ne s'appartient plus
devient mère et se couche en souriant
comme un verre renversé perd son eau

et les mots-flots envahissent la table
la maison le champ
le verre se multiplie par sa brisure
et le malheur devient transparent
semblable au matin qui entre
par le coin le plus mince d'un miroir sans tain.

299   *Roses et ronces*

À DENISE

Rosace rosace les roses
roule mon cœur au flanc de la falaise
la plus dure paroi de la vie s'écroule
et du haut des minarets jaillissent
les cris blancs et aigus des sinistrés

du plus rouge au plus noir feu d'artifice
se ferment les plus beaux yeux du monde

rosace les roses les roses et les ronces
et mille et mille épines
dans la main où la perle se pose

une couronne d'épines où l'oiseau se repose
les ailes repliées sur le souvenir d'un nid bien fait

la douceur envolée n'a laissé derrière elle
qu'un long ruban de velours déchiré

rosace rosace les roses
les jours où le feu rampait sous la cendre
pour venir s'éteindre au pied du lit
offrant sa dernière étoile pour une lueur d'amour
le temps de s'étreindre
et la dernière chaleur déjà s'évanouissait
sous nos yeux inutiles

la nuit se raidissait dure jusqu'à l'aube

rosace les roses les roses et les ronces
le cœur bat comme une porte
que plus rien ne retient dans ses gonds
et passent librement tous les malheurs
connus et inconnus
ceux que l'on n'attendait plus
ceux que l'on avait oubliés reviennent
en paquets de petites aiguilles volantes
un court instant de bonheur égaré
des miettes de pain des oiseaux morts de faim
une fine neige comme un gant pour voiler la main
et le vent le vent fou le vent sans fin balaie
balaie tout sauf une mare de boue
qui toujours est là et nous dévisage

c'est la ruine la ruine à notre image

nous n'avons plus de ressemblance
qu'avec ces galets battus ces racines tordues
fracassés par une armée de vagues qui se ruent
la crête blanche et l'écume aux lèvres

rosace les ronces!

rosace les roses les roses et les ronces
les rouges et les noires les roses les roses
les roseaux les rameaux les ronces
les rameaux les roseaux les roses
sous les manteaux sous les marteaux sous les barreaux
l'eau bleue l'eau morte l'aurore et le sang des garrots
rosace les roses les roses et les ronces

et cent mille épines!

roule mon cœur dans la poussière de minerai
l'étain le cuivre l'acier l'amiante le mica
petits yeux de mica de l'amante d'acier trempée jusqu'à l'os
petits yeux de mica cristallisés dans une eau salée
de lame de fond et de larmes de feu
pour un simple regard humain trop humain

rosace les roses les roses et les ronces
il y avait sur cette terre tant de choses fragiles
tant de choses qu'il ne fallait pas briser
pour y croire et pour y boire

fontaine aussi pure aussi claire que l'eau
fontaine maintenant si noire que l'eau est absente

rosace les ronces
ce printemps de glace dans les artères
ce printemps n'en est pas un
et quelle couleur aura donc le court visage de l'été.

JEAN-GUY PILON

b. 1930

300   *L'Étranger d'ici*

Il était d'un pays de corsaires dévots
Où l'on prenait l'inconscience pour le dogme
L'imbécile pour le maître
Le malade pour le voyant

C'était un pays de luttes inutiles
Et de ruines magnifiques
Un pays rongé par la vermine

Quand il a voulu crier sa rage
On ne le lui a pas permis

C'est à peine si on l'a laissé mourir

301   *Incendie*

J'ai retiré des eaux rapides
Des bois précieux
Venus de continents
Que nos siècles ne connaissent plus

J'ai cueilli dans un jardin déserté
Une unique fleur de poussière fragile
Protégée par des ronces tachées de sang

J'ai creusé au centre du miroir
Une alvéole secrète
Pour y mêler une goutte de parfum et du lait de femme

J'étais trop riche
J'ai mis le feu à ma maison
Sans regarder le bel incendie

Sur la cendre bientôt froide
Rebâtirons-nous
Avec un visage neuf

302   *L'Espoir qui triomphe*

Là-bas, au fond le plus mystérieux de l'espace, la main et
ses doigts émergent des tourbillons énormes de la terre.
Puis le corps entier se hisse sur les racines tordues et appelle
d'autres corps au-dessus du naufrage.

Soudain, par la couleur apprivoisée, les visages s'agrandis-
sent et s'élèvent, et les yeux aussi et les mains et les hommes
qui reprennent leur place dans ce matin de soleil trop blanc.

Dès lors, l'homme réapprend sa véritable taille au-dessus
des choses. Il est roi par son regard et son large front où
viennent mourir, comme des vagues, les approches du mal.
Domination pour vivre et force patiente de l'intelligence.

Si un jour vous vous égarez dans ces espaces méconnais-
sables et qu'au seuil du pays où les rochers s'entrechoquent
dans l'obstination de la foudre, vous voyez apparaître une
main qui s'élève, n'ayez plus peur, vous serez au pays des
géants qui sont vos frères en plus grand.

Étoiles et jonques

Étoiles et jonques
Happées par la nuit le mystère
L'adoration mortelle
Et les quatre saisons de nos petits malheurs

Ô silencieuse
Comme de la chair endormie
Pour la mémoire des oiseaux blessés
Et la triste promenade du pain durci

Fulgurante

La douleur hallucinante
Des portages
Des partages obligatoires
L'ennui du sang
Qui crée la plaie
Et ta robe
Sur ton corps de racines tordues
Qu'aucun feu n'a désiré

Étoiles et jonques
Renversées
Dispersées
Décimées sur le rivage sonore
Pour le grand soir de nos débuts
Pour la honte de nos sincérités

Et jette le masque
Et trahis l'amour

Nos journées d'homme à la boussole
De chercheurs de mousse
Nos songes noyés dans un étang visqueux

Seuls
Avec l'unique sanglot
Le dernier de la gorge
Qui sut dire les premiers mots d'amour
Il nous faudra joindre les mains
Et fermer les yeux
Car nous serons rejetés
De ce doux mais terrifiant jardin
Que notre obstination
Aura voué à la mort

JAY MACPHERSON

b. 1932

304   '*Go take the World*'

Go take the world my dearest wish
And blessing, little book.
And should one ask who's in the dish
Or how the beast was took,
Say: Wisdom is a silver fish
And Love a golden hook.

305   *Eurynome*

Come all old maids that are squeamish
And afraid to make mistakes,
Don't clutter your lives up with boyfriends:
The nicest girls marry snakes.

If you don't mind slime on your pillow
And caresses as gliding as ice
—Cold skin, warm heart, remember,
And besides, they keep down the mice—

If you're really serious-minded,
It's the best advice you can take:
No rumpling, no sweating, no nonsense,
Oh who would not sleep with a snake?

306   *The Innocents*

Bloody, and stained, and with mothers' cries,
These silly babes were born;
And again bloody, again stained, again with cries,
Sharp from this life were torn.

A waste of milk, a waste of seed;
Though white the forest stands
Where Herod bleeds his rage away
And wrings his bloodless hands.

307   *Eve in Reflection*

Painful and brief the act. Eve on the barren shore
Sees every cherished feature, plumed tree, bright grass,
Fresh spring, the beasts as placid as before
Beneath the inviolable glass.

There the lost girl gone under sea
Tends her undying grove, never raising her eyes
To where on the salt shell beach in reverie
The mother of all living lies.

The beloved face is lost from sight,
Marred in a whelming tide of blood;
And Adam walks in the cold night
Wilderness, waste wood.

308   *The Marriage of Earth and Heaven*

Earth draws her breath so gently, heaven bends
On her so bright a look, I could believe
That the renewal of the world was come,
The marriage of kind Earth and splendid Heaven.

'O happy pair'—the blind man lifts his harp
Down from the peg—but wait, but check the song.
The two you praise still matchless lie apart,
Thin air drawn sharp between queen Earth and Heaven.

Though I stand and stretch my hands forever
Till my hair grows down my back and my skirt to my ankles,
I shall not hear the triumphs of their trumpets
Calling the hopeful in from all the quarters
To the marriage of kind Earth and splendid Heaven.

Yet out of reason's reach a place is kept
For great occasions, with a fat four-poster bed
And a revelling-ground and a fountain showering beer
And a fiddler fiddling fine for folly's children
To riot rings around at the famous wedding
Of quean Earth and her fancy-fellow Heaven.

JAY MACPHERSON

The Boatman

You might suppose it easy
For a maker not too lazy
To convert the gentle reader to an Ark:
But it takes a willing pupil
To admit both gnat and camel
—Quite an eyeful, all the crew that must embark.

After me when comes the deluge
And you're looking round for refuge
From God's anger pouring down in gush and spout,
Then you take the tender creature
—You remember, that's the reader—
And you pull him through his navel inside out.

That's to get his beasts outside him,
For they've got to come aboard him,
As the best directions have it, two by two.
When you've taken all their tickets
And you've marched them through his sockets,
Let the tempest bust Creation: heed not you.

For you're riding high and mighty
In a gale that's pushing ninety
With a solid bottom under you—that's his.
Fellow flesh affords a rampart
And you've got along for comfort
All the world there ever shall be, was, and is.

b. 1934

310   *My Love Behind Walls*

This huge and purged trust I have
Under my suffering frequent as the thought
Befriends my fear boasting that I believe.
A truth I delude in this trust, more brave
Than birds, more bound to saviour God
Than all without or other of my life.
How was he when by the paper nurse
Under her white crisp hands careful of keys
He was caged that first outrageous day
In the room light bright which was worse
Than dark? and when by the dayroom door he
Stood all hours till they took him away?
How was he under the still sheets where
Too real for tragic he lay like sleep
By the squared sky and the walking ward all night?
What then in after hours by craft or care
Did they to delve him dare, how to heal
Him did they postured over his dreams preside?
I ride my trust like motion to his place
And praying break brick walls, but not his walls
Where he builds against my belief binding this
Silence around him, and oh his face
Wastes me in all mind, and he is mad,
And I do not know how he is.

There how they carved and capable mark
His mood and moving all the ward long
Where he in daylight ringed with cloudy world
Passes their listening, or by the barred
And raving dark evades their clocked intrusions.

He was strange to their will and by force the first
Terrible time they had to bind his hands
While they haltered him, and the bed
Was brittle under their cardboard eyes; till
They warred on his brain, and it broke; and
He did not know how he reeled and retched
In the bolt's wake, stretched or lurched his
Lovely body under their grasp, till he woke
With blood in his mouth and the gag gone sour
In a moaning room. And even then
What they had done, by his taut throat
And the thrashed sheets, or the shriek aloud
In a pushed past bed, he could not tell.
They took him back, when he could walk
To his own bed which he did not know
And left him drowsy and numb for a cure.
How bound and blasted week after week
He was, how watched—and now
He is building against them again, and is still obscure.

He is walled, who once on the loud wind
Laughed, whose limbs were the form of things
And touch was sweet to him, earth to his feet;
He is walled who went by the loved light
The air that embraced him, singing
Sense and sight which he did not fear.
Oh how or why was the blithe night turned
Treacherous to him, the teeming image
Raised to enrage him, that private dark
To appal him? why still he shunned
Them under his walls, and made his face
A foil to them, all the massed world marred
By him mad, fused to a fear and refused of him,

Him furtive and curved to his hurt? from all
Walled, welled, wombed till voice
Is vacant and shape is a void which moves, is
Mute and strange with meaning but has
No meaning, no sorrow, no noise.
He went from me wise as a dream, withdrew
The worlds of his eyes, and into his desolation
Passed with a twilight smile; it was
So lovely and otherwise; I am more cruel
To call him mad, to pursue my great trust
Troubling God, craving cure or cause.

But there the crude ward unmoved by beauty
Over his curled brooding drops
Ugly, discoloured hours; the impure clock
Requires him, that into iron time he
Wake and walk, to whom a time is lost,
And across his troubled body lays unreal stroke.
He is bruised by noise, confusion
In bleak dawn breaking among the beds
Impels him out of passive night, with the
Thorned keys to threaten his enclosures,
To sliver his stayed sleep with the day's wedge,
And chastise his peace with a charred sun.
Now by metal mouths when he will not take
Food he is warned of disturbed wards
And hoards his portion in sleek hands
Against their slander, until they quick
To quell him mark his rebellion. More
Forced he drifts to their influence, and
Down the dayroom rifts the silver air.
He is aware of their going, graves himself
In a gaunt chair among all haunted men,

Nor comprehends what hour, until their
Coming, nor moves in meanwhile world, till
They close him, to quarrel with his silence.

And I, in sheer sense a spender of days,
Descend a prayed passage, all old words
Now resound, and what I would ask is lost;
I am more than crossed, cursed for my trust, made
Small by someday hopes that prove me unheard.
And I not injure his fastnesses, I shake him not,
Him building at the boundaries of my grief,
Him past my grasp though I walk in the wields
Of God, walled all my toward him way.
And they, what good they gain who thwart him?
Is he more worth, more to be heard, be healed
That these should less abuse him, use him strange?
I crave them all my pain, to lose these
Clinic keys, to cleave with love his walled
In dwelling, lone beyond our knowing.
Yonder now in my kneeling night he sleeps
And with sleeved arms closes his stark head
From smite of stars, or harms of over him
Armoured eyes regarding; he fends his face
From light's ascending, guards against day.
God, lend me thus his image, to stir
Again this urgent trust, this fair faith
Thrust so sure forth over my prayers;
Suffer me thus secure, to his return.

311   *Prayer for Messiah*

His blood on my arm is warm as a bird
his heart in my hand is heavy as lead
his eyes through my eyes shine brighter than love
O send out the raven ahead of the dove

His life in my mouth is less than a man
his death on my breast is harder than stone
his eyes through my eyes shine brighter than love
O send out the raven ahead of the dove

O send out the raven ahead of the dove
O sing from your chains where you're chained in a cave
your eyes through my eyes shine brighter than love
your blood in my ballad collapses the grave

O sing from your chains where you're chained in a cave
your eyes through my eyes shine brighter than love
your heart in my hand is heavy as lead
your blood on my arm is warm as a bird

O break from your branches a green branch of love
after the raven has died for the dove

312   *Ballad*

My lady was found mutilated
in a Mountain Street boarding house.
My lady was a tall slender love,
    like one of Tennyson's girls,
and you always imagined her erect on a thoroughbred
in someone's private forest.

418

But there she was,
naked on an old bed, knife slashes
across her breasts, legs badly cut up:
Dead two days.

They promised me an early conviction.
We will eavesdrop on the adolescents
    examining pocket-book covers in drugstores.
We will note the broadest smiles at torture scenes
    in movie houses.
We will watch the old men in Dominion Square
    follow with their eyes
the secretaries from the Sun Life at five-thirty. . . .

Perhaps the tabloids alarmed him.
Whoever he was the young man came alone
    to see the frightened blonde have her blouse
ripped away by anonymous hands;
the person guarded his mouth
    who saw the poker blacken the eyes
of the Roman prisoner;
the old man pretended to wind his pocket-watch. . . .

The man was never discovered.
There are so many cities!
    so many knew of my lady and her beauty.
Perhaps he came from Toronto, a half-crazed man
    looking for some Sunday love;
or a vicious poet stranded too long in Winnipeg;
or a Nova Scotian fleeing from the rocks and preachers. . . .

Everyone knew my lady
    from the movies and art-galleries,

body by Goldwyn. Botticelli had drawn her long limbs.
Rossetti the full mouth.
Ingres had coloured her skin.
    She should not have walked so bravely
through the streets.
After all, that was the Marian year, the year
the rabbis emerged from their desert exile, the year
the people were inflamed by tooth-paste ads. . . .

We buried her in Spring-time.
    The sparrows in the air
wept that we should hide with earth
    the face of one so fair.

The flowers they were roses
    and such sweet fragrance gave
that all my friends were lovers
    and we danced upon her grave.

313   *Poem for Marc Chagall*

        Out of the land of heaven,
        Down comes the warm Sabbath sun
        Into the spice-box of earth.
        The Queen will make every Jew her lover.
            In a white silk coat
        Our rabbi dances up the street,
        Wearing our lawns like a green prayer-shawl,
        Brandishing houses like silver flags.
            Behind him dance his pupils,
        Dancing not so high
        And chanting the rabbi's prayer,

But not so sweet.
   And who waits for him
On a throne at the end of the street
But the Sabbath Queen.
   Down go his hands
Into the spice-box of earth,
And there he finds the fragrant sun
For a wedding ring,
And draws her wedding-finger through.
   Now back down the street they go,
Dancing higher than the silver flags.
His pupils somewhere have found wives too,
And all are chanting the rabbi's song,
And leaping high in the perfumed air.
   Who calls him Rabbi?
Cart-horse and dogs call him Rabbi,
And he tells them:
The Queen makes every Jew her lover.
And gathering on their green lawns,
The people call him Rabbi,
And fill their mouths with good bread,
And his happy song.

MYRA VON RIEDEMANN

b. 1935

314   *There are Places*

There are places between leaves
Where only the sun shines—
Flowers sitting
On the edges of their stalks;

And people walking
Like the bristles of mown wheat.
The sound of a hayfork,
Hard against a stone,
Tightly covered
By the flying wing of hay,
Makes a summer's end.
 There is a round mark
Made by a leaning tree;
Like a white arm carrying
A heavy bucket of tin.
A man drinks
From the water of a canvas bottle,
With his neck bent back,
And the five threads
Of a rumbling thunder
Storms over the river.
 A fly buzzes
Where something died last winter.
'I haven't seen him around,'
While the Alkali dries into dust
On the brown edges of a trough,
There is the child's voice
Of a coyote's crying.

315   *Horses*

A horse breaks glass
In the lift of an eyelid,
The nostrils blooming
Below a banking eye.
A stallion comes forward

With long steps slowly
The wind stands still
On his withers of crystal.
The flat hair slides over
Moving fingers of skin.
Many colours of manes
And the long, and separate
Hairs of tails
Are horses.

Horses' heads turn;
The reflection of their eyes.
The sun is a shine
Of the dust on the hairs
Of their sweat.
Horses,
Turning the wooden round
Of a small corral;
The funeral tilt of a hoof
With no iron nail;
Shadows like tipping trees,
And the closeness of dry earth,
Is horses.

316   *Last Will of the Drunk*

Lay me in the woodbox,
Pack me with kindling,
Feed me a doctor with pills in his hair.
My eyes are his olives; prick them with toothpicks.
Give me a drink;
Take down the emptiness,

And pour in the colour.
Blow the man down, with the popping of corks.
Lift up the window-pane, with the nail of your finger;
Give me the eating of the outside air.
Turn up your overcoat at open umbrellas;
Mine is the collar that needs no forgiveness.
I charge thee with murder, thou foul-smelling rat.
While you're awaking, whine for forgiveness.
Mine is the horse that wins on the racetrack,
Mine is the jukebox that takes in the loot.
Smile, with your hair turning grey as you bellylaugh.
I am the power, and I have forgiveness.
But you have a pony, a small little thing;
Break up its milknest, and pour out its wings.
The earth is empty, and the sky is blued over;
Paint out my eyes, and ink out the sentinels.
I am a packleader;
Give me a drink.

DARYL HINE

1936

317   *In Praise of Music
in Time of Pestilence*

The fall which twisted love to lust,
unfranchising the physical,
and made pleasure barren, lost
innocent magnificence, and all
things change, man and animal,
air and countryside, and temporal
forms change and are lost in flux.

Yet music, which is the musician's nightmare, can
to this dreamless body give relief,
charm the labyrinthine hearts of beasts,
melt marmoreal cruelty, and give
safe conduct to every Lazarus from the grave.

For time's bewitched, and all
her retainers sleep in attitudes
at once antique and baronial;
but this music is, alas, too valuable,
tempting the wounded spirit with green air,
green towers gleaming beyond compare;
there in vain the prince intrudes
and seeks the secret stairway to her room.
Most intricate music ends, while thorns again
imprison Eden and the pilgrim.

Or time is lost, and Venus comes
with empty hands and simple beauty there,
timeless lineaments shaped from the sea's foam,
and through the senses leads the sensualist home.
Where? In the hospital of the particular thing
eternal principles sicken and expire,
and under the deceitful lure of skin
the rebellious angels play with fire.

318   *The Doppelganger*

All that I do is clumsy and ill timed.
You move quickly, when it must be done,
To spare yourself or save your victim pain.
And then like the light of the sun you move away
While I come face to face with complex crime

Far from the moving of the mellifluous sea.
All that I do is clumsy and ill timed.
When you perform, my errors pantomimed
    Will give an example to the sun
    Of flight, and to shadows how to run.
You will in turn discover in my rhyme
Justifications for your simple crime.

Manifold are the disguises of our love.
We change, our transformations turn about,
Our shadowy forms become the doubles for
Affection or hatred. Yet a kind of growth
Is visible, and may be termed the heart,
Confused by the ambiguities of our art.
Manifold are the disguises of our love.
Contradiction of terms is all we have.
    To please the self and then the soul
    Is difficult and terrible;
Impossible to own a single heart
Lost in the double-dealing of our art.

Two edged is the doppelganger's tongue,
Malice and honey, and the prizes in
His logomachy, what lie near the heart:
Money, honour and success in love.
Harmonious ambiguities in a swarm
Burrow at the fulcrum of his speech.
Two edged is the doppelganger's tongue.
One side says Right, the other side says Wrong;
    One, Love is red, the other, Black;
    One, Go on, and one, Turn back.
One hopes for heaven, one for earth, and each
To strike a concord through cross-purposed speech.

So split and halved and twain is every part,
So like two persons severed by a glass
Which darkens the discerning whose is whose
And gives two arms for love and two for hate,
That they cannot discover what they're at
And sometimes think of killing and embrace.
So split and halved and twain is every part,
Double the loins, the fingers and the heart,
    Confused in object and in aim
    That they cannot their pleasure name,
But like two doubles in a darkened place
Make one obscure assault and one embrace.

For they were to duality born and bred.
From their childhood the powers of evil were
No less their familiar than the mirror,
Source of a comfortable terror now and then,
And romantic: What good is a fiend unless
I can think and he, my double, act?
Thus we were to duality born and bred.
If these two eyes could turn into the one head,
    Bright orbs by a brighter sphere enclosed,
    Mutually blind and self-opposed,
The right supplying what the left one lacked,
Then I can think, and you, my body, act.

In singleness there is no heart or soul
And solitude is scarcely possible.
The one-sailed ship, tossed on a divided sea
As lightly as cork is tossed, as blindly as
The partners toss on their oceanic bed
And rise and fall, is wrecked and lost away.
In singleness there is no heart or soul;

427

Thus he sees wrong who sees in halves a whole,
   Who searches heaven but for one,
   And not a double of the sun,
Forgets that, being light as cork, the day
Can rise or fall, is wrecked and lost away.

All that I do is careless and sublime.
You walk head downwards, now your opened eyes
Take comfort from the beauty of the site.
What if the vision vary in detail?
What are we but sleepers in a cave,
Our dreams the shades of universal doubt?
All that I do is careless and sublime.
You bore with patience to the heart of time,
   And though your rift of ore is small
   And my device yields none at all,
Still this two handed engine will find out
The complex reason of your simple doubt.

319   *A Bewilderment at the*
Entrance of the Fat Boy into Eden

'L'art ne me connaît pas; je ne connais pas l'art.'

CORBIÈRE

I

Not knowing where he was or how he got there,
Led by the gentle sessions of his demons,
Now in the right and now in the left ear,
The fat boy trod ungarlanded in Eden.
Perhaps he knew of nowhere else to go.
Affairs of the heart, concerns of money, too,

DARYL HINE

Deprived him of all choosing of his route.
Dreaming of disaster, he set foot
At midnight in the earthly paradise.
The ice around him shattered like a shot,
The gates swung open, and an angel stood,
(His bright sword averted and put up),
To watch the fat boy lollop from the wood
He couldn't see because he was asleep.

II

Within his head a rank and silent fortune
Gestured slowly. On the silver screen
Papier-mâché herds of buffalo
Pursued a cowboy over endless prairie,
While down his cheeks the glittering orbs of sorrow
Rolled their separate tracks to final ruin.
What password did his virtues and his powers
Whisper, that he awoke within the gates,
Preserved against his enemies the hours,
While we who, like the vultures near the towers,
Live at the expense of those who die of boredom,
Enchained by the strait enchantment of their longing,
Must pitch our camp beneath the walls of Sodom,
Detained within the sweet preserves of time?

III

Always through the badlands of the heart
The invisible posse kept a secret watch.
Across the desert of the intellect,
Murmured his persuaders, Forward march!
Lest mirage of thought too intricate distract
The sight, or sound amuse the hearing

Whose ignorance alone they might instruct,
They guarded their somnambulist, and laid
His ears in stillness and his eyes in shade,
And on his tongue the sesame of love:
A little word so common in the world.
All doors were opened to him. What he meant:
The sentiment, the purpose, or the act,
He couldn't say and never understood.

IV

A little word. Unconsciousness is all.
But all our wisdom is unwillingness.
We cannot blink the lightning of the wit,
Or sink the ego's fragile paper boat.
We think too much. Our selves are ponderous.
Only the fat boy bounces like a ball
The law set rolling into the lawless park:
Contemptible, unintroduced to art.
His demon is our muse, when, after dark,
Each must choose a mask and play a part:
I'll be Hamlet or Polonius,
Or the deuce, whichever face will fit.
And I, Ophelia, who, in her distress,
Interbound the bitter with the sweet.

BIBLIOGRAPHICAL NOTE

THE following list indicates the first appearance of the poems in volume form.

1–2	*The Emigrant, A Poem in Four Cantos*, Montreal, 1841
3–5	*The Rising Village, with Other Poems*, London, 1825, Saint John, N.B., 1834
6	*Life in the Clearings versus the Bush*, London, 1853
7	*Quebec, the Harp, and Other Poems*, Montreal, 1829
8–9	*Saul: A Drama in Three Parts*, new and revised edition, Boston, 1869
10–11	*Jephthah's Daughter*, Montreal, 1865
12–13	*The Emigrant, and Other Poems*, Toronto, 1861
14–15	*The St. Lawrence and the Saguenay, and Other Poems*, Kingston and New York, 1856
16	Uncollected
17–18	*Poésies complètes*, Montreal, 1882 (written 1858, 1862)
19	*De Roberval: A Drama*, Saint John, N.B., 1888
20–21	*Les Gouttelettes*, Montreal, 1904
22	*Dreamland and Other Poems*, Montreal and London, 1868
23–24	*Tecumseh: A Drama*, Toronto, 1886
25	*Dreamland and Other Poems*, Montreal and London, 1868
26–29	*Les Fleurs boréales et Oiseaux de Neige*, Paris, 1880
30–33	*Old Spookses' Pass, Malcolm's Katie, and Other Poems*, Toronto, 1884
34–35	*Les Aspirations*, Paris, 1903
36	*Les Fleurs de givre*, Paris, 1912
37	*Les Floraisons matutinales*, Three Rivers, 1897
38	*Patrie intime*, Montreal, 1928
39–40	*Lyrics on Freedom, Love and Death*, Kingston and Boston, 1887
41	*The Habitant and Other French-Canadian Poems*, New York and London, 1897
42	*New York Nocturnes and Other Poems*, Boston, New York, and London, 1898
43–44	*In Divers Tones*, Boston, 1886, Montreal, 1887
45–46	*Songs of the Common Day, and Ave*, London, Toronto, Montreal, and Halifax, 1893
47	*New York Nocturnes and Other Poems*, Boston, 1898
48	*The Book of the Native*, Boston, New York, and London, 1896
49–50	*Among the Millet and Other Poems*, Ottawa, 1888
51–52	*The Poems of Archibald Lampman*, Toronto, 1900
53	*Lyrics of Earth*, Boston, 1895
54	*The Poems of Archibald Lampman*, Toronto, 1900
55	*Alcyone*, Ottawa, 1899

BIBLIOGRAPHICAL NOTE

BIBLIOGRAPHICAL NOTE

126   *Laconics*, Ottawa, 1930
127   Uncollected
128–32   *Collected Poems of Raymond Knister*, Toronto, 1949
133–7   *Events and Signals*, Toronto, 1954
138   *Overture*, Toronto, 1945
139   *Poems*, Toronto, 1946
140   *The Strength of the Hills*, Toronto, 1948
141–2   *Poems*, Toronto, 1946
143   Uncollected
144   *Les Îles de la nuit*, Montreal, 1944
145–6   *Rivages de l'homme*, Quebec, 1948
147–9   *A l'ombre de l'Orford*, Montreal, 1930
150   *A l'ombre de l'Orford*, Montreal, 1948 (second edition)
151   *A l'ombre de l'Orford*, Montreal, 1930
152–4   *Viper's Bugloss*, by 'John Smalacombe', Toronto, 1938
155   Uncollected
156   *Deeper into the Forest*, Toronto, 1948
157–9   *News of the Phoenix*, Toronto and New York, 1943
160–2   Uncollected
163   *L'Immortel adolescent*, Quebec, 1928
164   *Ceux qui seront aimés*, Paris, 1931
165   *Je te fiancerai*, Paris, 1947
166   *Le Long Voyage*, Saint-Quentin, 1947
167   *David and Other Poems*, Toronto, 1942
168   *The Strait of Anian*, Toronto, 1948
169   *Now is Time*, Toronto, 1945
170–1   *Trial of a City and Other Verse*, Toronto, 1952
172–3   Uncollected
174–6   *Border River*, Toronto, 1952
177   *À travers les vents*, Montreal, 1925
178–80   *Suite marine*, Montreal, 1953
181   *Strophes et catastrophes*, Montreal, 1943
182   *Mes naufrages*, Paris, 1951
183   *The Mulgrave Road*, Toronto, 1951
184–5   *The Shrouding*, Toronto, 1933
186–9   Uncollected
190–2   *Hath not a Jew*, New York, 1940
193–7   *The Rocking Chair and Other Poems*, Toronto, 1948
198–200 *The Deficit made Flesh*, Toronto, 1958
201–3   *Flight into Darkness*, New York, 1944
204–5   To be included in *Rivers among Rocks*, Toronto, 1960
206   *Day and Night*, Toronto, 1944
207–8   *Selected Poems (1926–56)*, Toronto, 1957
209–10   *The Hangman Ties the Holly*, Toronto, 1955
211–13   Uncollected

BIBLIOGRAPHICAL NOTE

434

BIBLIOGRAPHICAL NOTE

295	*Even your Right Eye*, Toronto, 1956
296	Uncollected
297–9	*Les Armes blanches*, Montreal, 1954
300–3	*L'Homme et le jour*, Montreal, 1957
304–9	*The Boatman*, Toronto, 1957
310	*Asylum Poems and Others*, Toronto, 1958
311–12	*Let us Compare Mythologies*, Montreal, 1956
313–16	Uncollected
317	*The Carnal and the Crane*, Montreal, 1957
318	Uncollected
319	*The Carnal and the Crane*, Montreal, 1957

INDEX OF AUTHORS

References are to the numbers of the poems

INDEX OF AUTHORS

INDEX OF FIRST LINES

INDEX OF FIRST LINES

INDEX OF FIRST LINES

INDEX OF FIRST LINES

INDEX OF FIRST LINES

INDEX OF FIRST LINES